# NIGHTMARE

# NIGHTMARE

SANDRA SHULMAN

WITH 16 LITHOGRAPHS BY
JOHN SPENCER

MACMILLAN PUBLISHING CO., INC.
New York

To David

Copyright © 1979 by Sandra Shulman

All rights reserved. No part of this book may be reproduced or transmitted in any form or by any means, electronic or mechanical, including photocopying, recording or by any information storage and retrieval system, without permission in writing from the Publisher.

Macmillan Publishing Co., Inc.
866 Third Avenue, New York, N.Y. 10022
Collier Macmillan Canada, Ltd.

**Library of Congress Cataloguing in Publication Data**
Shulman, Sandra.
Nightmare.
1. Nightmares.
I. Title.
BF1078.S525    1979    154.6'32    79-11850
ISBN 0 02 610530 6

First American Edition 1979
Printed in Great Britain

The lithographs in this book are the work of John Spencer, a British artist whose distinctive style and idiosyncratic viewpoint have enhanced a number of notable books on folklore and mythology, among them *The Rusty Knight* by Richard Volkmann-Leander and *The Mistress of the Copper Mountain* by Pavel Bazhov.

    Their presence stems from the desire to illustrate the principal subject matter of this book: the fantasies, macabre and otherwise, that constitute nightmares. Unfortunately, no camera yet devised can record the images that pass through the mind of the sleeper: it is to be hoped, then, that John Spencer's lithographs will serve as the nearest that can be obtained to photographs of the mind.

# Contents

| | |
|---|---|
| Invitation | 9 |
| The Eighth Continent | 15 |
| The Demonic Tradition | 31 |
| Victims | 55 |
| Shadows in the Mind | 82 |
| The Pitiless Muse | 116 |
| Fearful Patterns | 143 |
| The Dark Prophet | 164 |
| The Pains of Sleep | 188 |
| Escape | 205 |
| Acknowledgements | 215 |
| Bibliography | 217 |
| Index | 221 |

# Invitation

Since the beginning of recorded time the dream has occupied a prominent position in every culture and has exercised a profound effect, not only on the individual but also over religions and history. Dignified as divine messenger, prophet, muse, problem-solver, route to the group unconscious, guardian of sleep, fulfiller of wishes, or signpost to psychological and physical ills, the dream has apparently opened a door into the unknown that could be of service to humanity. Its sister, the nightmare, enjoys equal significance but for quite other reasons. Her unsolicited visits are so miserable that human beings have always wondered what purpose could be served by this grim invader of sleep.

The nightmare respects neither age nor youth: a sixteenth-century writer on paediatrics gave it ninth place in a list of fifty-two childhood maladies. Anyone who has tried to comfort a small child in the toils of a bad dream will agree that this is one of the nightmare's most pitiless and cowardly onslaughts.

The nightmare recognizes no boundary of time or culture. It hounds both the sophisticated and the primitive. It scourges the healthy and the sick, the sane and the mentally deranged. It links the past with the future, for it comes unbidden to mock the outward self-assurance of the twentieth-century urban dweller (holding fast to the panacea of technology) just as it visited his prehistoric forebears, when all that was inexplicable was to be feared and darkness contained a multitude of terrors. No doubt it will continue to stalk our descendants even if they build themselves plastic castles on other planets for, like the dream, the nightmare is a universal and involuntary human experience.

Although frequently claimed to encompass the fears and

dilemmas of a person's earliest years, the nightmare may also enshrine those terrors and problems of humankind's childhood that lie at the heart of so many myths. Certain images, therefore, do not arise from the individual's conditioning but spring out of the vast cosmic sea of the shared unconscious.

The paperback dream manuals, available at any bookstand, are the mass-produced descendants of Babylonian and Assyrian clay tablets, describing dreams and nightmares and giving interpretations, that date back to 5000 BC. What we know of ancient terrors has been garnered from these earliest writings on religion, magic, and medicine; but we can be certain that, because of basic human physiology, similar nightmares were experienced long before any form of writing had been evolved to record them.

In those last isolated outposts where communities are totally ignorant of Western society, anthropologists have noted dreams and nightmares that are fundamentally the same. The real difference, however, is one of attitude. We may smile at the idea of South American Indians panicking and almost deserting a village because one of their number saw enemies stealthily approaching in a nightmare, but that is because we no longer allow the phenomena within a dream the same validity as actual events in the external world. For the child, the primitive and the superstitious, the drama in a dream is happening, or soon will, and therefore any warning or prophesy contained in it must be observed. After aeroplane and train crashes there are always those who claim to have seen it happen in a nightmare. Some have changed their plans and lived. Others have ignored their dreams and perished.

Human beings are paradoxical creatures. We may flinch from the personal nightmare but terror fascinates and challenges us. We both shun and court it. The *frisson* it evokes is akin to pleasure. It stretches our emotions, leaving us breathless and exhausted but strangely triumphant at having escaped with nothing worse than a fright. If terror did not exercise this extraordinary appeal, there would be no gruesome fairy stories, no vivid tales of witches, werewolves, vampires, and monsters, and certainly no horror and disaster films. Eager queues would not form at fairgrounds, waiting to enter the 'haunted house' or climb aboard the 'ghost train'.

Terror is something human beings need to experience, at least in fantasy, as if seeking to test their reactions by pitting themselves against it. When that terror is externalized for our entertainment—and admiration—we thrill to it, knowing it can be brought to a swift conclusion, explained away, or scoffed at.

The nightmare is quite different. It threatens to overwhelm and refuses to be harnessed or tamed. Despite its universality it remains a strictly individual experience. Each of us confronts it in the total isolation of our own sleep. We cannot walk out, close it up, or nudge our companions for reassurance. Our brush with it can be shared only *after* we have survived. That the nightmare is able to creep in and attack us in those surroundings where we feel safest underlines our innate vulnerability and the nightmare's apparent mastery.

Yet we remain obstinately intrigued by the nightmare's machinations, perhaps because it so often contains one or all of those great box-office attractions—shock, horror, violence, and sex—portrayed more subtly and expertly than in most late-night movies. Probably there is nothing new under the sun or in the darkness—only things waiting to be rediscovered and restated, for the libidinous aspect of the nightmare existed long before psychologists began to claim that deeply repressed sexual desires were its root cause.

Going back to its beginnings we find the nightmare regarded as an actual being, usually a female spirit or monster that attacked sleeping people and animals by night, crouching upon them to produce a feeling of suffocation. Gradually nightmare came to signify not only this unappetizing hag but also the actual dream with its attendant sensations. That the nightmare, like disease, is caused by certain kinds of demon, is one of our oldest traditions.

## INVITATION

To understand the nightmare's extraordinary reputation we have to pay special attention to the etymology of the word. The Anglo-Saxon for goblin or incubus is *mare*. This in turn derives from the Sanskrit *mara* meaning 'crusher'. *Cauchemar*, the French word for nightmare, contains the *mare* element and *caucher* further emphasizes the oppressive and sexual nature for it means 'to tread upon'. Somehow, and probably without much difficulty, 'mare' meaning female horse, which has an entirely different linguistic ancestry, became confused with *mare*, the goblin. No doubt a further complication was introduced because the Teutonic goddess Mara was said to change herself into a white mare when visiting male sleepers at night. According to Icelandic tradition Mara turned into a horse's bone after being exorcised by a bishop.

However, the nightmare did not have to rely on its equine connections for its sexual reputation. The incubus and his equally lubricious female counterpart were regarded as demons whose chief occupation was to have sexual relations with human partners. Sometimes these uninvited nocturnal visitors were diabolically beautiful, at other times ghastly. Whatever their guise they were apparently irresistible. They were blamed for involuntary arousal, spermatorrhoea, masturbation, and lascivious dreams and thoughts, particularly by young girls and holy hermits who were not supposed to let such ideas sully their minds.

The nightmare was a byword for lustfulness. Sometimes the fiend rode and charms were invented to prevent it from disturbing stabled horses by night; sometimes the nightmare was the horse and it could change its sex to suit the occasion—or the inadmissible sexual preferences of the dreamer. Its relatives included vampires, werewolves, witches, the devil, and other supernatural blackguards, all of whom might be invited to share its revels with the hapless human prey. Given the attitudes promoted by various philosophies of fear, guilt, repression, and morbid fascination surrounding all sexual matters, it is no wonder that the nightmare became the scapegoat for every conceivable forbidden appetite.

Apart from demonic agency, which satisfied popular opinion, the most widely held rationalist explanation for the nightmare's unwelcome manifestation was a disturbance in the stomach's mechanism: indigestion was the true, but internal, culprit that attacked adults and infants alike. The precursor of this prosaic gastrointestinal philosophy was the second-century Greek physician Galen whose rigid influence over medical science lasted a thousand years and discouraged much original investigation. Other medical theories as to the cause of nightmares have included sleeping in a supine position and respiratory and circulatory disorders. Yet all the herbs, potions, powders and special diets seem to have had as little permanent effect as prayers, amulets, holy water, and the Babylonian banishing rituals.

As long ago as the fifth century BC, Hippocrates of Cos, the ideal physician, took a surprisingly modern view of the nightmare's mechanics. In studying epilepsy he concluded that an excessive flow of blood through the vessels overheated the brain and he noted that during the nightmare's attack a similar condition occurred. Recent sleep researchers, armed with the most advanced gadgets, have compared those periods of sleep that are particularly associated with dreaming to epileptic seizures. Hippocrates also foreshadowed the theories of some psychologists that an individual's nightmares and dreams could point to serious mental conflict, perhaps arising from forbidden or criminal tendencies. Plato, too, shared such ideas for he considered that in sleep those actions that are normally repressed might break through to produce violent and lustful dreams of murder, unlawful sexual activity, or sacrilege.

Twentieth-century psychology tends to regard dreaming as the product of mind and body and sees the nightmare as an individual's struggle to integrate the internal and external world frequently harking back to buried childhood memories and impulses. In recent years physiologists, biologists, and chemists have focused their attention on the workings of sleep, dreams, and nightmares. Sophisticated laboratory techniques now mean that the nightmare's actual course through brain and body can be minutely charted. At long last, it seems, the dark hunter is being pursued.

As fresh facts about dream and nightmare emerge we seem tantalizingly close to the heart of the ancient enigma but each discovery reveals yet another puzzle to be solved. Perhaps in our lifetime the nightmare will finally be pinned to the work bench so that its intricate pattern and structure can be observed as if it were no more deadly than a death's-head moth; or perhaps it will defy all attempts at explanation and retain that elusive quality which has always terrified and intrigued.

Does the nightmare tell us something of humankind's eternal fears and murmur, to those prepared to listen, warnings of future catastrophe, or are all those dread images merely the product, as D. H. Lawrence suggested, of 'pancakes for supper?' Is the nightmare simply a biochemical action in the brain or the result of repressed taboo desires? Can drugs finally banish the nightmare or do substances such as alcohol and LSD give fresh strength to its attacks?

In an attempt to answer these questions and to trace the nightmare's character, habits, history, and victims, you are invited to join an expedition into the obscure continent where the nightmare dwells undisturbed. In making this journey you may throw a beam of light into our shared darkness but the nightmare has retained its secrets for too long to allow the inquisitive to penetrate them without a struggle. Be warned: when you threaten our oldest foe it may turn and begin chasing you!

# The Eighth Continent

> *. . . the innocent sleep,*
> *Sleep that knits up the ravell'd sleave of care,*
> *The death of each day's life, sore labour's bath,*
> *Balm of hurt minds, great nature's second course,*
> *Chief nourisher in life's feast.*
> *Macbeth* WILLIAM SHAKESPEARE

Most of us share this Shakespearian view of sleep although our reasons, like his, are based on empirical assumptions rather than proven fact. There is an underlying belief that a good night's sleep will be beneficial, so it is all the more distressing that the so-called remedy can produce further ills in the grotesque guise of the nightmare and the anxiety dream.

While anthropologists and sociologists collected detailed studies of the customs and beliefs surrounding sleep, the scientifically-minded remained singularly incurious about its mechanics. Over the centuries they delved into every facet of the human organism in an attempt to pinpoint just what makes men and women tick. Apart from those who regarded sleep as the necessary vehicle for the dream, most tended towards the opinion that it was a rather negative function where nothing occurred and needed only in order to rest mind and body after the day's fatigue. In effect, such an attitude discounted one-third of our existence. The creative and superstitious have always adopted a more reverential attitude to the mystery. Any human activity that permitted dream and nightmare could not be dismissed as mere quiescence.

Sleep has frequently been regarded as so akin to death that

prayers had to be recited to prevent the individual from slipping irrevocably into the final resting place. For many disparate cultures sleep was the dark time when the human soul left the body to explore those domains of time and space inaccessible during consciousness. Whatever transpired in dream and nightmare was the soul's actual experience. In some parts of Ireland a belief existed that on St John's Eve (23 June) souls visited the place on land or sea where one day the body must meet its death. To ensure the soul's successful return was a matter of some concern among primitive peoples and it was considered imperative not to disturb a sleeper's body or to alter its appearance. An attempt to arouse someone too abruptly could even incur an attack by the infuriated soul. Sleeping in a house where there had been a recent death was ill-advised for the living soul might encounter the ghost of the dead and be tempted away; and in some communities the very sick were prevented from falling asleep in case the soul took the opportunity not to return.

In contradiction to this sleep has long been employed as a therapy. A remote ancestor of modern psychotherapy was incubation, the sacred dream treatment practised by many ancient civilizations and still to be encountered today. The afflicted attended temples, caves, grottoes, or groves where special priests and priestesses induced sleep with ritual, incantation, and drugs. During sleep, a god or the spirit of an ancestor was supposed to appear to indicate treatment and ailment and it was the priestly task to interpret this dream. Actual healing seemed more dependent on a dream event than on any subsequent medication so we can regard incubation as a form of faith-healing, based on the earnest wish of a patient to be cured. The treatment seems to have been remarkably efficacious—unless the records do not choose to give the full failure rate.

Many of the illnesses must have been of a hysterical, psychosomatic, or self-induced nature and the very fact of having the priest's undivided attention in sympathetic surroundings, and following a positive régime, would prove therapeutic. Incubation was a particularly widespread remedy for sterility and this suggests that, in every community, matrimony need not always be a bed of roses but can contain some thorny psychological problems.

Sleep can be described as the largest and most mysterious continent but the one that we are all bound to visit. Although we spend on average a third of our life there, we know far less about its characteristics than about those of many a far-flung land which we may never see except on a television screen.

The accoutrements available for this apparently unremarkable sojourn are as varied as anything recommended for other sorts of longer, specialized expeditions. Vast industries have grown up to foster and cater for our sleeping habits. Consider the evolution of the bed—from heap of straw, through four-poster to the most avant-garde water couch. Think of the fortune spent annually on bedding and nightwear, to say nothing of all those sleep-promoting drugs and beverages. Then there are those accessories invented to make sleep more efficient or entertaining: alarm clocks and radios, automatic tea-makers, cassettes and records to educate us while we doze, and of course, books to teach us how to improve our sleeping patterns and interpret our dreams. Hotels, inns, and camp-sites make their fortune out of providing sleeping accommodation for those away from their own beds. Nor is our interest in resting purely selfish: we give our dogs and cats baskets, boxes, and cushions, wishing to make their nocturnal voyage as comfortable as possible.

You might care to accept the premise that the sleep factor lies at the heart of many civilizing behaviour patterns. Asleep, mammals are totally vulnerable to outside attack, especially during the hours of darkness. While animals huddled in their lairs, humankind gradually stepped from the communal cave to evolve dwellings, villages, and then complicated civilizations, to contain safe, warm places in which to sleep undisturbed.

Yet what precisely is this state that leaves us so helpless?

You will find many a lyrical description in dictionaries of quotations but a modern and rather prosaic definition may be given: sleep is an easily reversible, periodic condition, characterized by relative physical inactivity and a decreased awareness of external stimuli.

Until the middle of the twentieth century sleep was an unexplored region so statements as to its function and mechanics could not be supported by empirical evidence. If you had been asked to sketch a map of the imagined continent of sleep you would probably have insisted that there was nothing much to the chart only a flat, dark wasteland, with a twilight zone at each end. Precise methods of research now show the real picture to be far more fascinating and full of high peaks and deep troughs.

In the early fifties the researches of Nathaniel Kleitman, Eugene Aserinsky, William Dement and others led to an amazing and revolutionary discovery: all mammals, including human beings, experience two separate types of sleep. The brain that everyone had assumed to be idling at night is in fact attending to complex cyclical duties arising from a physiological-biochemical process. That darkest of continents could no longer be described as a featureless desert.

The two states of sleep are categorized by the eye movements associated with them: REM (rapid-eye-movement, sometimes called D, de-synchronized or dreaming sleep) and NREM (non-REM, sometimes called S or synchronized sleep).

Today it is not a vain abstraction to say: 'How I wish I knew what was passing through your mind.' For in a sleep laboratory the electrical activity of the brain (EEG or electroencephalogram), eyes (EOG or electrooculogram) and muscles (EMG or electromyogram) can be monitored. Electrodes attached to the scalp and face transmit impulses to a polygraph, which automatically records them as undulating lines on graph paper. These patterns provide the contours for the map and demonstrate through which territory the sleeper is passing.

NREM is characterized by even breathing, a steady pulse rate, and slow rolling eye movements. Although known as 'quiet' sleep, this is the condition in which any snoring occurs. The body is capable of movement but, because the brain is not issuing commands, it usually remains inactive. In NREM the individual is virtually detached from the external world for the senses are not relaying messages to the brain. If a sleeper should turn over, the EEG records a brief patch of wakefulness. You may have noticed that small children do not sleep peacefully and during NREM they either remain relatively still or jerk about quite violently.

REM sleep produces brain patterns similar to those belonging to wakefulness. Experiments on animals suggest that this phase does not stem from the cerebral cortex—the outer layers—but from the primitive areas of the brain. REM has paradoxically been termed 'active' sleep although this is the time when the body's larger muscles are virtually paralyzed, while those in the face and fingertips may twitch convulsively. During its course the pulse and blood pressure rise and are irregular. Respiration is sometimes very fast and shallow, at other times so laboured as to cease altogether. Beneath the eyelids the eyes dart about just as if their owner were wide awake and watching something but there is nothing to suggest that these movements are associated with a dream. In infant and adult males the REM phase is punctuated by penile erection but this need have no relation whatsoever to the dream's content.

It seems natural to envisage going to sleep as a gradual drifting-off process but the EEG demonstrates a fairly abrupt change from wakefulness to NREM. The first steps on to the continent lead gently downwards as if you were walking through the shallows away from the beach. This is Stage 1. If, on going off to sleep, you have ever experienced a sensation of floating or falling curtailed by a sudden jerk into consciousness, it would have occurred during those first five minutes. The 'false start' seems more prevalent among highly strung people but it can also be triggered off by some very faint external disturbance which you may not even recognize.

After a brief stay at Stage 1 you descend to Stage 2. A few more minutes are spent here and then you move into Stage 3. Ten minutes later you reach Stage 4. Each phase puts more and more distance between you and your external environment, so that complete arousal would require greater stimulus.

After sleeping for thirty to forty minutes, various body movements show that you are beginning to emerge from this deepest valley. Another thirty or forty minutes of climbing leads you back up to Stage 1. This time, however, there is a radical difference in the landscape. NREM yields to the first REM phase, which will last for about ten minutes. Curiously enough, although REM always coincides with what is termed 'light sleep', it is particularly difficult to rouse sleepers at this point.

A whole NREM/REM cycle lasts about ninety minutes. (It has been suggested, although not proved, that a similar underlying pattern of sleep-wakefulness exists in the human organism throughout the twenty-four-hour period.) The early part of the night is devoted to a high proportion of NREM sleep, particularly at Stages 3 and 4. Gradually the REM periods lengthen until they can last up to an hour, with the sleeper descending only as far as Stage 2 for a snatch of NREM.

REM has to be preceded by NREM so if a sleeper is disturbed and the break in REM lasts longer than five minutes, NREM takes over, and it will be about half-an-hour before Stage 1 is regained. It has been mooted that a systematic attempt to deprive the individual of REM sleep results in irritability, hunger, paranoid tendencies, hallucination, and aggressive behaviour. However, the evidence available is insufficient to prove this. Attempts to prevent REM always produce a 'rebound'—an extraordinary increase in REM once the inhibitor is removed. Therefore REM sleep plays some vital part in our total psychological-physiological drama.

One of the torture techniques beloved by certain states where human rights are not of prime importance is to deny captives sleep. This can induce psychotic behaviour and cause the individual to break down. Although such a result may well be related to the prisoner's social isolation and mental and physical anguish, it might also be due in part to the prevention of REM.

Laboratory tests into sleep deprivation suggest that a subject's reaction depends on mental and physical health, plus basic motivation. Some people have suffered hallucination and paranoid psychosis, while others have shown no impairment, except when performing repetitive tasks, and seem perfectly capable of dealing with anything requiring concentration, albeit brief. More thought-provoking are those sleep-depriving experiments carried out on animals; some have died but the autopsy revealed that nothing untoward had happened to the brain.

Before you relegate what you have just read to the very back of your mind as being applicable only in laboratory conditions or police states, it should be pointed out that various substances generally accepted by society can have a profound effect on REM sleep. Alcohol, barbiturates, reserpine (used as a tranquillizer and to reduce high blood pressure) and monoamine oxidase inhibitors do surpress REM if used over a long period. Withdrawal results in a greatly increased percentage of REM sleep and nightmares.

Sleeping badly, as any self-diagnosed insomniac will tell you, is worse than a nightmare. Pills seem the perfect answer but, used regularly, they build up a psychological and physiological condition as unwelcome as the one they are supposed to be remedying. A doctor consulted by a patient who claims to have little or no sleep usually accepts this statement and prescribes accordingly. Tests in sleep laboratories on such individuals have revealed that sometimes their sleeping record is not nearly as bad as they imagine. Basing one's treatment on such a proof can eradicate an individual's sleep problem—by removing the anxiety surrounding it. The trouble is, of course, that there are not enough sleep clinics to cope with the volume of people requiring attention.

One of the causes of hypersomnia and insomnia can be an extraordinary disorder known as sleep apnoea. The sufferer may never know of the condition but on falling asleep respiration ceases. Clearly this has a swift arousing action. Some people may wake up literally hundreds of times in a night without being aware of the fact but next day will complain of feeling constantly sleepy; others never become accustomed to the suffocating sensation but do not connect it with being unable to sleep.

Another chronic sleep disorder—narcolepsy—presents a bizarre close-up study of REM and brings the nightmare into the world of wakefulness. The symptoms of this complaint are cataplectic seizures, where the victim is suddenly fully or partially paralyzed while remaining awake, and uncontrolled attacks of sleeping. On falling asleep the narcoleptic immediately experiences sleep paralysis and hypnagogic hallucinations—lurid and usually scaring dreams. Their content is often a highly distorted continuation of whatever was happening just before sleep. Research has shown that this is REM breaking through the waking barrier, which is something that does not happen to non-sufferers even if undergoing severe REM deprivation. Cataplexy blocks the body's movements so that the individual cannot jump up and try to deal with the vivid experiences within the dream. In sleep, narcoleptics do not journey through the regular NREM phases but find themselves straight away at REM. It is to be hoped that research in sleep laboratories will eventually effect a cure, other than drugs, for a condition that brings its sufferers so much misery and risk.

The most fascinating aspect of REM sleep is its coincidence with dreaming. Even those who proclaim they *never* dream would, if roused during an REM period, recall that they had just been doing so. This means that the dream can no longer be regarded purely as a psychological response for it is also part of an innate biochemical-physiological patterning, probably inherited through our evolutionary pedigree. It has to be stressed, however, that the purpose of REM may not be solely to produce dreams.

Leaving sleep disorders aside, an average night's sleep for an adult contains about twenty-five per cent of REM. Your dream programme has been compared with going to the cinema and watching several trailers and short movies before ending up with one long feature. Dreams have the evanescent quality of morning mist which disappears as the sun rises. Consequently, you can often recall only a few unintelligible scraps from two hours' dreaming. You may remember quite clearly on waking at least part of your last REM phase but this, too, will vanish before long unless a special effort is made to keep it in mind. Subjects woken during REM phases in a sleep laboratory revealed that their dreams through the night were often related to each other, albeit vaguely. Similar tests on nightmare sufferers have shown that when two or more nightmares occurred in a single night the themes were similar or interrelated.

A popular misconception about dream material relates to the effect of external stimuli during an REM period. In the nineteenth century informed minds, inspired by the general craze for scientific research, rejected any irrational explanations for dream and nightmare: heat, cold, external noises, or indigestion were the proper progenitors of dreams, rather than gods and demons. For many years the experiments carried out by the Frenchman Alfred Maury were widely cited to uphold this theory.

In his book *Le sommeil et les rêves*, published in 1861, Maury described some fascinating tests that he had carried out to prove that external stimuli unlocked forgotten memories, thus giving the foundations to dreams. A feather tickling his face provoked dreams of ghastly facial torture; the aroma of eau de cologne induced a dream of a perfume shop in Cairo; the faint ringing noise made by striking tweezers held close to his ears gave him a dream of bells sounding the alarm during the Paris Revolution of 1848. Maury dreamed of the French Revolution, of his being tried and condemned to death. He felt the guillotine descend—and awoke to discover the bed rail had fallen across his neck. This seemed to demonstrate, at least to him and his supporters, just how swiftly—almost instantaneously—a stimulus could be transformed into a full-scale dream fantasy.

Maury was mistaken, but then he lived a long time before the discovery of REM sleep. Experiments in the sleep laboratory demonstrate that the dream is not an instantaneous manifestation. Someone may in fact have been dreaming for half an hour but, on being woken up, will recall only the last few minutes of a dream. An external stimulus, as long as it does not actually waken the sleeper, is cunningly incorporated into the existing dream, whether it is pursuing a nightmare course or a perfectly mundane one; and any resulting activity will take as long as it would in real life.

Awakening a child too abruptly from deep sleep may sometimes provoke a nightmare attack, as if the senses, alerted to some outside disturbance, stimulate the alarm circuit. With this sort of 'bad dream', the child can scream, jump out of bed, suffer hallucinations, and fail to recognize familiar surroundings, although he may not be able to describe very effectively just what it was that terrified him. Perhaps this kind of reaction, unnerving both to witness and sleeper, accounts for some of the primitives' apprehension about angering a sleeping person's soul by too sudden an arousal.

The theories about the functions of sleep, REM, and NREM are various and some or all may eventually prove to contain the definitive answer. Our sleeping habits are acquired and conditioned by environmental and social factors but these do not radically alter the autonomous functioning of that ninety-minute cycle. If sleep were not necessary then it is unlikely that our evolutionary development would have permitted the continuation of a practice that so incapacitates the human organism.

No doubt our earliest ancestors *had* to sleep during darkness. The night contained more than imagined terrors: it was less dangerous to go to sleep than to wander around, practically sightless, and perhaps encounter a truly nocturnal wild animal that was better equipped to cope with night-time conditions. Recent researches into circadian rhythms also demonstrate that sleep normally occurs when most of us are at our least efficient, mentally and physically. At four o'clock in the morning you will find yourself colder, more depressed, and less capable than at four o'clock in the afternoon, even if you have not been deprived of too much sleep.

If REM sleep exists only to provide dreams then we are forced to conclude that newborn babies—and all mammals—enjoy a vivid dreaming life. Obviously we cannot begin to guess at the contents of our babies' dreams, any more than we can imagine those of a monkey or an elephant. However, as soon as the infant can speak we learn about its dreams and nightmares. Sometimes this can happen as early as eighteen months. Just because a child is a late speaker, however, there is no reason to believe that he or she is not dreaming. The same consideration may apply to the tiniest infants and might sometimes explain why they wake up crying so bitterly. Since the nightmare is known to afflict children between the ages of two and five, might it not begin to rear its grisly head even earlier?

At birth an infant's sleep contains fifty per cent REM and it enters this state immediately on falling asleep. In the case of premature birth, seventy-five per cent of a neonate's sleep is of the REM variety and many experts subscribe to the hypothesis that within the womb the foetus actually has nothing but REM sleep. Such an idea is not inconsistent since newborn puppies, kittens, and hamsters have been shown to have only REM sleep.

When we watch the sleep of a tiny baby, a puppy, or a kitten, we are observing REM at work. It reveals a far from tranquil state: the mouth makes sucking movements, the muscles in the face produce all sorts of expressions, and the extremities twitch. Some current thinking tends towards the theory that, in the young, REM may have something to do with stimulating the cortex towards proper maturation, and that only vestiges of this process remain in adults. The ubiquitous guinea-pig adds a certain credence to this for it has very little REM sleep at birth but is born 'mature'.

As an interesting sidelight on the sleep of the newborn, a baby boy appears to undergo greater NREM after circumcision. This suggests to certain experts that NREM may sometimes have a psychic defence role. NREM may also be involved with growth and the regeneration of body tissue. People suffering from minor illnesses, colds, and 'flu are subject to increased NREM sleep.

How long any individual requires to sleep is a topic of endless debate. Babies average around sixteen hours a day; this period decreases with maturity, reaching its lowest point in old age. If sleep's chief function is the restoration of mental and physical processes then this falling-off pattern is easily comprehended. While there seems to be no accredited testimony of people who never sleep, there are reports of individuals who manage quite healthily and happily on only three hours a night, while others feel exhausted unless they get a regular nine or ten hours. Good news for short sleepers: studies show that you tend to be less prone to anxiety. Consolation for long sleepers: you worry more and therefore need the extra sleep.

Sleep requirements can vary in the same individual. When life is pleasant, stress minimal, and work either undemanding or going so well that you are enjoying the extra effort required, then your sleeping-time is likely to decrease. However, when you are going through a bad patch emotionally, changing jobs, or involved in new and difficult work, your sleeping-time increases. In this instance it is highly likely that what you require from sleep is longer REM.

There is some evidence to support the theory that 'naps', which include a high percentage of REM, lift depression and increase energy. Perhaps those highly successful people who claim the ability to 'cat nap' whenever they choose are actually benefiting from a swift burst of REM, which reduces strain. This would certainly make sense in the case of babies and little children, whose every waking hour is bombarded by fresh experiences, which must create enormous turmoil and anxiety. We are inclined to smile fondly at the thought of carefree childhood but we have conveniently forgotten all the stresses that we had to endure as we were forced to adapt to an already structured environment over which we had no control.

Women suffering from premenstrual tension often feel better if they can get more than their normal quota of sleep and tests show that at this point in their monthly cycle their sleep contains increased REM. This tends to suggest that there is a basic need for REM sleep and that it somehow releases tension. Certainly the onset of a period can be accompanied by remarkably vivid bouts of dreaming. Pregnancy, too, requires additional sleep, perhaps due to hormonal changes, but this could also signify the necessity for extra REM.

REM sleep is frequently thought to be connected with learning and remembering. It is postulated that, during REM, new information is stored and some moved from a 'short-term filing system' to a 'long-term' one; this activity may also include discarding useless data acquired during the day in order to leave room for fresh information. An analogy popularly used to describe this process is reprogramming a computer. The learning theory seems particularly applicable in the case of children and it has been noted that among certain mentally deficient youngsters a lower proportion of sleep is devoted to the REM state.

What is perhaps most daunting about the two kinds of sleep is that both permit the intrusion of nightmare, although each moulds it to its own basic characteristics. Initially NREM was regarded as a barren patch where no dreaming took place but then research revealed that dreams of a sort do in fact grow there. They have been compared to background or secondary thinking in waking life, when there is neither a problem nor a daydream occupying the attention.*

NREM dreams are described as sensible and conceptual, more concerned with ordinary daily life than with playing complex charades. At the lighter levels of sleep the NREM dream is pleasant, unfraught and undemanding. However, it is even more ephemeral than its REM counterpart, so you may be left with the feeling that you only dreamed you were dreaming! When fragments are remembered these seem to relate to the rest of the night's dream cycle, rather as if during NREM the mind is trying to work out what the preceding REM fantasy intended.

Some evidence exists to support the theory that people with analytical minds, who generally repress the more fantastic aspects of dreaming and living, tend to recall a dream if woken during NREM, as if this is the sort of mental exercise they prefer to cope with. The same individuals will deny knowledge of REM dreams, possibly because these are too extraordinary to be rendered into sense.

---

* I am sure you recognize this condition: perhaps while sitting in a train with nothing to read and feeling a host of commonplace thoughts flowing through your mind, although you are making no effort to shape or impel them.

Sleep disturbances, such as somnambulism, sleep-talking, and bed-wetting can occur at the NREM state, especially during the first descent into that deep valley—Stage 4. These are afflictions associated chiefly with childhood but some researchers believe sleepwalking is a family complaint. One sleep expert reported a slightly 'black-humoured' episode: at a Christmas reunion a whole family gathered in the dining-room one night—but while they were all *asleep*. Surely the perfect setting for a spine-chilling movie.

Other manifestations during one's time at Stage 4, or just as one is waking from it, are the nightmare and the night terror. The latter—*pavor nocturnus*—attacks children and resembles hallucination or a 'waking dream'. It lasts for several minutes, whereas the nightmare is of briefer duration. Both are typified by their overwhelming sensation of terror and a distinct dearth of reportable content. Sufferers feel themselves to be the victim of violent persecution and may shriek wildly and jump out of bed. On waking they are not easily reassured. Confusion reigns so absolutely that familiar faces, objects, and environment are not immediately recognizable and the individual may continue to hallucinate. Although the NREM nightmare is a truly horrific experience, fortunately it is one that can be forgotten next day. Small children may have no recollection whatsoever of their sleep being ferociously wrecked—while the adults who came to their aid remain bleary-eyed from lack of sleep!

One of the purposes proposed for REM dreaming is to ensure that a person remains asleep at the lightest level. The thread provided to weave the fantastic dream tapestry is so rich and variable that repressed fears, thoughts, and desires can be transformed into dramatic situations less likely to disturb and arouse. The NREM nightmare may possibly have such an overpowering impact because it cannot use symbolism to disguise or temper underlying hates, dreads, and painful memories but allows them to erupt undisguised—'red, in tooth and claw'—and something unbearable to a sleeper of any age.

The nightmare or adult 'anxiety' dream haunting REM sleep is another species of monster and, on the whole, one the dreamer seems better equipped to cope with, perhaps because it is especially rich in hallucinatory content. Daylight, however, does not banish memory of that particular intruder but its effect depends on the basic psychological state of the adult and, for children, their ordinary lives; naturally, where these are unhappy, the nocturnal experiences will leave a deeper and longer-lasting impression on the infant mind.

One of REM's chief features is the inhibition of motor activity and this may well account for those horrendous fantasies of being rooted to the spot while being pursued by some dreadful creature, or that suffocating sensation of the incubus crouching on the sleeper's chest. Lying in the darkness, unsure whether you are dreaming or awake, and finding you can't move an inch or breathe properly, is a most appalling experience. Though it lasts no more than a few seconds it feels like a lifetime—and one that is about to be brought to an unholy conclusion by some murderous assailant! In that twilight zone of sleep, an awareness of this actual physical condition must be more than sufficient to over-emphasize a dream's terror content. Interestingly enough, the experiences of some narcoleptic sufferers may throw a little light on this dark tale: they relate how, during those 'frozen' hallucinatory sessions, they often sense themselves to be victims of intruders who have broken in, and against whom they cannot lift so much as a finger in self-defence.

Since the nightmare occurs at the same times as other sorts of dream that fail to awaken the sleeper, the cause appears to be a mixture of physiology and psychology. If the dream's role is to keep us asleep, then the nightmare's should be the exact opposite: to arouse us to fear and danger. Of course, by the clear light of day, it is easy for an adult to rationalize these dangers as coming from within and to believe that the fear they induced has no sound basis. For a child, however, the borderline between the imaginary and the real is very hard to define so it is hardly astonishing that the nightmare is such a feature of childhood: the stage when we are unrelentingly made aware of our helplessness in the face of every real or imagined threat and peril. In one sense the brief years of immaturity mirror those eons that represent humankind's childhood. The nightmare's alerting and awakening mechanism may well be part of our evolutionary inheritance, dating from the time when the senses violated the organism's sleep in order to arouse it to an actual external danger which threatened its life.

We have completed the map of sleep and marked in the roads used by dream and nightmare. Now it is time to investigate how other ages and cultures have viewed this continent. Although some of their beliefs and practices may cause us to smile disparagingly, the tradition to which they contribute is as much part of our heritage as is the physiology of sleep and dreaming.

# The Demonic Tradition

*That fiend that goth a-night*
*Women full oft to guile,*
*Incubus is named by right;*
*And guileth men other while,*
*Succubus is that wight.*
FROM CAXTON'S CHRONICLE

Once upon a time—although exactly when is debatable—humankind came into existence. Unless you are a stickler for one or other of the creation myths you will agree this could not have been an overnight transformation but was a long evolutionary process. From then onwards there could be no completely fresh beginnings for successive communities and civilizations; indeed, memories and traditions must also have remained from the primeval state which, although not passed on by word of mouth, were already a part of the physiological, instinctual, and dream heritage.

Of course, theologians, philosophers, and reformers—whatever the century or society—need to believe that their current ideas will provide a totally new start but at best they can only superimpose upon whatever went before, so in turn to supply the base for what comes next.

Cultures restructured by others have a remarkable knack of melding the indigenous with the alien, be it to trick out African deities in the guise of Spanish Catholic saints or to imbue a conquering political dogma with the very definite flavour of the 'liberated' (or 'subjugated') people. Christianity not only absorbed its founder's Jewish customs but also took on some of the practices of converts, and in its earlier centuries accepted dream incubation within churches to promote healing as well as the more sinister doctrine that on witches and demons lay the responsibility for the nightmare's invasion of sleep. By doing this the followers of the teachings of the Galilean carpenter were actually preserving the magical beliefs of all the most ancient recorded civilizations.

Consequently, what even the best educated and adjusted among us believe may be compared to a vast palimpsest. Confronted by irrational and highly personal terror occasioned by the nightmare, most individuals will briefly pierce the veneer of up-to-date scientific and psychological explanations to confront the complex archaic designs beneath. Thus, to realize a better perspective on the 'mare', ancient and modern, we need to peel away the tidy twentieth-century façade and gaze far beyond into the dark and intricate patterning of the shared past.

Wake abruptly from a disturbing dream and the borderline between fantasy and reality seems very indistinct. You will not immediately sieze upon the reassuring knowledge that it is all the fault of your digestive system, or that your personal problems are rearing their many heads, or even that you were travelling through a particular area of sleep. For a second, you may believe there is a malign something lurking in the darkness around your bed. Unable to make sense of the phenomenon, you might, next day, insist that what happened could not have been a dream but was a real visit by a supernatural being. Then you will be in a position to empathize with all the preceding generations of sleepers who have encountered the fiends that walk the night.

Even in this century, under certain circumstances, the nightmare can exercise a vivid and lasting effect. An Algerian clerk gave himself up to the police for murdering his adored wife and children. When the authorities investigated this crime they were amazed to find the victims alive and well, albeit anxious as to why husband and father had left home so early. Imagine the 'murderer's' shock and joy: he had confessed to a crime committed only in a dream. Sometimes this false sense of reality can have

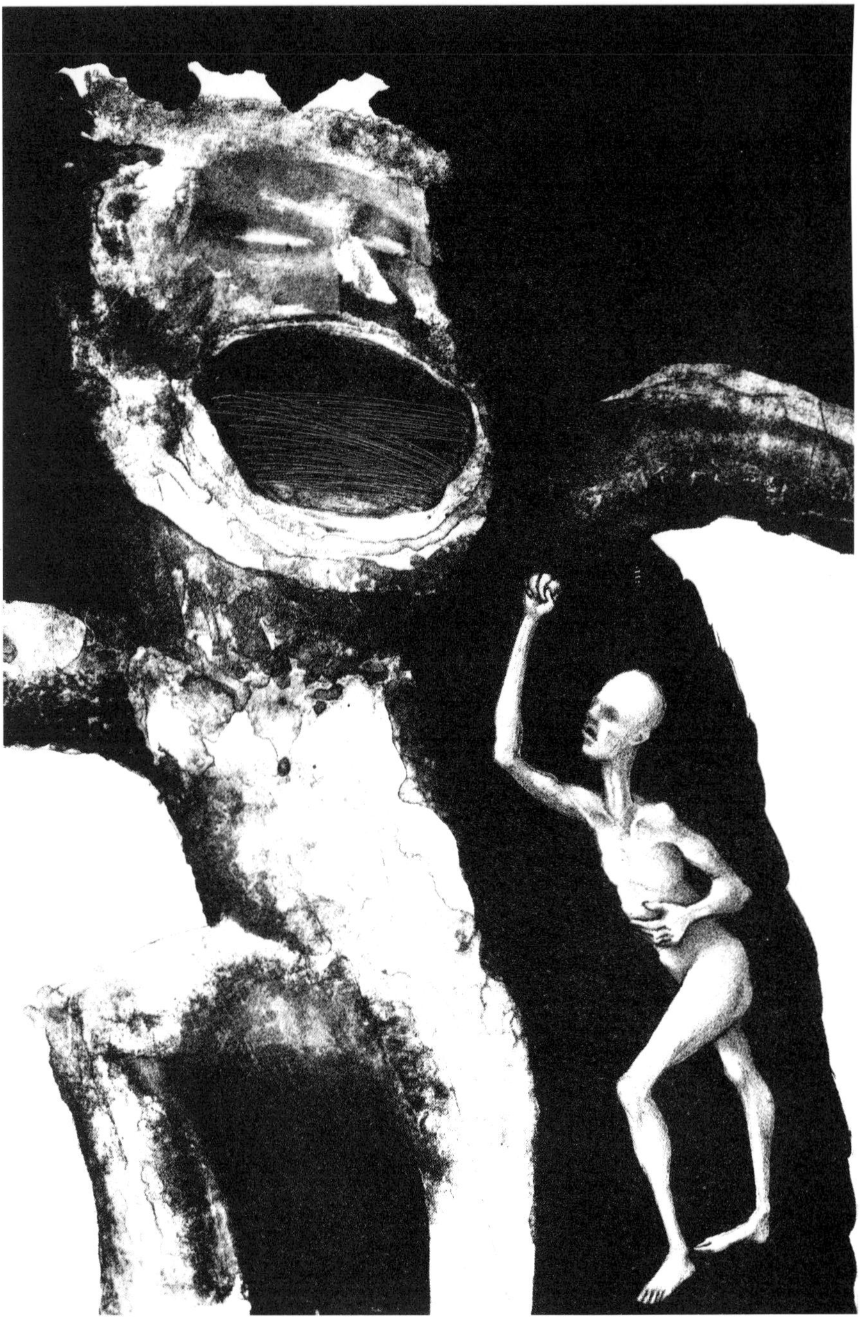

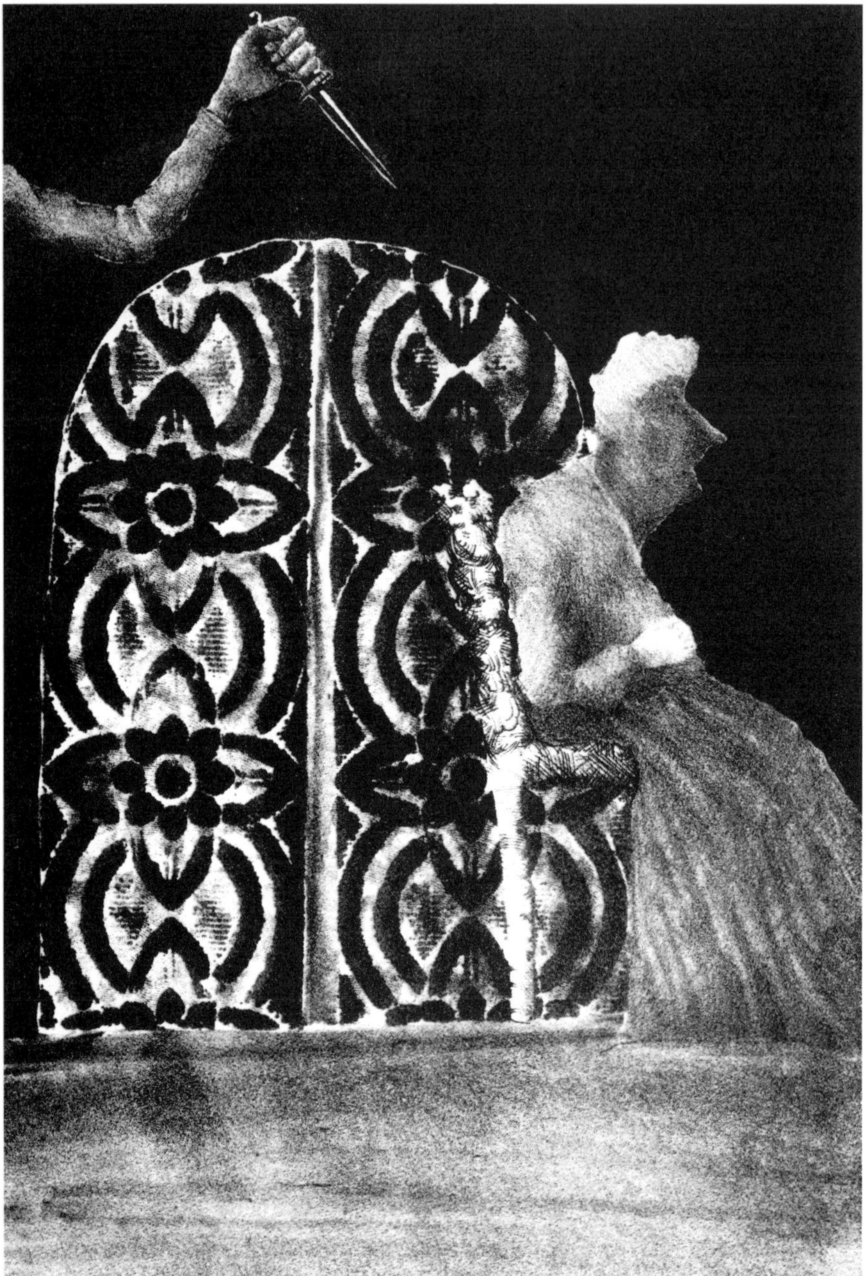

more ghastly results, like the young Frenchman who, in the grip of a violent nightmare, threw himself to his death from a fifth-floor window, despite his distraught wife's attempts to pacify him.

The average modern dreamer, fortunately, does not usually consider dreams or nightmares to be real, predictive, or of particular value in the daytime existence of individual or community. Occasionally, when someone's disaster or assassination nightmare comes true, the majority of us choose coincidence as the logical explanation or suspect that the original account was tampered with to give it greater veracity. In these attitudes we differ from ancient, primitive, or superstitious peoples who believe that the events in good and bad dreams genuinely occur during the night, or will do soon, and therefore must be taken quite as seriously as any waking occurrence.

While modern parents soothe away a child's nightmare with 'It's only a nasty dream ...', one Mexican Indian tribe encourages even its youngest members to recount their dreams, which suggests to the sceptical mind that some of the little dreamers may embellish their accounts to impress peers and elders. For, where the dream plays such a significant role, its most relevant aspects will be learned early, along with basic myths and skills.

It is worthwhile to point out at this juncture that the importance placed on certain types of dream is conditioned by a society's deepest fears and beliefs. If you dream of a dead relative the effect will probably depend on your feelings for the deceased, but if you belonged to one of the communities which hold that those who have passed on use dreams to advise, warn, or even carry off the living, your reactions would not be merely sorrowful or sanguine.\*

Certain preoccupations never quite change for human beings, primitive or sophisticated. What purpose do we serve by living

---

\* Personally, I am relieved not to live among the Zinacantecs of Mexico, who take their dreams seriously enough to rouse the entire household to discuss them and to be advised on how they should be treated. It would be surprising if a trivial report in the middle of the night did not provoke the family's sleepy wrath!

and what happens to us when we die? These questions are the cornerstones of all religion and, together with myth, ritual, and even dance, are the fruits of humanity's oldest spiritual experience—the dream.

If dreaming offers a positive vision of light then the nightmare provides the very antithesis. In its shackles all are forced to make the acquaintance of fear, evil, and cruelty. Surely the concept of damnation, in every sort of faith, was fathered by the nightmare.

It is relatively safe to assume that humankind has always dreamed but to say what form those nocturnal fantasies took, and how they were regarded, is more speculative, at least until some method of recording them was evolved. Our only method of determining the possible contents of prehistoric dreams is to examine those tribes that are unaffected by our customs and knowledge and are therefore closer to the Stone Age in outlook. Some may argue that the nightmare is a product of guilt and repression, particularly about sexual matters, and so was unlikely to disturb that blissful Golden Age enjoyed by our earliest forebears. To support this theory they will cite the 'happy savage' who, unscarred by the burdens of our jet-propelled age, is free of the anxieties and conflicts that wrack the civilized mind during sleep. However, an inspection of the dreams of these so-called 'happy savages' yields a rich crop of nightmare material and suggests that the cave dweller must have been equally in awe of the dark dream's power.

Although names, details, and rituals vary, not just from continent to continent but also among tribes sharing the same landmass, the most common primitive nightmare themes involve spirits, ghosts of dead relatives, animal-headed humans, or monstrous animals. These chase, attack, suck blood, or try to devour their victims. Even if a deceased ancestor proves friendly and keeps paying nocturnal calls, this is considered just as hazardous as more menacing behaviour for it signifies that the ghost is attempting to lure the sleeper away to join the dead. An American Indian medicine man will recommend that the sufferer from this sort of nightmare be daubed with ashes, refrain from food and drink, and live in a special little house for a few days to convince the ghost that the victim is already dead. This treatment seems efficacious—at least for members of the same tribe.

There is no reason to doubt that our earliest ancestors experienced similar nightmares and practised various apotropaic rites. Although we do not have contemporary reports to substantiate this theory, the prehistoric artists may have bequeathed us clues more telling than words. Clearly paintings and carvings discovered on cave walls, or on stone and bone artefacts, were executed for reasons more significant than decoration; yet did they always mirror the practices and aspirations of real life or did some of them depict nocturnal experiences invisible by day?

The renowned 'Sorcerer' from Les Trois Frères in the Pyrenees may be a portrait of an actual shaman, clad in animal skins, but it could as easily be a representation of the monstrous half-human figure that has pursued countless generations of sleepers in the nightmare. Indeed, the dream may have engendered reality, its power and terror copied by priest or leader to command the tribe. Are all those curious engravings of distorted and bestialized human faces merely the products of a prehistoric cartoonist's sense of satire, or are they phantoms conjured from sleep?

Exactly why those nightmare images were fashioned must remain an enigma. That the artist was compelled to spend long hours in the cave's chill, black depths seems obvious, and surely sleeping in such a highly charged atmosphere, where the soul must have felt itself completely at the mercy of the darkest forces, would have been sufficient to initiate the most alarming fantasies (with or without the hallucinatory substances which some anthropologists believe were ingested or inhaled as part of the ritual associated with painting). Indeed, the artist may have been not just a craftsman but the official tribal dreamer and visionary who, in sleep, visited that unseen plane from where all power stemmed. Inspirational dreams, resulting in paintings and designs, are quite common in many cultures and feature particularly in ancient Chinese art; and there seems no sound reason why this practice did not commence at the dawn of history.

The invention of the various forms of writing puts our hunt for the nightmare's genealogy on a less hypothetical basis, as well as giving us an opportunity to compare archaic beliefs with primitive and superstitious ones existing in our own time. Those ancient papyri and tablets chronicle not only contemporary dreams, their interpretations and causes, but also far older material inherited orally from the unlettered ages.

They show, too, a rough consensus of opinion on the nature of the nightmare, which could be any one of the following, or a permutation of all or some: a malign, supernatural entity crouched on the bed, like the Teutonic *alp* or **mara**—its shape and behaviour dependent on the beliefs of the community; the work of dark gods, goddesses, and demons, pursuing their own nefarious ends; ghosts of the dead with equally unhallowed intentions; or the result of enchantment by witches and magicians, acting out of personal malice and jealousy or at the request of an ill-wisher. The nightmare's power was never to be underestimated, and always dreaded. Magical and religious countermeasures—as complex as a particular religion's structure—were in the hands of powerful priests and shamans, the ancestors of medical practitioners.

Later civilizations, and a host of disparate tribes, were to share these views and use the same cures. Indeed, you can still discover traces of ancient beliefs in areas that are accessible to the ordinary holiday-maker. In rural Greece, *ephialtes* (the old Greek word for incubus and nightmare and a term used by medical men well into the last century) is considered a supernatural visitation and one which particularly afflicts 'light-shadowed' folk. Such people are thought of as 'second-sighted', and consequently more prone to see visions of pre-Christian spirits. Given the superabundance of Greek mythology, they must find every sacred pagan site crowded. Not only do the 'light-shadowed' have nightmares, they also suffer from insomnia and talk and cry out when they are asleep. One Greek Orthodox priest's ingenious explanation for their problem is that somehow they were not baptized properly.

If you feel that something went wrong at your own christening that makes you see and hear things at night, perhaps you'd care to try out a Greek remedy: before going to sleep tuck some bread and rue beneath your pillow. Should this prove ineffective, you could attempt an ancient Babylonian cure. You require a special amulet decorated with a picture of the devil causing the nightmare—always supposing you have pinned down which one it is. You also need a priest (Babylonian, naturally) skilled in rituals that expel the disease demons, who must recite:

> That one which has approached the house scares me from my bed, rends me, makes me see nightmares. To the god, Bine, gatekeeper of the Underworld, may they appoint him by the decree of Ninurta, prince of the Underworld, by the decree of Marduk who dwells in Esagila in Babylon. Let door and bolt know that I am under the protection of the two Lords.

Although the proper names sound alien to our ears, the wish contained in the incantation is much the same as in the old Cornish prayer:

> From ghoulies and ghosties and long-leggety beasties
> And things that go bump in the night, Good Lord, deliver us!

The orgiastic characteristics of many nightmares can be traced back to ancient Greek mythology. Ephialtes (meaning 'he who leaps upon') was the leader of the Titans—the monstrous earth-born giants who attacked the Olympians. One myth states that these monsters can be overcome only through a magical herb—ephialton—a remedy against the nightmare. Another ancient tradition urged anyone threatened by an erotic nightmare to invoke the Saviour Heracles. This rite arose from the story that Apollo aimed an arrow at Ephialtes' left eye while invoking Heracles, who put another arrow in the giant's right eye which vanquished him utterly. The nightmare contains the attributes of individual Titans: one was a fierce wind that brought bad dreams and inclinations to murder and rape; another, the 'stampede of horses' seems a link with the Mare-headed goddess, the bringer of terror dreams in Nordic mythology.

Tradition also has it that the nightmare in ancient mythology and British legend is associated with the number nine, hence Shakespeare's reference in *Lear* to: 'He met the night-mare, and her nine-fold', which curiously enough Coleridge was later to misquote as: 'The Night-Mare, and her nine foals'.

Not only has the nightmare always inspired a dread that does not fade with daybreak, it has frequently been seen as the harbinger of disease and death as well as unwelcome sexual sensations, its effects making the healthy sick, and worsening the condition of anyone already ill. The handsome and friendly young man who appears in Indian dreams and tickles the sleeper is not a desirable erotic fantasy but the bringer of leprosy; and a particularly loathsome female ghost attacks with rheumatism the joints of those who dream of her.

While terror, suffocation, and a sense of total helplessness characterize the nightmare proper, we have to bear in mind that the images associated with the different sensations vary according to culture. Your idea of an ogre will not be the same as that described by an African bushman but both are terrifying. As if deliberately to confuse us, not all nightmares appear as instantly alarming but some of the pleasant ones are as malevolent as the openly hideous.

In one North Borneo tribe the nightmare incubus—regarded as a monkey or some other evil animal—transforms itself into an attractive man to have intercourse with sleeping women. Not only is the nightmare believed to cause miscarriages and all sorts of misery and havoc, it also possesses the ability to fertilize so it is no wonder that a master shaman is called upon to cope with it.

Should an Indian dream of a man dancing in the middle of a road, wearing a crimson turban, dhoti, and feathers, this colourful entertainer would be most unwelcome. He is the god of night, who turns his victims into buffaloes before devouring them. Sometimes the dancing deity prefers to send a monstrous emissary

(also a cannibal), who overlays and stifles the sleepe[r]
beginning its feast on human flesh. When such a nightma[re]
the victim is warned that there is no time to consult a s[...]
black animal must be sacrificed immediately in darkne[ss]
cultures share an Indian belief that the overwhelming sense of
oppression and terror is sometimes the work of gods or devils of
storm.

In contrast, Australian Aborigines' nightmares do not seem quite so horrific but obviously they are for the dreamers. One spirit creeps close to the fire and anyone seeing it in sleep is advised to jump up, sieze a lighted brand, and hurl it towards the nightmare while uttering various imprecations. If the spirit has manifested only for the purpose of stealing light it should promptly depart, well satisfied.

Koin is another nightmare demon that disguises itself as an Aborigine, painted with pipe-clay and carrying a fire stick. Unless the sleeper's companions recognize his true identity and drive him off by shouting, Koin will drag his victim to his own fireside in the bush. In true nightmare fashion the dreamer is prevented from struggling or crying out for assistance by the strangling sensation. Presumably the terror of this dream arises from a belief that the sleeper will not return to the living world. With daylight Koin vanishes and mysteriously the dreamer finds himself back among his own people—rather like the African and European witches who admitted flying off to unholy nocturnal revels but who woke in the morning in their own beds, unable to distinguish dream from reality even to save their skins.

The image of nightmare that has provoked widespread controversy (to say nothing of prurient curiosity) is the incubus or succubus: here a grotesque dream is accompanied by feelings of voluptuousness mingled with dread. The demon lover whose outrageous attentions are impossible to repel still exercises a universal appeal, so it is hardly surprising that this is the side of the nightmare that has most fascinated demonologists, writers, and artists down the centuries.

From the current plethora of erotic books, magazines, movies, and mind-boggling accessories you might be forgiven in thinking that we, the twentieth-century inhabitants, actually pioneered the wilder shores of sex. Not a bit of it. Although the concept of coition for the sake of procreation only has been vociferously recommended in every age, it has never won humankind's basic allegiance. Taking the prehistoric cave drawings as the earliest evidence, we have to accept that sex—in all its possible *and* impossible deviations—has occupied a good deal of our thoughts from the outset, even when this did not conform with official dictates.

For the secular and religious, it was the nightmare's highly charged erotic associations and effects—whether disguised or overt—that excited fascination, repugnance ... and the imagination. Remember, most of them were seeing it not as a fantasy within the sleeper's mind but as an actual happening. Modern purveyors of 'sex aids' and under-the-counter pornography would be amazed at some of the frankly obscene capabilities medieval and celibate clerics ascribed to incubus and succubus—and went on to describe in almost loving detail.

It was not a pornographer but the sixteenth-century Inquisitor, Sylvester Prierias, who produced the ingenious theory of an incubus possessing a double penis 'so that he abuses himself simultaneously with both organs'. Given such an unfair advantage over mortals, there was no sexual feat that these diabolical bedmates could not perform—at least in a nightmare—which was why they were often as welcome as they were feared. One man claimed to have slept with the same succubus for forty years, obviously to their mutual satisfaction, for he said he preferred to die in prison rather than renounce her. Priests acknowledged, too, that some of the young girls who came to them for spiritual aid, and described in the greatest details how an incubus entertained them, were not always overly enthusiastic to be severed from the demon lover.

... I came to the opinion that in spite of her denials she had given

> the demon some indirect encouragement. Indeed, she
> always forewarned of his coming by a violent over-excita[tion]
> of the sexual organs ... instead of having recourse to pra[yer]
> she ran straight to her room and threw herself on her bed

We do not need to be told that the more forbidden the fruit the more enticing it begins to appear. Medieval churchmen seemed blissfully unaware of this fact, which shaped their own motives and judgements. They were like doctors suffering from a disease with which they infected those they insisted they could cure. While claiming to do battle against the incubus they were its best publicity agents. All the sermons and writings on demonic depravity fostered morbid fascination. In an age when physical and mental suffering was commonplace and no outlet existed for the energies or fantasies of most folk, little wonder that men and women were continually plagued with these nightmares: to travel by broomstick to a feast presided over by the devil, eat as much as you want, dance, and engage in every sort of sexual commerce—although only in a vivid dream—might be terrifying and damning ... but it was also thrilling, especially if your daytime existence was just a rural treadmill.

If we accept that too much sex and violence on our television screens has a deleterious effect on the impressionable, and that small children often suffer nightmares after a scary story or movie, then we can better comprehend how people fed on an almost undiluted diet of diabolical deeds and witchcraft were bound to dream and fantasize about such things, especially when there was no authority to consult except equally superstitious theologians who continued to provide the details. In view of the painstaking lengths some of these celibate gentlemen went to in order to get confessions of sexual encounters with demons from, for the most part, young girls—and what salacious accounts they were—we are bound to wonder about their own inhibitions ... and nightmares.

We might enjoy a good Rabelaisian laugh at the expense of the credulity of those centuries, when if there were not an incubus in your bed then there was probably a witch under it, were it not for the terrible fate meted out to those who aroused envy or suspicion in their neighbours. In 1468 at Bologna a man was condemned to death for running a brothel full of succubi.

The testimonies of those accused of witchcraft were crammed with details suggested by their inquisitors; since one of the requisite pieces of proof was sexual intercourse with a demon, pathetic creatures were tortured until they confessed; no doubt some of the victims believed in the authenticity of their confession on the evidence of their own nightmares.

During the three centuries that the witchcraft mania disgraced European culture, those men and women accused of being witches were caught by what we would now call a 'Catch 22': even if it could be proved that the confessions extracted from them were based only on a nightmare, the very fact that they recalled the details made them as guilty as if the events in the dream had been reality. In *Leviathan* Thomas Hobbes seemed to sum it up:

> As for witches, I think not that their witchcraft is a real power; but yet that they are justly punished for the false belief they have that they can do such mischief . . .

Those were not times to raise your voice too loudly in rational dissent; to insist that the incubus was nothing but a dream could lead to a charge of heresy—or of being in league with the devil, for why else come to his defence?

Where society has transformed a very basic human activity into something dirty and shameful, the emotionally unstable and suggestible are bound to suffer from some type of sexual nightmare. This need not contain anything recognizably erotic but can be filled with sadistic and masochistic images, and creatures emanating cruelty and inhuman strength, such as vampires, werewolves, and other monsters. That such a dream may waken the sleeper with some of the symptoms associated with intercourse—such as palpitation, sweating, and genital secretion or an emission of semen—is not unusual, but totally inadmissible in the individual who believes that sex is evil and is torn between desire for and dread of it.

The most popularly held theory about the incubus or succubus type of nightmare is that it is always a manifestation of repressed sexual appetites, yet this does not allow for terrifying dreams that have no erotic content, which this theory insists are cunningly disguised. Nor does the longing to make love inspire horror in all men and women, whatever society has tried to tell them, although this may well result in explicitly sensual dreams; current research reveals that sex is the most common topic of our contemporary dreaming.

Undoubtedly the lascivious nightmares and visions of early Christian ascetics must be seen as the outcome of rigorous repression. With their bodies and minds weakened by fasting, isolation, and every kind of physical privation, it was no wonder that natural instincts surged past the censorship mechanism in sleep to erupt in the most extraordinary dreams. Ignorant of their own unconscious, these holy hermits could only believe a diabolical external force was endeavouring to corrupt their chastity. Fearful of their own desires, and even more so of the power of the female to excite them, it is not surprising that the naked woman was a recurrent feature of their nocturnal fantasies.

Poor St Anthony of Egypt complained that the devil kept throwing filthy thoughts in his direction at night, as well as assuming all the characteristics of a woman. As soon as his disciple, St Hilary, shut his eyes to sleep, he found himself surrounded by nude beauties. As long as you were sufficiently strong-willed and devout you could get the better of these unclothed nymphs: St Hippolytus had the presence of mind to throw a chasuble over one nymph, who promptly became a corpse, demonstrating how the devil had animated a lump of dead flesh to ensnare the righteous. Nor were pious females immune from such attacks: St Margaret of Cortona was followed about her cell by a devil singing dirty songs and encouraging her to join in. Eventually her tears and prayers expelled the unholy gleeman.

History asserts that only one of those sorely tempted saints actually yielded to the blandishments of the demon lover, and he died within a month, worn out by her excesses! Yet their fight with temptation was obviously often a closely fought contest and fear of defeat inspired the Ambrosian hymn: 'Let all dreams and phantasms of the night . . . fade away, lest our bodies be polluted.' More explicit was the seventeenth-century prayer composed by the Franciscan Father Candidus Brognolus that the devil 'would not be able to molest me in phantasies, either in the imagination or in the flesh, especially in those members designed for procreation'.

Many of the young men and women who took religious vows had little or no vocation but were confined to a cloistered existence for family or economic reasons. With all this involuntary stifling of youthful instincts, houses of religion proved ideal hunting grounds for the nightmare. Paracelsus, who believed demons were a by-product of menstrual blood, stated firmly that convents were seminaries of nightmares!

Only *after* she had been handled over-familiarly by a certain Father Picard did Sister Marie-du-St-Sacrament, a nun of Louviers, experience the strangest fantasies, and in sleep felt that a

> tremendous weight rested on my shoulders so that I thought I was going to choke. I dragged myself . . . to the cell of the Mother Superior, and I felt this weight fall to the ground with a large noise . . . I myself was thrown down and injured, with blood gushing from my nose and mouth . . .

That all the accounts of nuns being visited by incubi, so that in the morning they found 'themselves polluted as if they had commingled with a man', were occasioned purely by nightmares fuelled on repression and hysterical imaginings, is difficult to accept. Since nobody could interrogate the demon, it was pretty safe for one fifteenth-century bishop to explain how an incubus had *borrowed* his appearance to climb into bed with a young nun, and 'in lickerish language declared lyingly that he was the bishop'. Given the climate of opinion then existing, the convent never queried the bishop's alibi.

Not for several centuries were many seriously prepared to regard the incubus as partly a product of an over-stimulated fancy, partly the perfect excuse for illicit relations and gross perversions. Thomas Aquinas came up with an ingenious theory: as demons were not human, they could not procreate along normal lines, but collected semen (another authority insisted only of the best quality) from young men in their dreams and used this to impregnate young women during theirs.

Such examples of sexual repression were scarcely to be found in many ancient civilizations where fertility rites played a significant part in religion. Yet Babylon, which recognized temple prostitution as a normal practice, also feared the nightmare succubus. This was Lilitu, a female spirit who visited men in their sleep and forced her libidinous attentions on them. From such couplings were born faceless and destructive nightmare monsters. Christian demonologists also believed that monstrous births resulted from union between demon and human—which must have made it traumatic for those delivered of less than perfect babies.

According to Cabbalistic teaching, much of which was inherited from Mesopotamian and Egyptian sources, man's erotic dreams were caused by the succubus. Hebrew tradition has it that offspring born of this nightmare hovered about a man's sick bed waiting to greet their father on his death. For the Jews, who absorbed many of their neighbours' and captors' customs, Lilitu became Lilith, traditionally Adam's first wife, and also 'the terror by night' mentioned in Psalm 91, against whom God's truth 'shall be thy shield and buckler'.

The Vulgate Latin Bible translated Lilith into Lamia—an ordinary Latin word for 'witch', but her antecedents and later associations made the actual meaning far more complicated. The original Lamia seems to have been a Libyan queen seduced by that Olympian playboy, Zeus. His jealous consort, Hera, killed the children of this love affair and transformed Lamia's beauty into ugliness. Consequently the wretched creature began slaying other people's children and could resume her former loveliness only when lying with men and drinking their blood.

Those indefatigable demonologists confused matters and interchanged Lamia with vampire, nightmare, and the eternal fatal woman—figures that can be found throughout the world's folklore and literature. One or more of her attributes constantly crept into accusations against women standing trial during the long night of the European witch hunt: pacts with the devil to gratify monumental sexual desires, the stealing and eating of children, draining blood and semen from men—even extremes in beauty and ugliness could be grounds for suspicion. Wherever a belief in witchcraft still obtains you will find similar charges levelled at women.

It was a pity that other experts did not imitate the down-to-earth approach of the thirteenth-century writer Gervais of Tilbury, who identified Lamia as a 'simple nocturnal hallucination ... which disturbs the minds of sleepers and oppresses with weight ...' Clearly he could distinguish between nightmare and reality when he wrote:

> Others assert they have seen such imaginations in dream so vividly that they seemed to be awake. But I am moved against this because I know women, my neighbours, who have told me they had seen with shame at night the naked organs of males and females.

Not even today's most arrant misogynist would hint that nightmare was somehow woman's fault or that she, being the weaker in moral fibre, was more prone to this night-time affliction. Yet in earlier times nightmare went scaly hand in velvet glove with that very curious misogyny which culminated in the persecution of so-called witches, who were credited with sending nightmares to others and consorting with the devil in their own.

For the celibate, the female was always suspect, liable to be led astray by Satan and take men with her. She had, it was alleged, a more licentious appetite and thus was easily seduced by the nightmare—hence the incubi having to outnumber succubi by nine to one! The extension of such an argument was that, were it not for females—mortal and supernatural—men could the better resist temptation, therefore it was in society's interest to keep her in a subservient position. It is impossible for us to pursue the provenance of the nightmare without attempting to discover how this suspicion against women arose, long before Christianity adopted and enlarged upon it.

Initially, woman exercised one incontestable talent—the ability to procreate. For a long age the fertility of humans, crops, and domestic animals and all the associated crafts and rituals were under her aegis, so that the perpetuity of society depended on her. The gradual awareness that babies were the fruit of sexual intercourse began to diminish female status. Male deities unsurped the goddesses' supremacy but many of the early civilizations continued to demonstrate remnants of the older beliefs in retaining priestesses and goddesses chiefly concerned with the interests of women and children.

Although she was no longer supreme, man was still shackled to woman's sexual allure. What had once been a magic to revere became feared as a potential threat to the new order. Men might be overthrown by the exciter of passions over which they lacked absolute control. As Hobbes pointed out in *Leviathan*, the 'reputation of power is power'.

Judaism strove to preserve its sternly monotheistic and masculine philosophy by execrating the rituals of its pantheistic neighbours. None of Israel's daughters were to be allowed religious responsibility lest they bring back the bad old ways. Christianity followed this lead, particularly in deploring the sexual laxity of pagans. It eulogized as saintly those who embraced chastity, which became so prized that anything other smacked of sin.

We have to understand that these concepts, which took centuries to evolve, were not being consciously considered in individual minds but became locked into the human 'computer' along with far older instincts.

Attitudes to the nightmare, to women, and even to witchcraft might have been quite different from what we have already glimpsed because, until the thirteenth century, the Church theoreticians took what can only be called a balanced view. They held that the belief in witchcraft was pagan and consequently heretical—and, anyway, acts of witches were only illusions or fantasies, originating in dreams. At last the nightmare was being seen for what it was.

But, alas, not for long.

Rationalism was obliterated by those whose reputations as scholars might have led us to expect better. Thomas Aquinas was one of the authorities who bequeathed to later ages the justification for treating witch and nightmare as real. Witchcraft, night-flying (especially by broomstick), intercourse with demons, transformation into animals—in fact all those ancient images and beliefs that are reflected time and again in nightmares—were held to be true. Anyone who suffered bad dreams and then became ill or died in mysterious circumstances, as did the Earl of Derby in 1594, had to be the victim of a witch. Indeed, you had to believe in these delusions or run the risk of being accused of heresy. The Church had effected a complete about-turn. The negative powers had triumphed and the nightmare stalked abroad in all its dark and terrifying majesty for it had been granted an irrefutable permit.

This link between nightmare and witchcraft has to be part of humankind's common heritage because similar beliefs are paralleled in so many unrelated cultures. Accounts and explanations of bad dreams in such divergent areas as Africa and Mexico could have been taken straight out of the confessions and depositions from sixteenth-century European witch trials. The nightmares of children and adults are not only the evidence of witchcraft but actual experiences of it. Any untoward behaviour in a sleeping child is feared as a symptom of bewitchment. In West Cameroon there is a taboo against waking a child too suddenly from a very deep sleep—lest it be caused by witchcraft. This ties in neatly with what we know about the physiology of sleeping: a child roused too abruptly from Stage-4 sleep may well exhibit violent

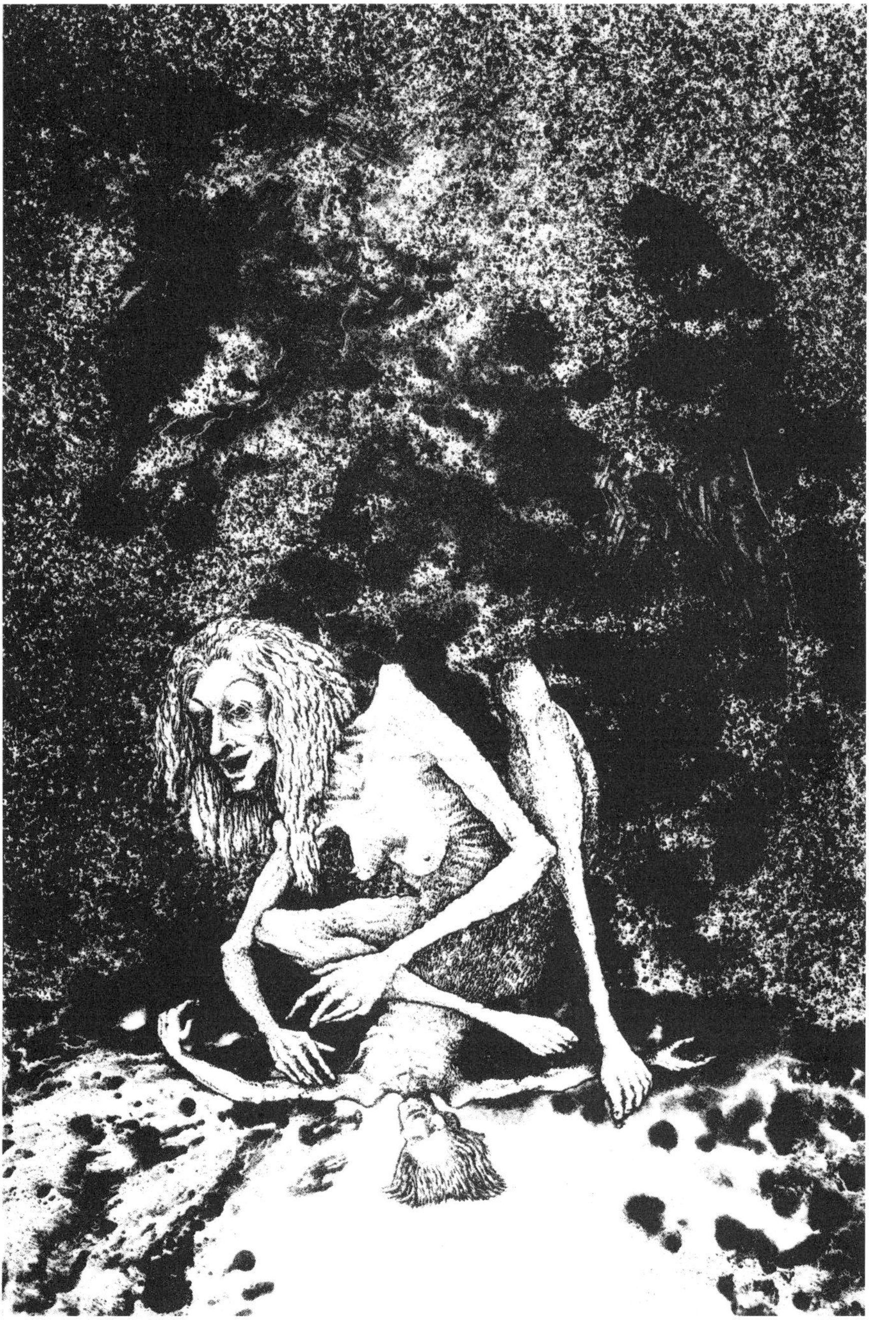

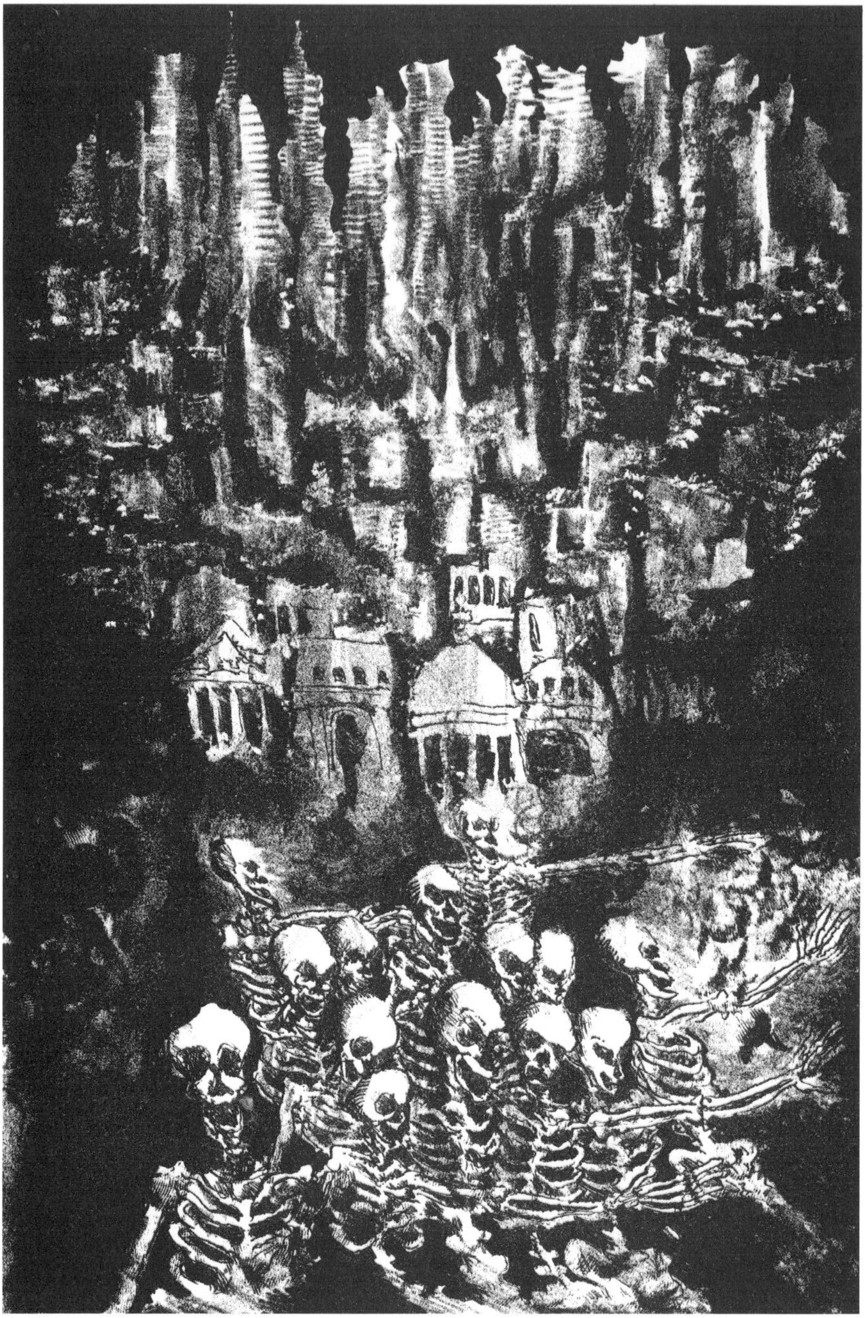

night terrors—proof enough of witchcraft to another age or society.

An almost fanatical dread of witchcraft sends people to the witchdoctor, shaman or medicine man, for many believe that witches are trying to force them to join their company through the medium of the nightmare. Yet for an African to see witchcraft in a dream may prove a positive waking peril, since it could invite the suspicions of neighbours that the dreamer is actually a witch. This applies particularly to women, some of whom confess, on the strength of their bad dreams, to flying off to feast on human flesh with their sisters. Like the self-confessed European witches they may enjoy temporary notoriety and awe-filled respect but these admissions, frequently fired by impotent aggression, result in punishment, exile, or even death.

Anyone dreaming of being stabbed or speared, chased by animal-headed men or wild beasts—fantastic ones like water leopards and rainbow snakes, or recognizable, like black dogs and goats—knows that this must be the work of a witch trying to devour the soul. One West African nightmare fiend is a great black bird-shape that flies down from trees to stifle its victim. The image is not confined to Africa, however, for I know several Europeans who have experienced a similar unnerving nightmare.

The Zinacantecs say that, in order to confuse and frighten, a witch's soul rolls over three times and changes itself into an assortment of creatures. Since this kind of dream visitation can be made only by a shaman, the victim must request someone equally powerful and adept to repel the attack. A dream duel results. These Mexican Indians have another interesting theory that nightmares occur when you have a new possession because some resentful or envious individual may ask a shaman to employ his malevolent art against you so that your soul 'shrinks' and your body 'slackens'. The acquisition of anything enviable, such as a new house, probably does inspire nightmares—whether or not any shaman is to blame—for the Zinacantecs' conditioning must produce anxiety dreams about the imagined machinations of jealous neighbours.

I can almost hear somebody muttering: 'That's all very well for people who lived long ago, or belong to a primitive community, but nobody in my street would begin to think they could conjure up a nightmare ...'

Are you quite sure?

Modern practitioners of black magic, often highly sophisticated if rather warped personalities, sometimes try to invoke a serpent goddess who emanates from shadow-women like the succubus or the lamia. The ceremony hinges on the use of sexual techniques to gain power and culminates in a nightmare where the sleeper has intercourse with a 'shadow'. In order to maintain complete control the dreamer must not allow himself to reach orgasm. As long as he holds out the nightmare will take him on a journey into an infernal world to encounter those who dwell there. How many have completed this dark dream voyage I cannot know but I do not doubt that it is as real for them as were the sabbats to the witches—and some will argue that both are more than mere nightmares ...

# Victims

*But yester-night I prayed aloud*
*In anguish and in agony,*
*Up-starting from the fiendish crowd*
*Of shapes and thoughts that tortured me:*
*A lurid light, a trampling throng,*
*Sense of intolerable wrong,*
*And whom I scorned, those only strong!*
*Thirst of revenge, the powerless will*
*Still baffled, and yet burning still!*
*Desire with loathing strangely mixed*
*On wild or hateful objects fixed.*
*Fantastic passions! maddening brawl!*
*And shame and terror over all!*
*Deeds to be hid which were not hid,*
*Which all confused I could not know*
*Whether I suffered, or I did:*
*For all seemed guilt, remorse or woe,*
*My own or others still the same,*
*Life-stifling fear, soul-stifling shame.*
*The Pains of Sleep* S. T. COLERIDGE

Some nightmares are so bizarre as to be downright amusing . . . *afterwards*, in the telling. Caught up in this sort of nocturnal 'black comedy', the unfortunate individual feels quite as anxious and miserable as if embroiled in a distinguishably terrifying situation.

The humorist Jerome K. Jerome experienced one of these 'funny' nightmares. He dreamed of going to the theatre where an attendant insisted that he leave his legs in the cloakroom. This curious rule, which sounds as if it came straight from the Red Queen in *Alice*, had been introduced to help people reach their seats without stumbling over the usual rows of legs. In the dream Jerome K. Jerome indignantly vowed to write and complain to *The Times* but nonetheless was persuaded to remove his legs, the attendant obligingly showing him how these unscrewed. As with many dreams, frightening and commonplace, rationality was temporarily suspended to allow for the intricacies of the plot so the action seemed neither surprising nor impossible. What marred Jerome K. Jerome's enjoyment of the actual play, and increased his agitation, was the apprehension that there might be a mix-up with the cloakroom tickets and that someone else would be given his presentable legs, leaving him with a vastly inferior pair!

Enjoyable as an after-dinner anecdote but not as an experience was a nightmare experienced by E. S. P. Haynes, a solicitor and man of letters. He dreamed he was in a country where a strict law dictated what you might drink: having chosen one kind of ale or wine you could touch no other. The dreamer had the overwhelming fear that a wily policeman would discover a bottle of claret hidden in the chimney, when he had a licence to drink only Moselle.

Dreams about death usually offer little entertainment but in a letter to a Professor Felton, dated 1 September 1843, Charles Dickens described one that is comical, or perhaps it is the storyteller's skill that makes it so.

> I dreamed that somebody was dead. I don't know who ... It was a private gentleman, and a particular friend; and I was greatly overcome when the news was broken to me (very delicately) by a gentleman in a cocked hat, top boots, and a sheet. Nothing else. 'Good God!' I said, 'is he dead?' 'He is dead, sir,' rejoined the gentleman, 'as a door-nail. But we must all die, Mr. Dickens, sooner or later, my dear sir.' 'Ah!' I said, 'Yes to be sure. Very true. But what did he die of?' The gentleman burst into a flood of tears, and said, in a voice broken by emotion, 'He

christened his youngest child, sir, with a toasting-fork.' I never in my life was so affected as at his having fallen a victim to this complaint. It carried a conviction to my mind that he never could have recovered. I knew that it was the most interesting and fatal malady in the world; and I wrung the gentleman's hand in a convulsion of respectful admiration, for I felt that this explanation did equal honour to his head and heart.

Generally, nightmares, however absurd, cannot be recounted with such humour. Daylight cannot dispel their innate menace. Most people's grisly accounts of their bad dreams normally induce our pity, or a chilling echo of fellow-feeling ... a kind of 'I too have been in that hell-hole', but there are some whose sleeping torments must strike us as richly deserved. At least they suggest that even an utterly inhuman creature cannot quite get away with every iniquity. Nero definitely fits this category of dreamer. To describe his character and behaviour as disturbed would be an understatement. Like other emperors, he entertained a healthy respect for the warnings contained in dreams, omens, and auspices so he could hardly have dismissed his own nightmares with a shrug of the imperial shoulders.

According to Suetonius these vivid and ominous dreams began only after Nero had ordered his mother's murder. He dreamed that he was being dragged into some threateningly dark place by his wife, Octavia; that the national images set up near Pompey's theatre surrounded him and prevented his advancement; that a vast army of winged ants swarmed over him; and that the body of his favourite Spanish horse was transformed into an ape, although it retained its equine head and recognizable neigh. Perhaps most significant was the nightmare where Nero steered a ship and the rudder was forced from him.

Caligula was undoubtedly as mad as he was bad yet whether the following nightmare was an instance of the imperial subconscious rearing its troubled head or a divine warning I leave to your discretion. The night before his assassination, so it is told,

Caligula dreamed of being in heaven (not so unusual, for someone who had already declared himself a divinity) standing before Jupiter's throne. With the big toe of his right foot, the king of the gods sent the Emperor of Rome tumbling headlong down to earth. Subsequent events proved Caligula subject to the usual rules of mortality!

The nightmare was frequently employed by the gods to point out the folly inherent in certain acts. In *On Divination* Cicero recounted how Hannibal bored a hole into a column of the temple of Juno Lacinia, suspecting it was pure gold but wanting positive proof. Having reassured himself that the pillar was solid gold, the Carthaginian general decided to appropriate it. Then, in a nightmare, Juno appeared and threatened that if he went ahead with his scheme his one good eye would be forfeit. Wisely, Hannibal forsook this 'golden opportunity' and, no doubt to ensure that he could not be found guilty of stealing even a scruple, used the gold already removed by the boring to fashion a heifer which was placed on top of the column.

The gruesome monster is not confined to the nightmares of seven-year-olds: it featured also in another of Hannibal's nightmares. He dreamed of being summoned to a council of the gods, where Jupiter ordered him to carry the war into Italy. One of the other gods was appointed to accompany him but warned Hannibal not to look back. In true Orpheus fashion he disobeyed and saw a huge and terrible creature, surrounded by writhing serpents, that destroyed everything in its path. The divine guide explained that this monster signified the desolation of Italy and commanded Hannibal to advance without delay, ignoring whatever evil lay behind . . .

Clearly, nightmares appear different in detail but many contain an underlying theme that evokes a similar emotion in people of quite disparate cultures and centuries. The space-age youngster's dream of being chased by a Venusian wielding a ray gun and the tenth-century child's dream of fleeing from a terrible figure armed with an axe are both nightmares where the dreamer's existence feels threatened. Whatever the contemporary explanation, stark terror is almost certainly the response.

Sometimes terror is made all the more unbearable by being undefined. How can flesh and blood fight against ever-changing shadows? Sometimes a dream can provoke face-burning embarrassment and the wound to self-esteem still hurts in waking life. Violence, blood, and death are some of the entertainments lovingly devised by the nightmare. How it treats them can vary, not only from person to person but also from dream to dream in the same individual.

The art critic and author John Ruskin had two decidedly grim although unrelated nightmares about death. In December 1872, he dreamed of looking after a little girl who sat eating at a table with the spirits of Wisdom and Death. Both were beautiful, but dreadfully cold, and Ruskin feared lest the child touch either of them. Untroubled by any such misgivings, the little girl asked the spirits why they never smiled. Whereupon Death did smile, and showed more of his teeth than seemed right. Apparently the child did not notice this . . . and Ruskin awoke, in dread that she would.

The second dream, on his own admission the 'ghastliest' he had ever experienced, also occurred in December, three years later. This involved him going to rest in a room hung with fine old pictures. On examining one very large canvas, he discovered it depicted a surgeon 'dying by dissecting himself! It was worse than dissecting—*tearing*; and with circumstances of horror about the treatment of the head which I will not enter . . .'

To dream of a dead loved one is the classic harrowing nightmare, and we have already seen how primitives react to this sort of nocturnal visitation. The concept of burying the deceased with his or her prized possessions may actually have arisen as an attempt to prevent the ghost from returning to repossess them.

Such considerations hardly apply to the nineteenth-century poet Coventry Patmore. He was paid what most of us would consider a tragic and spiteful visit by the nightmare. He dreamed his beloved wife was dying and awoke with that enormous sense of relief which always accompanies the realization that thankfully it was all only a dream. Then, almost instantly he recollected reality: his wife had indeed died six weeks before.

For 29 June 1667, Samuel Pepys confided to his famous diary: 'Up, having had many ugly dreams tonight ...' He, too, was a victim of the nightmare about a departed relative. In the dream he and his wife were leaving his office, dressed in mourning for his mother, when who should they meet but Pepys' father, sister, *and* mother. His mother said she needed a pair of gloves and Pepys, remembering a pair of his wife's in his own room, resolved to give her these. Then it dawned upon him that he had made a mistake in believing her dead and, to save embarrassment all round, arranged that if anyone enquired as to whom they were mourning, the answer would be that it was his wife's mother. At first glance this does not sound a particularly alarming dream, yet obviously it upset the sleeper, who wrote: 'This dream troubled me and I waked.'

Death, as portrayed by the nightmare, is not only heartrending but frequently hideous and macabre. Sometimes the dreamer is allotted the role of victim, at other times forced to be the murderer. Walter de la Mare, whose imaginative writing explored the dream world, related a particularly gory nightmare. He dreamed that he was in one of those Gothic chambers so beloved of makers of horror movies. Precisely why he stabbed in the back the old lady sitting silently in a chair he had no idea; but there was no alternative to murder. The woman's blood trickled onto the flagstones to form puddles; some seemed to be flowing towards the gap under the door, which could alert others to the fact that a dreadful crime had been committed. The dreamer panicked. His dream considerately provided a leather bucket; as the poet put it, 'dreams leave little to chance'. Feverishly he started mopping up the blood, wringing the cloth into the bucket. Not only had he to keep at this horrid chore, he had also to be alert for the slightest noise. A sound of footsteps in the corridor so alarmed him that he knocked over the bucket. Vivid red washed over the flagstones. At the same time the whole room began to glow a brilliant pink from the break of day ...

Only then did de la Mare waken to discover himself in his own room, which was bathed in the light of the rising sun.

In another nightmare he was forced to play the victim: a condemned prisoner awaiting execution. He made one desperate bid to escape the guard, only to confront another figure in uniform. Calmly, this newcomer levelled a gun; de la Mare stared along its barrel into his executioner's eyes. He could only presume the gun was fired for, in that moment, came a blinding yet soundless explosion of light.

The characters who attack, or are attacked by you, in your worst dreams can be famous contemporary or historical figures. The man of letters, poet, and historian Robert Southey recorded his dreams in a diary. During a particularly patriotic one he found himself in Bonaparte's palace. The Frenchman attempted to kill him but Southey struck the Emperor with an axe, dragged him into a public hall, and proceeded to complete his vengeance by beheading the tyrant. It was the first time in a dream that Southey had ever killed Napoleon in self-defence, although he admitted: 'I have more than once done it upon the pure principle of tyrannicide.'

Another of Southey's dreams, while lacking such urgent activity, is much more in the true nightmare genre. He was haunted by evil spectres and dead bodies which could not be seen yet were not to be ignored. Terrified beyond any measure he had known in his waking life, Southey still reasoned that delusion was the root cause. However, the terror increased, and eventually an elongated hand appeared through a half-open door. Determined to prove that this was no more than a figment of the mind, Southey caught hold of that hand ... to find it lifeless. Dragging at it produced a shapeless body, on which he trampled, screaming aloud in his terror. Naturally these cries awoke his wife Edith 'who immediately delivered me from the most violent fear that ever possessed me'.

Remember your own childhood and how the dark at the top of the stairs (or anywhere else isolated from family hubbub and light) was inhabited by nameless horrors waiting to pounce, which the insensitive adult world insisted were nothing but your own fantasies. This same terror of the invisible and unknown during sleep is the genuine stuff of nightmare, when horror is heightened by the very intangibility of its cause.

Recently a young woman told me, almost shamefacedly, how she was a victim of a dream of this sort which has recurred since childhood and has not diminished in its terror with the advent of her maturity. It is always the same. She is lying in bed, sensing that something terrible lurks outside and will enter her room at any moment. At the same time, she knows it is all a dream and so tells herself that the terror will vanish as soon as she wakes up. She wakes with a sense of relief at having escaped ... only to discover that the 'thing' is brooding outside. Gradually the awareness dawns that this is still the dream. Once more she fights to waken. And does so. Only to find herself caught in that same nightmare. It seems to her that there is no eluding whatever unknown horror is contained in the dream.

When, eventually, she does wake into the real world, it always takes time for her to be convinced that the nightmare has departed —at least for the time being.

The nightmare seems to take perverse joy in forcing the unwitting sleeper to perform deeds that would be anathema in daily life. Here is one that is particularly apposite since the nineteenth-century diarist Francis Kilvert was a clergyman also. Like a painting within another painting, he *dreamed that he dreamed* that Mr and Mrs Venables were trying to poison him. Aware of their malign intent, he managed to evade them but finally they succeeded and he felt the poison begin to burn in his neck.

This dream so infuriated Kilvert that in his outer dream he determined to murder Mr Venables. He lay in wait for him and then made a terrible hole in Venables' head with a pickaxe, afterwards kicking the face until it was mutilated beyond recognition. This extremely bloodthirsty crime was perpetrated on the vicarage lawn! Suddenly the dream changed (as we all know how it can) and there was a pacific but reproachful Mrs Venables asking: 'Wasn't it enough that you should have hewed a hole through his head, but you must go and kick his face so that I don't know him again?' The Vicar of Hay also made an appearance to remark: 'You have made a pretty mess of it.' An understatement if ever there was one.

All this while Kilvert was going about his parochial duties; but on noticing how his flock reacted, the reverend dreamer suspected they knew of his heinous crime. Stricken with remorse, he gave himself up to a policeman, who clapped him in prison. It was then that he knew this was no dream from which he could wake to comfortable reality. He had definitely committed murder, would be tried at the Spring Assizes, and hanged early in April.

When, at last, poor Reverend Kilvert did wake up, he was so convinced of the reality of *both* dreams that he felt for the manacles on his wrists and still could not believe he was safely home in bed until he heard the clock on the stairs strike five.

Equally unlikely, but nevertheless disturbing, was Mary Baker Eddy's dream of being assaulted by a strange man while she was with a Christian Science congregation. She managed to disengage herself from this unwanted lover and ran into a house—which unfortunately turned out to be one of ill-repute. The man followed, locked the door, and laughed. Only when Mrs Eddy understood her predicament did the nightmare dissolve. A couple of centuries before, such a dream might have been viewed as an attempted assault by an incubus.

The dread of being eaten or gorging yourself on flesh—human or otherwise—is a well-known feature of childhood and adult nightmares in both primitive and developed societies. In many communities such dreams are regarded as unlucky—even predictions of death—perhaps because meat is included in any burial feast. These flesh-eating, cannibalistic themes may also be dim echoes from our savage ancestry.

A particularly ensanguined example assailed the creator of Madame Bovary. Gustave Flaubert dreamed of lying in a curtained bed. He was aware of foosteps on the stairs and, at the same time, a breath of foul-smelling air wafted into his room.

Then seven or eight black-bearded fellows entered with daggers held between their teeth. They approached the bed; their teeth made gnashing sounds. Each finger left a tell-tale bloodstain on the white bed curtains. For a long while seven or eight pairs of lidless eyes gazed down at Flaubert. The typical prisoner of nightmare, he could neither shout nor move. When at last they drew back, he saw that one side of their faces was skinless and bleeding. They lifted all his clothes, leaving blood on every item, and sat down to eat. As they broke bread it spurted and dripped blood, and their mirth was the rattle in a dying man's throat. The apparitions vanished to leave the whole room smeared with blood. Flaubert knew a choking sensation and felt as if he had swallowed flesh. Then he heard a long cry . . .

How many other people's dreams, I wonder, have been infiltrated by such grisly details just from reading this nightmare?

In this poem, Thomas Lovell Beddoes describes a dream of being devoured in his grave.

>         . . . *then I was dead;*
> *And in my grave beside my corpse I sat,*
> *In vain attempting to return: meantime*
> *There came the untimely spectres of two babes,*
> *And played in my abandoned body's ruins;*
> *They went away; and, one by one, by snakes*
> *My limbs were swallowed; and, at last, I sat*
> *With only one, blue-eyed, curled round my ribs,*
> *Eating the last remainder of my heart* . . .

Graveyards are settings much favoured by the nightmare for staging its spectaculars. The devoutly religious poet Christina Rossetti dreamed of one filled with innocent-faced sheep, under a clear greyish night sky. In the midst of the flock lay a satanic-looking goat. There were also some long-haired white dogs; one had a flattering face, another wore an expression that was both sensual and, to the dreamer, 'abominable'.

A much more personal graveyard nightmare was that of the

nineteenth-century German dramatist Christian Friedrich Hebbel who dreamed that he was simultaneously both in and out of his coffin. A priest whom he had known since his youth informed him that he was soon to be interred but that the coffin was to be kept in a vault with others until a grave could be dug. Hebbel pleaded to be allowed to spend the remaining time in the open air, explaining that anyone must shrink from the idea of being buried beneath the earth. Eventually the priest consented, pointing out, however, that this was contrary to all the rules, since it was unsuitable for the dead to go about among the living; Hebbel was bidden to return as soon as the bell struck.

Quite a few notable people have left us accounts of dreams in which they walked around *after* death. Dr John Dee, astrologer to Elizabeth I, led a remarkably up-and-down life. He began his career as a mathematician but became involved in the less precise science of necromancy. Not all of his relationships with royalty were under auspicious stars: Queen Mary had him clapped into prison for 'using enchantments' against her life and King James declared him 'an ally of Satan', although he was too canny to go as far as putting Dee on trial. So it is hardly surprising that occasionally the extraordinary doctor's existence was made the darker by a visit from the nightmare.

For 24 November 1582, Dee wrote in his diary:

Saturday night I dreamed that I was dead, and afterwards my bowels were taken out and I walked and talked with diverse, and among others with the Lord Treasurer who came to my house to burn my books when I was dead, and thought he looked sourly on me.

It has been proposed that this dream proved that Dee suffered from colitis: whatever element of truth lies in that premise, he eventually died in 1608, *aged eighty-one*.

Henrik Ibsen's vision of mortality within a nightmare is more apocalyptic than personal. He and some friends had been walking in the mountains and, surprised by the coming of night, were forced to sleep outdoors. Like Jacob, the Old Testament dreamer, they rested their heads on stones, which maybe explains why an angel appeared in Ibsen's dream, saying: 'Arise, and follow me . . . I will reveal to you human existence in its true reality.' Filled with misgivings the playwright followed his guide. They descended some stairs so that the rocks seemed to tower above like giant arches. Spread out before them

> lay a vast city of death with horrible remnants and tokens of mortality and transient existence—a perished grandeur, an immense, sunken world of corpses, death's silent subjects. Over all hovered a withered, ghastly twilight that enveloped churchyards, graves, and sepulchres. In a stronger light row upon row of white skeletons reflected a phosphorescent glow.

Fear gripped the dreamer and the angel said: 'Here, you see, all is vanity.' There came a roar as if a storm were breaking; it grew into a raging hurricane until the dead stirred and extended their arms towards Ibsen, who awoke with a cry to find himself wet from the cold night's dew.

Another Scandinavian, Emanuel Swedenborg, the founder of a religious sect, whose soul's journeys through hell, purgatory, and heaven formed part of the foundation for his scriptures, also experienced a nightmare about the infernal regions. He dreamed that an executioner was cutting off heads and roasting them in an oven. These were his 'food', and somehow the oven never seemed filled. The executioner appeared as a gross laughing female and was accompanied by a little girl. The dream altered, and the Devil carried Swedenborg into the depths and bound him in hell.

To dream of being in a narrow and stifling place, or of being buried alive, is a fairly familiar nightmare that loses none of its terror through its ubiquity. It may arise from a perfectly normal instinctive fear of being smothered, or it may hark back to the trauma of birth. It is, therefore, not surprising that so many generations assumed the sensation to be caused by the presence of the 'nightmare' itself crouching on the sleeper's chest. However, it seems unlikely that someone of Adolf Hitler's disposition would have accepted this theory to explain away a nightmare which convinced him that he had been entrusted with a divine mission which subsequently, and most horrifically, affected the world.

On 22 September 1938, the French magazine *Match* published an account of this dream, which occurred in 1917 when Hitler was a corporal in the Bavarian Infantry on the French front. He dreamed of being buried under a great mound of earth and molten iron and could feel the warmth of blood spilling down his chest. The nightmare woke him abruptly.

The area of the Somme that the Bavarian troops were defending appeared very quiet but Hitler still felt anxious and restless. He left the trench and wandered towards the open country, telling himself he was being stupid because there was certainly more danger, from shrapnel or a stray bullet, outside the trench. Yet the impact of this nightmare seemed to hold him captive and he could only continue walking. At a burst of gunfire Hitler threw himself to the ground. The dream and its effects forgotten, he rushed back towards the trench—but it had disappeared completely: all his comrades were buried alive.

What does such a nightmare suggest? Prescience? Not necessarily. In similar situations soldiers must always suffer presentiments that the trench walls could cave in and these fears would naturally colour their dreams.

Bad dreams during warfare are scarcely astonishing. Recall how Shakespeare portrayed Richard III's nightmare-ravaged sleep on the eve of Bosworth Field. The ghosts of those he had destroyed to secure the crown visited this unhappy monarch as he slept in his tent; on the morrow he declared: 'I have dream'd a fearful dream . . .' and 'By the apostle Paul, shadows tonight have struck more terror to the soul of Richard than can the substance of ten thousand soldiers . . .'. Evidently this nightmare was not a neat example of dramatic licence to highlight Richard's thousand-tongued conscience for the history books also record how the King was afflicted by a terrible dream so that 'he did not buckle himself to the conflict with such liveliness of courage and countenance as before'. Richard recounted his dream to many in the morning in order that his followers should not imagine that fear of the enemy influenced his mood. To enter battle with such a dark shadow weighing him down hardly boded well for a victory.

You are never in control of the nightmare and it presents diabolical *tableaux vivants* just to highlight your helplessness. The helter-skelter dream is a particularly unnerving example of this. One woman dreamed of being aboard a train where all the other passengers were sentenced to death although they were innocent of any crime. It was darkest night. The train hurtled towards a chasm. The locomotive was driverless . . .

Often in such dreams you are immobilized as the terror bears down on you. The critic and novelist Sir Hugh Walpole dreamed of being in a busy, cheerful market place when suddenly everything seemed to change: the air chilled, the noise ebbed, the light faded, and everyone else disappeared. Although he felt dreadfully apprehensive, he could not move.

Then a procession entered the square. Two men in black carried a stretcher on which lay a woman. Behind them followed a small group of silent people. Before the pall-bearers walked a thin man with a yellowish face twisted to one side as if his neck were broken. Walpole was standing directly in the path of this retinue; although he was convinced that if the sallow-faced man so much as laid a finger on him something frightful must happen, he could not stir. The group drew nearer, and nearer. The terror was agonizing. Walpole awoke. Hardly surprising that his pyjamas were soaked with sweat.

Most of us do not recall nightmares with pleasure: some people, as we shall see later, use their inspirational qualities for the purposes of art; others regard nightmares with ghastly fascination or even puzzled amusement. Yet there are those who would gladly forego all experience of dreams. For them, Thomas Carlyle's pronouncements must seem peculiarly apt. When asked by William Allingham if he dreamed a lot, Carlyle replied:

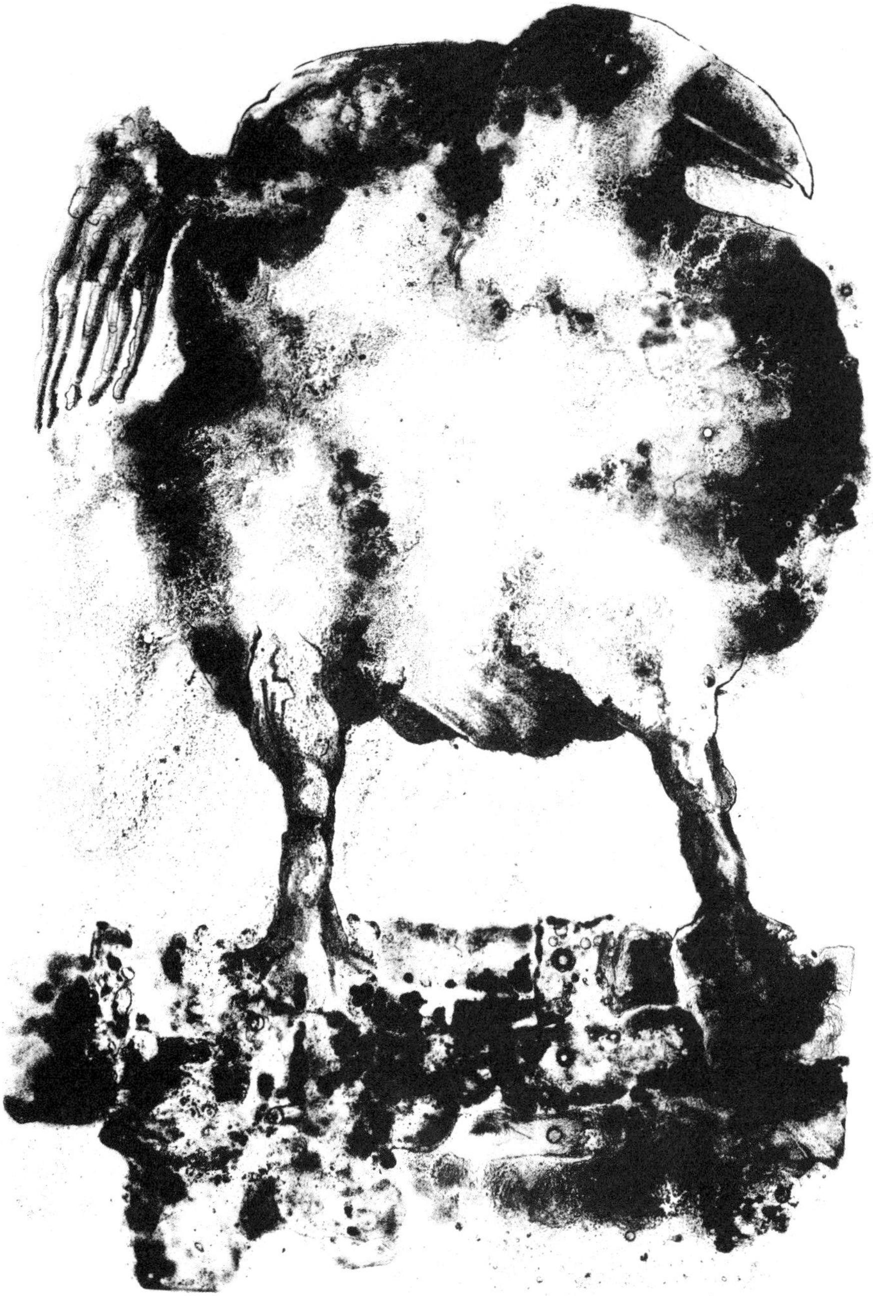

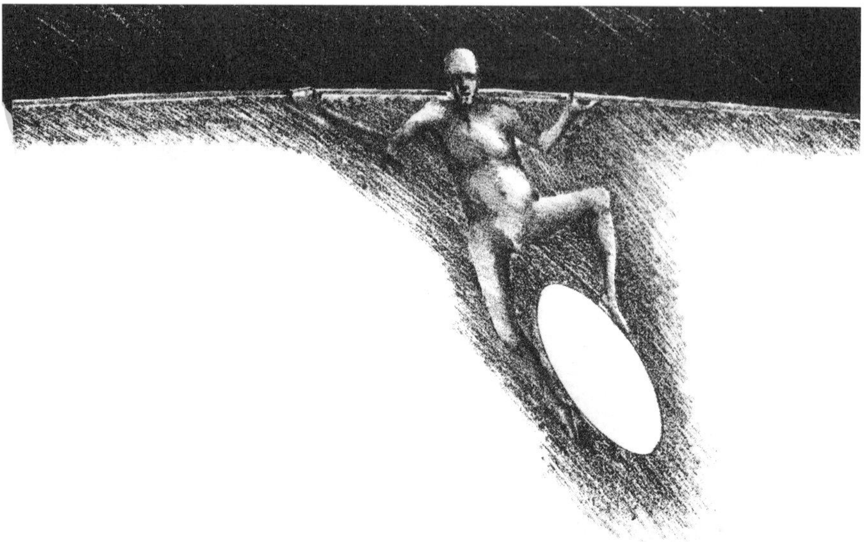

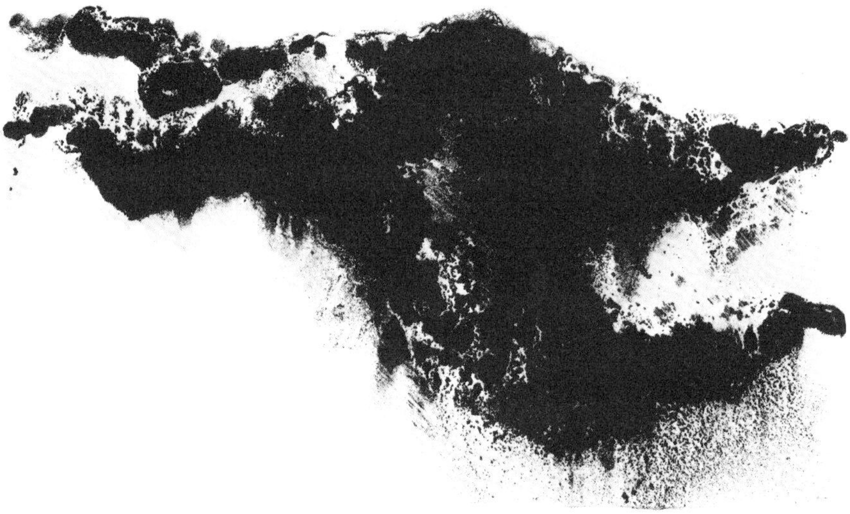

Dreams! My dreams are always disagreeable—mere confusions—losing my clothes and the like, nothing beautiful. The same dreams go on night after night for a long time. I am a worse man in my dreams than when awake—do cowardly acts, dream of being tried for a crime. I long ago came to the conclusion that my dreams are of no importance to me whatever.

Unimportant to him, perhaps, but significant to others who want to know more about this great man's character. Were dyspepsia and depression the only initiators of Carlyle's disagreeable dreams —for most of his life he was subject to both disturbances—or had they a deeper cause? We do know that when his wife, Jane, died, Carlyle suffered dreadful pangs of guilt for having neglected her. Anyone who underwent the incredible catastrophe of having the only manuscript of *The French Revolution* accidentally destroyed seems a likely candidate for anxiety dreams, and deserves our sympathy. For any writer, whatever the calibre, this is the ultimate nightmare.

I always experience the most uncomfortable dreams whenever a manuscript is due to be delivered to a publisher. The nightmare is set in an editorial office and around a table sit innumerable editors, some whom I know, others quite unfamiliar. They circulate copies of my book and make scathing comments about it and the writer. When eventually I catch a glimpse of what they're reading I understand their scorn: the pages are either quite blank or are covered with 'Jabberwocky' nonsense.

It is some comfort, I admit, to learn how the famous and respected encountered similar miseries in their nightmares. John Clare, the countryside poet, dreamed of looking at one of the proofs of his new poems sent from London. It crumbled like dust in his hands and he took this as an ill omen for the fate of the book.

The nightmare visited the German poet Heinrich Heine in the guise of an incomplete hexameter, which limped to his bed on five feet and, with dire threats, demanded the writer give it its missing sixth foot. Ruefully, Heine related how 'he appealed to his primitive classic right, and left me with horrible gestures only on condition that I would never make another hexameter'.

Imagine what consternation this nightmare caused to a historian like Thomas Babington Macaulay. He dreamed that his niece, Alice, confessed she had forged Pepys's *Diary*. 'What!' exclaimed Macaulay, 'I have been quoting in reviews, and in my History, a forgery of yours as a book of the highest authority. How shall I ever hold up my head again?'

The burning embarrassment that the nightmare delights in inflicting to topple our self-confidence can overtake prelate as well as poet. Edward White Benson, Archbishop of Canterbury, dreamed that he had invited a school examiner to lunch. When he entered the dining-room the table was set for a meal but his official guest was leaning as far out of the window as possible to inhale fresh air. And, no wonder. The only available food was a dish containing two roast ducks which were blue with putrefaction!

William Archer, a friend of George Bernard Shaw, had the sort of nightmare that anybody who does any public speaking must dread. He dreamed that he was at a dinner held in his honour and, rising to reply to the toast, discovered to his chagrin that he could neither remember who had proposed it nor what had been said. As Archer began to speak he noticed the other guests slip away. Then, as he turned to leave, a waiter handed him the bill. Mortification and indignation woke him.

Often the nightmare takes a happy event and, by turning it head-over-heels, transforms it into something distressing. The poet Thomas Hood was happily anticipating his wedding day. On its eve he dreamed of where he and his bride would pass their honeymoon. Everything proceeded with admirable smoothness. He found a pretty seaside villa and an elderly woman (in decayed sables) agreed to take care of the honeymooners at a reasonable cost. Then 'incoherent fancy crept in and confounded all' for Hood discovered himself married off to the old woman of the house!

Besides intimidating, embarrassing, or scaring us half to death, the nightmare has, very occasionally, performed practical functions. Like the cure-all medicines that quicksalvers used to purvey at fairs, the nightmare has been known to make the dumb speak and bring the guilty to book.

The following remarkable event was recorded by Archdeacon Squire in *Philosopical Transactions* for 1748. Henry Axford, a gentleman from Devizes, Wiltshire, suddenly lost his speech at the age of 28; all the efforts of the physicians to cure him were in vain. About four years later, in 1741, he was riding home and, being somewhat the worse for drink, fell from his horse three or four times. A kindly neighbour took charge of the inebriated traveller and put him to bed in a roadside house. Mr Axford slept and dreamed that he had fallen into a furnace of boiling malt. In an agony of terror he struggled to cry for help and succeeded in calling aloud *in reality*. From that moment he recovered his vocal powers and, we are reliably informed no hoarseness or alteration in tone remained to suggest his previous incapacity.

Guilt of as much as murder has actually been exposed by wild babblings during nightmare-ridden sleep. This was true of one Helen Dougal, a prostitute who was involved in the resurrectionist atrocities of 1828 in Edinburgh that made the names of Burke and Hare for ever infamous exhibits in history's black museum. The unfortunate Helen was Burke's 'woman'; the hue-and-cry occasioned by the body-snatching murders forced her into beggary, and to move to Carlisle. The inmates of the common lodging-house where Helen first stayed had no inkling of her true identity, until her screaming nightmares revealed her awful knowledge and complicity. Afterwards, even that brotherhood of outcasts refused to keep her in their midst.

The nightmare's chief infamy lies in its treatment of the very young for it delights in cruelly sporting with those least able to defend themselves with reason and experience.

It is paradoxical that society's views of childhood as a carefree garden should exist while writers give us such vivid descriptions of their own dreadful childhood nightmares. One of the best accounts of these torments can be read in Charles Lamb's essay

*Witches and Other Night-Fears* which was published in 1823. A picture of the Witch of Endor raising the dead Samuel, found in *The History of the Bible*, had shaped the nightmare that persecuted the young Lamb from his fourth to around his eighth year. Nightly the hag sat on the boy's bed and even in daylight he dared not enter his room without turning away from that witch-ridden pillow.

Of course, people could dismiss this account as being typical of only a highly imaginative child, so no doubt a lot of informed eyebrows were raised when, in 1834, R. Macnish, an early writer on troubled sleep, questioned the widely accepted view of untroubled childhood:

> Many of the dreams experienced at this early period leave an indellible impression on the mind. They are remembered in after years with feelings of pain, and, blending with the more delightful reminiscences of childhood, demonstrate that this era ... had, as well as future life, its shadows of melancholy, and was not untinged with hues of sorrow and care. The sleep of infancy ... is far from being that ideal state of felicity which is commonly supposed. It is haunted with its own terrors, even more than of adults, and, if many of the visions which people it are equally delightful there can be little doubt that it is also tortured by dreams of a more painful character than often fall to the share of after-life.

Because the nightmare is experienced by very young children, many experts now believe that it is not the product of emotional disturbance, as earlier psychologists hypothesized, but arises from some powerful instinctive forces which fuel the inner conflict associated with bad dreams.

Charles Lamb, who had already arrived at much the same conclusion, considered that, had he never set eyes on the Witch of Endor illustration, his night fears would nonetheless have materialized, but probably in some other guise, such as 'headless bear, black man, or ape'. He cited the example of one small boy brought up uncontaminated by any superstition or scary tale of ghost and goblin, who 'from his little midnight pillow ... will start at shapes, unborrowed of tradition, in sweat to which the reveries of the cell-damned murderer are tranquility'. For Charles Lamb, like C. G. Jung in our own time, the individual contains eternal archetypes, terrors that 'date beyond body—or, without the body ...'.

It is significant that in adulthood Lamb admitted that, although he had only the occasional bad dream, 'I know them for mockeries, even while I cannot elude their presence, and I fight and grapple with them'. Given his own mental instability, and the fact that he took care of his sister, Mary, who had fatally stabbed their mother in a fit of mania, one might have supposed the matured nocturnal visions would have been far more horrific than those of childhood.

It was Robert Louis Stevenson who coined that marvellously evocative phrase 'the raw-head-and-bloody-bones nightmare, rumoured to be the child of toasted cheese'. A most prolific dreamer himself, possibly as a result of tuberculosis which through its fevers may introduce more than an average percentage of REM into sleep, Stevenson was eventually to learn how to harness these dreams so that the muse which rode across his sleep could be transcribed into the written word on the following day.

In *Across the Plains* he described his own dreams in the third person singular: we learn that as a child Robert Louis was

> ... an ardent and uncomfortable dreamer. When he had a touch of fever at night, and the room swelled and shrank, and his clothes, hanging on a nail, now loomed up instant to the bigness of a church, and now drew away into a horror of infinite distance and infinite littleness, the poor soul was very well aware of what must follow, and struggled hard against the approaches of that slumber which was the beginning of sorrows. But his struggles were in vain; sooner or later the night-hag would have him by the throat, and pluck him, strangling and screaming, from his sleep. His dreams were at times common-

place enough, at times very strange, at times they were almost formless: he would be haunted, for instance, by nothing more definite than a certain hue of brown, which he did not mind in the least while he was awake, but feared and loathed while he was dreaming; at times, again, they took on every detail of circumstance, as when once he supposed he must swallow the populous world, and awoke screaming with the horror of the thought ... the practical and everyday trouble of school tasks and the ultimate and airy one of hell and judgement were often confounded together into one appalling nightmare. He seemed to himself to stand before the Great White Throne; he was called on ... to recite some form of words, on which his destiny depended; his tongue stuck, his memory was blank, hell gaped for him; and he would awake, clinging to the curtain-rod with his knees to his chin.

I have quoted Stevenson's experiences *in extenso* because I doubt that anyone has presented a more vivid picture of what many children suffer during their nightmare years.

Although the generally accepted age for the nightmare to begin its devilries is five, there are plenty of examples of the fiend crouching over unhappy three-year-olds. I see no reason why we should doubt that, long before a child is even able to articulate, it does not confront the awful spectre in what we fondly imagine is the warm haven of its crib. Five-year-olds have difficulty in relating their bad dreams and incline towards jumbling up fantasy and reality until it is hard for them—or a sympathetic listener—to sort out the two. The nightmare rouses and so terrifies the child that he or she fights against returning to sleep and, like the young Stevenson, would willingly be parted from the power of dreams.

The shapes adopted by the fiend at this time of life include fierce animals like wolves and bears—although, oddly enough, six months earlier the child may dream quite happily of wolves. *Strange* and *bad* people of weird colouring and appearance also predominate and they, like the wild beasts, bite and hunt the small dreamer as if intending to devour life. The fatal effects of fire and water are other frequent features.

Recently one small boy kept dreaming that he was drowned in a river close to his home and that his body was trapped and mangled under the bridge; a local drowning accident had provided the bare bones of his nightmare. During the day, however, there was no sign to show that the child thought the incident particularly distressing. His father explained that the only way to comfort the terrified boy was to cuddle him and have a 'man-to-man chat about this-and-that', rather than dwell on the events within the dream. Contact and a warm, loving relationship, while not preventing the nightmares, at least countered its daytime hangover effects.

Long before the advent of child psychiatrists and 'advice to parents' columns, Charles Lamb had advocated much the same compassionate treatment of the hag-ridden child. 'Parents do not know what they do,' he wrote with obvious feeling, 'when they leave tender babes alone to go to sleep in the dark. The feeling about for a friendly arm—the hoping for a familiar voice—when they wake screaming—and find none to soothe them—what a terrible shaking it is to their poor nerves!' He also suggested that to keep the child up late would be preferable to sending it off to bed, to lie quaking in the darkness, knowing the terror must soon pay its nightly call.

At around the age of five and a half the dreams begin to change and tend to be less disturbing, probably because the child seems better able to report the bad ones. There are still wolves, bears, foxes, and snakes to chase and bite the child and these often attack the pet dog if the family owns one. Now we hear of 'things' in the bed. In such circumstances it makes sense for the parent to go to the frightened child rather than the other way about. Who would wish to walk through a pitch-dark home having just escaped from the nightmare's clutches, shades of which seem to lurk in every corner?

Many experts counsel the use of night-lights and a banishing bedtime ritual or a special cuddly toy that the child accepts as defending it against the tormentor—creating a charmed circle which the fiend has difficulty in penetrating. The ancient Egyptians had magical spells for driving off the ghosts that afflicted their children with night terrors; witnessing a child's pitiful struggle with the nightmare gives one sufficient evidence for one not to smile condescendingly at what sounds like quaint superstition.

At the age of six there are fewer nightmares but those that do occur still contain chasing, biting animals, and also fire, thunder, and war. Ghosts and skeletons begin to put in a macabre appearance. It is perhaps significant to Freudians that, at this age, girls especially will dream of *bad men* trying to get into their room. A particularly painful dream is of mother going away, or being killed or injured. But at least by now the child can freely describe its nightmares.

Sometimes the seventh year marks the final nightmare phase and, quite often, even in the grip of a dream, the child will recognize it as only a dream. Being chased and rooted to the spot occurs in the nightmare now, as do those universal motion sensations, such as flying, swimming, diving, and walking on air. The child also experiences within the dream embarrassing daily situations, such as an 'accident' in its pants, only to waken and find one has actually happened—a humiliation for anyone whose pride insists they are long past babyhood. Burglars and all sorts of supernatural figures shape the nightmare and themes borrowed from television and the cinema start to manifest themselves.

The Victorian art historian John Addington Symonds had no such modern techniques for sparking his nightmares, which nonethless were numerous, recurrent, and hideous. The dreams of this highly nervous child sound like marvellous plots for Gothic tales but at the time the little boy could hardly take so sanguine a view. One frequent dream was of a coffin containing a corpse that was directly beneath the child's bed. He would wake, believing that the dead person was just about to throw a sheet over his small body. Not only were his nights broken by strange sounds but, whenever he opened his eyes in the dark, lights seemed to move about and he felt forced to gaze at them until 'I either sank back hypnotized or rushed from the bed, and sat in my nightshirt on the staircase'. Interestingly enough he, like Robert Louis Stevenson, was later to be the victim of consumption.

Nine to ten is another age where the nightmare may predominate. Dreams are grotesque and menacing, showing the dread of being chased, kidnapped, injured, or murdered. There may also be a fear of dying during sleep so that the child lies in the dark listening to the beating of its own heart. At this age, a less egocentric approach to life shows that the dreamer is learning to relate to others more, and in the nightmares the victims may be those he or she loves (and, paradoxically, hates at the same time). There are lots of motion sensations and a curious disorientation where space is so distorted that the child feels everything is far, far away.

However, as well as being able to talk about the nightmare, the child is conscious of outside influences—for example, that the horrible nocturnal adventure mirrored something from television or a film—and a certain wit at evading the fiend demonstrates itself. The youngster will avoid looking at disturbing pictures or at certain books when alone, or close to bedtime.

I doubt that the Devil and hellfire play such a large part in children's nightmares now as they did in other centuries, since religion no longer sways popular imagination as it did before the onslaught of the mass media. When he was only six Robert Southey dreamed that the Devil paid a visit to his governess, Miss Palmer, who was clearly delighted by its presence. The infant Southey sat trembling on a flat-bottomed mahogany chair and witnessed Miss Palmer saying: 'Be seated, dear Mr Devil'. The recollection of Old Horny's villainous eyes and nose, and diabolical tail, stayed fresh in grown-up memory as if the nightmare had occurred only the day before.

Perhaps it is not at all odd that the man who gave us *The Pilgrim's Progress* should have written this of his own childhood nightmares:

Often, after I had spent this and the other day in sin, I have in my bed been greatly afflicted, while asleep, with the apparitions of Devils and wicked spirits, who still as I then thought, laboured to draw me away with them; of which I could never be rid.

Tell a child 'the bogeyman will get you if you're naughty' and, sooner rather than later, it will dream of some sort of retributive 'bogeyman' if a small mischief lies heavy on its conscience.

Older children's nightmares resemble adults' anxiety dreams and may demonstrate fears and worries over school, exams, and future careers. There is a very ancient example of one such dream. The second-century Greek writer Lucian stopped going to school and instead became apprenticed to his uncle, a stoneworker.

My uncle gave me a chisel, and bade me use it gently . . . I hit too hard, and broke the marble. My uncle enraged . . . belaboured me in such a manner as made me shed many tears, and gave me no great stomach to the trade . . .

Possibly, Lucian cried himself to sleep and then the nightmare appeared to decide his future. Two females—Sculpture and Learning—tried to pull him in opposing directions. Each argued the case for her respective discipline. Eventually the dreamer at the centre of this spectral tug-of-war was persuaded to follow Learning.

We have witnessed how nightmare attacks the weakest yet there is still a greater enormity it perpetrates—its pitiless treatment of those deprived of one or more of their senses. Anyone who becomes blind after their seventh year usually has 'visual' dreams but those who lose their sight in early childhood or who are born blind 'see' nothing in their dreams. They hear and feel the terrors that invade the dark kingdom, from which daylight can never release them. In dreams the same rule applies whatever the disability: the remaining senses contrive a drama to lighten or rend sleep.

A young girl, born deaf and blind, would wake abruptly from nightmares, feeling her blood rushing about and her heart beating rapidly. She described a frightening dream as 'hard, heavy and thick'—adjectives that the sighted and hearing would least employ to relate their nightmares.

The most famous blind and deaf dreamer must be the remarkable Helen Keller, who lost these senses at the age of nineteen months. Until she was seven, when Miss Sullivan came to teach her, Helen Keller admitted that her dreams had been devoid of any emotion save fear.

> I would often dream that I ran into a still, dark room, and that, while I stood there, I felt something fall heavily without any noise, causing the floor to shake up and down violently; and each time I woke up with a jump.

Possibly as a result of the tale of 'Red Riding Hood', the young Helen dreamed about a wolf rushing towards her and burying its fangs in her body.

No matter how pleasant the day, Helen Keller's dreams at night were more often than not unpleasant and were obviously shaped by what she had read or heard at some time, which in turn would be coloured by her own highly developed emotions and warm sympathies. What surprised her most in the middle of a nightmare was her conscious longing to wake up.

> Something seems to hold my senses tightly, and it is only with a spasmodic movement that I can open my eyes. Even then I feel, or I think I feel, a rapid motion shaking my bed and a sound of light, swift footsteps. It seems strange to me that I should make such an effort to wake up, instead of doing it automatically.

Anyone, whatever their age or capacities, who has ever done battle with the nightmare, must immediately sympathize with what Helen Keller experienced.

# Shadows in the Mind

*And I will show you something different from either*
*Your shadow at morning striding behind you*
*Or your shadow at evening rising to meet you;*
*I will show you fear in a handful of dust.*
         *The Waste Land* T. S. ELIOT

The jargon of psychology is so much a part of everyday vocabulary that we are apt to forget just how revolutionary the concept of 'the unconscious' was to an earlier generation. Here was a whole uncharted area of the mind, apparently beyond the individual's control, where lurked ideas, impulses, and memories that few would wish to acknowledge as part of their make-up and which, apparently, ruled our motives and our dreams. This recognition is comparatively recent; after all, the systematic study of mind and behaviour in order to alleviate mental ailment and nervous disease began only in the latter part of the nineteenth century.

 For the fathers of psychoanalysis, dreams and nightmares were the keys to unlock their own and their patients' hidden and forgotten memories which might be arresting development or causing psychosis. This was not quite the first time that nightmares had been regarded as a signpost—albeit one near-impossible to decipher—to the individual's underlying mental and physical state. Most ancient thinkers accepted the dream as an external manifestation introduced by gods or demons. But not all. Unlike his contemporaries, Aristotle believed dreams and the terrible *ephialtes* were the result of the brain continuing to think during sleep. He also noted that the faint sensation experienced by the body at rest, such as heat and cold, could be magnified by dream situations and therefore might provide clues to some as yet undetected physical condition.

Much later, the English philosopher Thomas Hobbes, who blamed the nightmare for the widespread acceptance of superstitious and unhealthy beliefs in fairies, goblins, witches, and their like, upheld the Aristotelian view. In *Leviathan* he pronounced:

> ... And seeing dreames are caused by the distemper of some of the inward parts of the Body; divers distempers must needs cause different Dreams. And hence it is, that lying cold breedeth Dreams of Feare, and raiseth the thought and Image of some fearfull object ...

Because we belong to a post-Freudian era, and are governed by the knowledge that the rigorous suppression of anything can produce distortion in thought, behaviour, and dream (and usually breeds that which it is attempting to deny), what we have learned about the lubricious nightmare experiences of the chaste does not seem very extraordinary. Even in the seventeenth century some enlightened souls had already reached much the same conclusion. In the *Anatomy of Melancholy* Robert Burton drily commented that marriage would often eradicate the nightmare!

Nor was his the lone voice of reason in a superstitious wilderness. A case history cited in the mid-eighteenth century, in the first study of the nightmare to be written in English, supports this theory.

> A robust servant Girl, about eighteen years old, was severely oppress'd with the Nightmare, two or three nights before every eruption of the Menses, and used to groan so loudly as to awake her Fellow-servant, who always shook or turn'd her on her Side; by which means she recover'd. She was thus afflicted periodically with it, 'till she took a bedfellow of a different sex, and bore Children.

Dr John Bond, the author of this 'Essay on the Incubus, or

Nightmare', sounds an admirably sensible man. Wishing to dissociate himself from all the usual old wives' explanations, he declared forthrightly:

> I have not introduc'd anything in this Essay that did not appear serious or probable. I have therefore omitted an enquiry into the origins of many old epithets and quaint names, commonly given to this Disorder: such as Hag-riding, Wizard-pressing, Mare-riding, Witch-dancing, and etc., nor did I think it requisite to mention particularly the curious charms adapted to each superstitious name . . .

The unsuperstitious Dr Bond had also observed his own nightmare attacks in collecting evidence on its origins and so it was with some feeling that he wrote:

> I have often been so much oppressed by this enemy of rest, that I would have given ten thousand worlds like this for some Person that would either pinch, shake, or turn me off my back; and I have been so much afraid of its intolerable insults, that I have slept in a chair all night, rather than give it an opportunity of attacking me in a horizontal position . . .

These observations led him to a totally rational conclusion that the nightmare was some complication in the blood circulation aggravated by lying on the back. The bad dream was nature's method of rousing the sleeper in order to alter the body's position, 'and by that means avoid the approaching danger'.

Yet Dr Bond went much further than this in his deductions and showed himself to be an early precursor of those psychoanalysts who view the nightmare's origins as repressed sexual appetites or underlying conflicts. Here is another of his anecdotes illustrating how fear of and desire for sex may erupt in true incubus guise:

> A young lady, of a tender, lax habit, about fifteen, before the

menses appeared, was seized with a fit of this disease, and groaned so miserably that she awoke her father, who was sleeping in the next room. He arose, ran into her chamber, and found her lying on her back, and the blood gushing plentifully out of her mouth and nose. When he shook her, she recovered and told him that she thought some great heavy man came to her bedside, and, without further ceremoney, stretched himself upon her. She had been heard moaning in sleep several nights before; but, the next day after she imagined herself oppress'd by that man, she had a copious eruption of the menses, which, for that time, removed all her complaints.

Not only is this a perfect example of the libido conflicting with rigid upbringing in a pubescent dreamer but, like the servant-girl's attacks, it is particularly interesting in the light of modern research which suggests that girls dream more intensely before the onset of the menstrual cycle. Undoubtedly Paracelsus would have concurred with this, although for somewhat 'unscientific' reasons, since he believed that phantoms in the air were engendered by the menstrual flux.

Only when those old beliefs in the embraces and machinations of a demon lover (of either sex) were shed could it be recognized that the nightmare is sometimes a symptom of psychosis as well as a mirror to it. In 1834 François Leuret remarked:

The descriptions given by the insane in our hospitals resemble those given earlier by saints and mystics . . . only the names are different. Thus, to understand the incubus, it is only necessary to listen to one of these sick people who complain they are visited during the night. The incubus still is just what it was in times past, and acts in just the same way.

We may add: only the explanations as to its causes are different.

A haunting description of how a mental state can escalate is contained in Dostoevsky's phrase 'a dream, a nightmare, a madness'. Not only has the comparison between the dream and certain kinds of insanity been made by writers, philosophers, and theologians from the past but certain twentieth-century psychiatrists and psychoanalysts, through their clinical studies, have noted similarities between schizophrenia and the infantile nightmare state. Both are conditions where the individual feels in jeopardy, marked by overriding terror, panic, total vulnerability, and the inability to distinguish between imagined and internal aggressors and external reality. However, the nightmare is a reversible state while the psychotic is trapped in a 'waking' nightmare.

Of course the sporadic childhood nightmare need not be regarded as the nucleus of a psychological disorder but it does point to an underlying stressful situation, either current or recalled. As long as the problem is resolved and integrated into the personality, a development stage is successfully achieved. However, where these nightmares are recurrent and are mishandled by adults, there is the danger that a later neurotic or psychotic condition may arise.

It was Sigmund Freud who dubbed dreams 'the guardians of sleep', and explained that they were concerned with wish-fulfilment; we can readily understand why the nightmare and severe anxiety dream do not neatly dovetail into his philosophy so that he was forced to treat them as problems of neurosis rather than as straightforward dreaming.

Freud's theory about dreaming was the all-important kernel to his studies of psychoanalysis for he believed that, by discovering the original cause for the dream, the dreamer's basic problems might be dispelled. At a time when the medical establishment was claiming that dreams were mere 'froth', or only induced by external stimuli, this Viennese doctor chose to risk his professional reputation—made the more precarious by being Jewish—in expounding an idea which corresponded with the popular belief of his own and all other ages: that the dream *does* contain a meaning. Others may have anticipated some of his views, and provided the basis for certain concepts, but Freud was the first

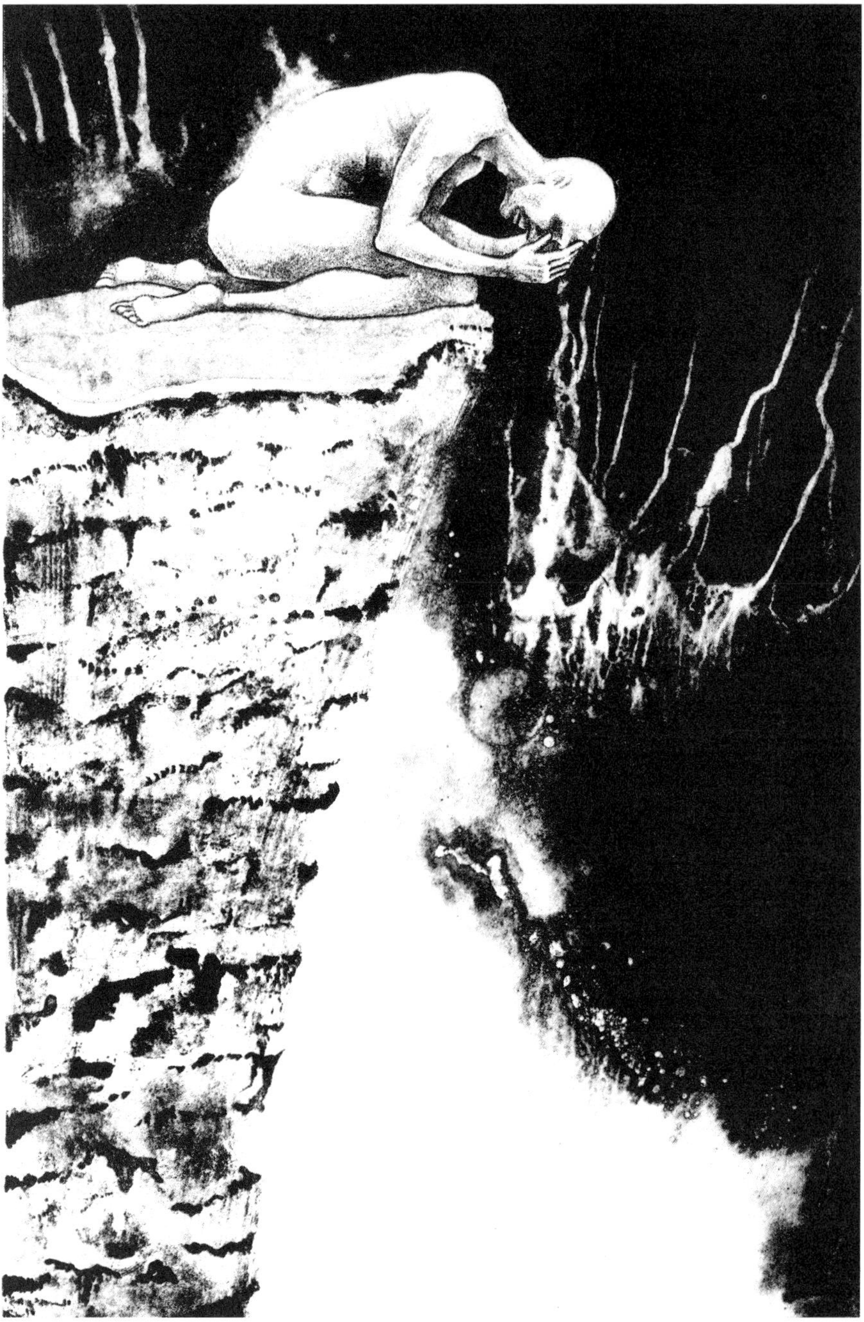

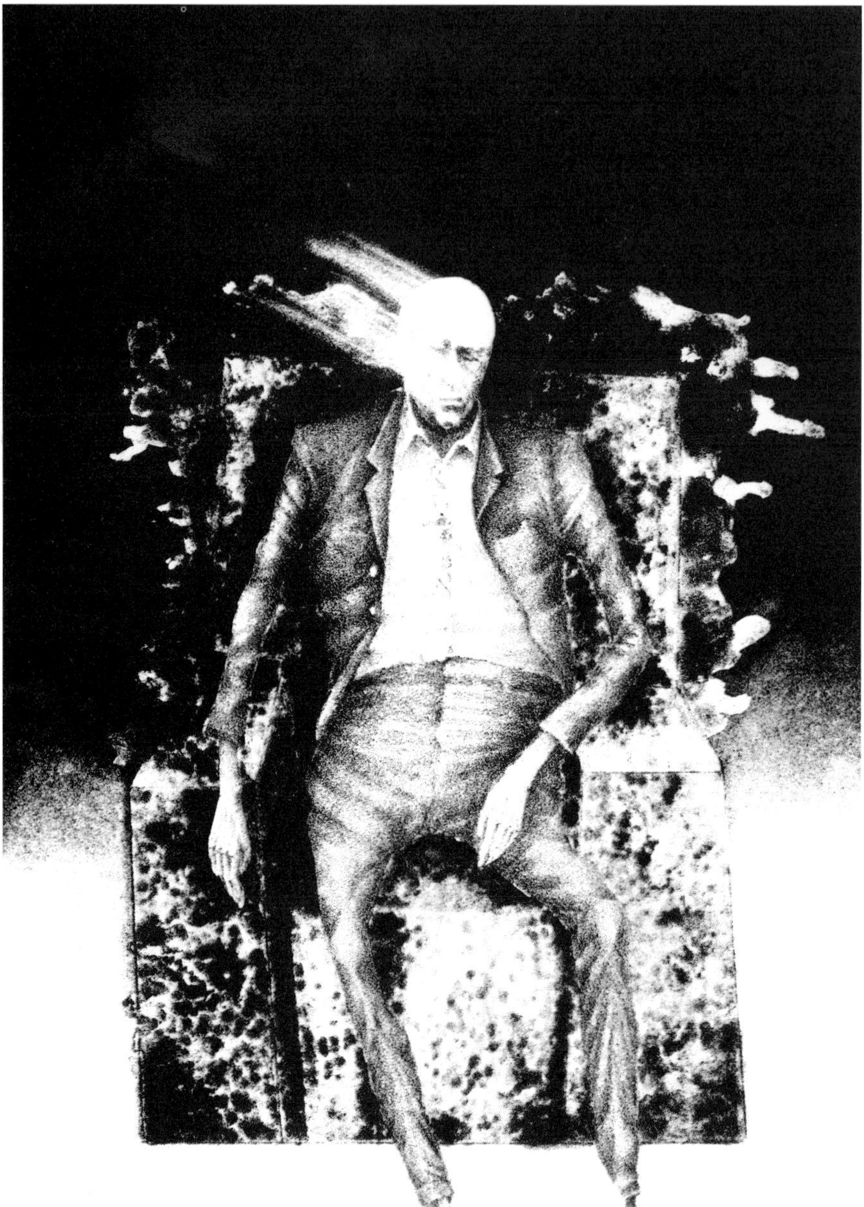

to attempt to present a comprehensive reason for the dream, its process, use, and how it could be understood.

First published in 1900, *The Interpretation of Dreams* may be seen not only as Freud's greatest work but also the cornerstone of psychoanalysis. Subsequently, many of its theories formed the foundation for others, or were modified—or flatly rejected in favour of later ideas. But, however far we progress in our understanding of the mind and its mechanism, Freud's influence on the world of dreams must never be underestimated.

The enormous book still makes intriguing reading, even where it seems old-fashioned or where we perceive paradoxes, discrepancies, and inconclusive areas—or notice that Freud chose to answer only the questions *he* was prepared to ask, and skated over certain factors for personal reasons. We are bound to admire the author's humanity, wit, and sincere enthusiasm, as well as his reasoned arguments.

Freud presents people as ultra-human and includes himself in that description by testing his own theories to discover the roots of his personal neurosis—a painful process for any person who is really aware. In studying and interpreting his dreams, Freud rediscovered hidden childhood memories that provoked thoughts and feelings he had not been aware existed in himself, including a 'dark, plainly sexual' infantile craving for his mother and an ambivalent attitude towards his own father.

We are so accustomed to some of Freud's best-known ideas that it is a hackneyed joke to say something is full of tremendous Freudian implication if the slightest sexual innuendo can be traced in an object, word, or action. Thus one of his most important concepts has been adopted and familiarized, and consequently has lost much of its first significance and impact, which may mean it has served its original purpose by making us aware that in the mind anything can be other than it seems by conscious or unconscious association. In much the same way we are not overly shocked by the idea of oedipal urges and infantile sexuality.

However, Freud's contemporary opponents vociferously insisted that his approach was unscientific, applicable only to patients suffering from neuroses, and even downright disgusting! The strength of this opposition suggested in fact that he was on the right track. For Freud was claiming that everybody possesses a mind with a conscious, a pre-conscious, and an unconscious, and that the last two areas repress painful memories and feelings. In attempting to reject these new ideas, medical men demonstrated how nobody wants their hidden longings made known, or even to admit to having any or learn that beneath their schooled adult façade lurk unrequited desires and childhood frustrations.

The greater the hostility they provoked the more dogmatically Freud defended his ideas—ideas that poured light onto a lot of dark, distressing corners of the mind and tore down the cobwebs of hypocrisy snarling up middle-class thoughts. In our sort of society it becomes increasingly difficult to imagine anyone being antagonistic to Freud's theories because they contained references to universal sexual desires and problems.

It is worth bearing in mind, while considering what Freud thought about repression, that he was dealing with patients (and physicians) who had been rigorously conditioned about their bodies and emotions. Sex was not then a fit topic for discussion or thought, so perhaps we should not find it too extraordinary that 'respectable' people could have been shocked when Freud suggested that sharp, pointed, apparently sexless objects seen in dreams symbolize the penis, while everyday containers, ships, and buildings represent the female genitals. Such critics were equally horrified by Freud's theories on infantile sexuality for he considered babies and little children, instead of being doll-like creatures devoid of the so-called baser instincts, to be human beings and therefore capable of loves, hatreds, frustrations, feelings of rejection, and pleasurable sexual sensations.

We must remember Freud never claimed that *all* dreams have a sexual interpretation but he did write: 'The more one is concerned with the solutions of dreams the more one is driven to recognize the majority of dreams deal with sexual material, and give expression to erotic wishes.'

In dealing with his patients' neuroses—anxiety, phobias,

obsessions—and hysterical symptoms—dizziness, paralysis, and heart spasms—for which there was no physical cause whatsoever, Freud had discovered that these were physical and mental expressions of some deeply hidden, unbearable memory. As long as the patient was plagued by the neurosis the real anguish, which Freud believed had its source in some childhood experience, and generally involved something sexual, would not be recalled. Since we know how the Victorians felt about that subject we cannot be too astonished that a mind so strictly conditioned must do anything to prevent the painful memory from manifesting, and thus employs the pre-conscious—a personal censor—to prevent this irregular material from introducing itself into the conscious.

Freud's concept of the unconscious was not new. However, unlike his predecessors, he believed that the conscious was only the tip of a huge iceberg concealed by deep, dark waters. The large hidden area was the unconscious, which really controls thoughts, actions, and dreams without the knowledge and consent of the conscious mind.

In this unconscious, thought is divested of all its civilized training and is ruled by instinctive and sexual forces. This means that the unconscious reverts to the uncontrolled childhood state . . . rather like the time before we had been taught not to kick, bite, scream, or empty our bowels and bladders wherever we chose. Freud argued that the unresolved problems and unfulfilled desires of early childhood continually patrol the unconscious, forever seeking opportunities in everyday life when they can reappear to seek out the unattained gratification. Between the unconscious and the conscious is the pre-conscious that tries to prevent material from escaping, or at least to distort it.

During what he termed periods of 'free-association' Freud encouraged his patients to talk freely, which meant allowing the mind to wander as it chose, so that the subject could relate whatever suggested itself. Often this led people back among their memories to trace the original source of problems. During 'free-association', patients recalled dreams and nightmares—and these touched off further avenues of recollections for exploration.

Like later psychoanalysts, Freud felt it rare that any single dream could point the way, nor should dreams be interpreted out of context; that is, without a knowledge of the dreamer's background, character, and overt troubles—which means that those books promising to tell you the meaning of all your dreams are at best a hotch-potch of dream traditions.

From his observations Freud was unable to accept that a dream has an entirely physiological source. He considered that those basic desires dwelling in the unconscious tried to attain the conscious during sleep. In order to prevent them from disturbing the sleeper physically and psychologically, the dream is the process of 'venting' instinctive impulses. These are further masked with symbols, and also through the censorship device of the pre-conscious.

According to Freud the 'guardians of sleep' borrowed any external stimulus that might affect the dreamer and wove it into the dream to prevent awakening and to prolong sleep—if only for a moment. How many of us have overslept, simply because our dreams have adopted the insistent ringing of the alarm clock, so that some part of the mind can think: 'Oh well, it's only a dream. I don't have to get up yet . . .'

Sometimes, if we are hungry, thirsty, or deprived of tobacco, or are desperate to go to the lavatory, we dream of favourite meals, long cool drinks, stacks of cigarettes, or that the visit to the lavatory has been accomplished—this last, occasionally, with distressingly *real* results. Here is wish-fulfilment at its most straightforward, which is often demonstrated in children's dreams: the chocolates they were made to give as a present without tasting became theirs, the postponed visit to the fair was made . . . and a little child may have some difficulty in distinguishing between dream and truth.

However, most dreams do not seem to fit so snugly into Freud's wish-fulfilment category. How about those that have a comprehensible content but hardly tie in with our waking thoughts? For instance, a dream of some well-liked relative dying, when there is no reason to expect, fear, or assume such an event.

And what about the majority of dreams, in which events are disconnected and apparently meaningless?

To understand how Freud arrived at his interpretations of these 'unintelligible' dreams we have to examine the way in which he thought the dream functions. It is worthwhile remembering that those who consider the unravelling of the dream and nightmare to be of benefit to the individual's mental well-being may refer to one or more of Freud's terms, even if they cannot accept all his theories and findings.

For Freud the dream contains two distinct areas: the manifest and the latent. The manifest is what we recall. The latent is the repressed or unconscious wish that produces the manifest—it is the dream thought.

This is most easily demonstrated with those unambiguous wish-fulfilment dreams. The manifest content is, for example, that we have arrived at the holiday destination. The latent is the longing for that arrival. In overtly erotic dreams we are often surprised by the manifest, which shows us indulging in activities involving other people that we would not normally accept during waking life. According to Freud, that dream is the fulfilment of a desire that we could not consciously admit to having.

Freud believed that some part of the manifest always relates to an event in the near past, usually from the previous day. If it seems very trivial then free-association reveals its nature. Further, deeper association gradually uncovers its links with a more deeply repressed experience belonging to the distant past. This is possibly why some apparently unexciting dream can make us as anxious as a distinctly frightening one.

When a dream does not appear to make much sense, the images should be read as if they were parts of a charade composed of pictures. Two images that have no relation to each other at first glance may be pictorial syllables forming the name of a place, person, or even some book or film which has a significant bearing on repressed memories.

For Freud, incoherent dreams are the result of five special mechanisms: condensation, displacement, representation, symbolization, and secondary elaboration. The following is a summary of how each concept is imagined to work.

*Condensation*  It usually takes little more than half a page to describe the manifest content of even a quite complicated dream or nightmare. Once interpretation begins, however, the content expands as the latent factors are revealed. Meanings appear behind meanings until what had first seemed like random bits of jigsaw becomes an epic film, which might start with your own birth and range over countless experiences that you were not consciously aware of having.

*Displacement*  In order for the repressed memory to get past the mind's censorship, it adopts an unrecognizable form. Unpleasant or hurtful feelings are attached to a substitute object instead of the original one. The unconscious presents childish violent wishes in undisguised terms, so the adult might have a dream about smashing a doll, which makes the dreamer feel unaccountably miserable or worried, although on waking the incident would seem too trivial to merit serious attention. Freud believed that anxiety in dreams is often aroused even by the disguised fulfilment of a repressed wish, especially if the original repression was necessary to spare the individual guilt, fear, or pain.

As a child the dreamer might have had a wild urge to kill the parent who prevented it from doing something that seemed vitally important. If that parent 'went away' through illness, death, or divorce, it is easy to understand the child believing its 'murderous' impulses had caused the disappearance; but these feelings remain in the unconscious of the adult who remembers nothing of its infantile fury and the ensuing guilt.

*Representation*  Dream images represent specific ideas rather than abstractions, which is another reason why the manifest may seem bizarre. Perhaps you know someone you like a lot, but who doesn't respond and acts coldly towards you. In your dream the abstract characteristic you attribute to this person becomes a reality and you see his or her image standing in the snow.

Visual images are unable to express the ideas conveyed in words like 'as if', 'because', 'although'. Cause and effect may appear as one scene following on another. The dream cannot explain that the second happened just because of the first. Only interpretation can reveal just what the unconscious is trying to indicate in these instances. All kinds of essential expressions and feelings are incapable of being presented pictorially. 'You make me sick' would have to be shown quite literally as the dreamer suffering a bilious attack. 'I feel trapped' might be communicated by depicting the dreamer within some imprisoning situation, perhaps lost in a maze, behind prison bars, or manacled to a wall. The concept of something beyond our control might appear in a dream as driving a car along a winding road with a deep ravine on one side and a high cliff on the other: as you drive you find that neither steering nor brakes respond; you are imprisoned in a crazily jolting vehicle hurtling you towards destruction.

*Symbolization* This is perhaps the most abused, misunderstood, and misapplied of Freudian concepts, although probably the best known. According to Freud, in order for a dream's erotic content to evade the censor, the images must be replaced by apparently non-sexual symbols. He did warn that the interpretation required great caution for the symbols frequently contained more than one meaning, which made their translation a tricky and ambiguous task, especially when you consider that the genitals can be represented by another part of the body. Freud was anxious, too, that an interpreter should use the dreamer's own free-association together with the reading of the symbols: the two methods were intended to be complementary. To rely on an arbitrary application of a list of symbols would mean regressing to the world of the ancient dream book.

Freud damned any such mechanical interpretation as 'unscientific', although it has to be admitted that the whole theory of symbolization relies on art rather than science since it is impossible to prove reliably that the replacement images do have identical connotations in all minds and societies. An orthodox Jew or Moslem might have a nightmare about eating pork—whether this indicated a secret wish or the pork symbolized an even more taboo activity—yet a dream of eating pork for someone of a different social conditioning would scarcely share the same significance or induce such horror.

*Secondary Elaboration*  This is the final stage in the dream work. On waking, the mind tries to recapture the dream but adds or subtracts certain elements. This process is continued when the patient recounts the dream. The area where particular details vary with each retelling is the one that both dreamer and analyst are advised to examine most carefully.

Obviously these interpretative mechanisms can be applied to nightmare as well as dream. However, the wish-fulfilment explanation, especially of concealed erotic desires, while being satisfactory for some dreams, fails to recognize how a dream often contains also the conflict created by that wish—and it scarcely offers an adequate interpretation for all nightmares and anxiety dreams which rend sleep and terrify the dreamer. How, then, did Freud apply his theories to encompass these?

Initially, by sticking to his sexual guns.

> I maintain that neurotic anxiety has its origin in the sexual life, and corresponds to a libido which has been deflected from its object and has found no employment ... From it we may deduce the doctrine that *anxiety-dreams are dreams of sexual content, and that the libido appertaining to this content has been transformed into anxiety*. [my italics]

Rather uneasily, or so it seems, Freud admitted that, where an attempt at wish-fulfilment in the unconscious disturbs the censor so deeply that it can no longer maintain a state of rest, the dream becomes the disturber instead of the guardian of sleep. He explained that the anxiety dream—a neurotic symptom—acts as a compromise in the conflict between the unconscious and the preconscious by bringing it to an end.

Although Freud contended that most children's dreams are simple matters of wish-fulfilment, where he was compelled to face the fact of his own and his patients' infantile bad dreams he produced sexually orientated interpretations.

Little Hans, who awoke in terror having dreamed his mother had gone away, was suffering a repression and punishment dream; the anxiety producing it arose from the child's fear of his forbidden oedipal impulses. That is Freud's reading of the dream, although most of us might conclude that this is a typical example of the childhood nightmare of being abandoned by the person relied upon for love and protection.

The four-year-old's cannibalistic nightmare of wolves sitting around a walnut tree sounds like another fairly usual nasty dream but Freud identified it as being caused by a profound terror of castration, a pre-birth fear of being eaten, and an anal-homosexual fixation. Admittedly, this dream occurred after the child had been the victim of sexual seduction and in fact the nightmare contained the seeds of a later psychosis: in adulthood the unfortunate patient developed paranoia and persecution delusions.

An adolescent's recurring bad dream of being chased by a man with a hatchet and rooted to the spot is a quite common nightmare, as many of us can testify. To interpret it Freud worked his way through many recollections to the patient's childhood memory of his parents making love, which in his mind was associated with violence, fighting, and the shedding of blood.

These sex-ridden interpretations may well have applied to the cases in question but, as a comprehensive explanation of the nightmare phenomenon, they seem singularly unsatisfactory. Sex and fear are two of our deepest drives. We do have others— and those two are not related in every instance. That depends on the individual's experience. To use 'sex problem' case histories as a foundation for a general theory seems to be building on quicksand.

It must not be forgotten that Freud was anxious to point out he had never said that *all* dreams are about erotic desires; but he did insist that those night terrors with hallucinations—the bugbear of childhood—

> can only be due to misunderstood and rejected sexual impulses, which, if recorded, would probably show a temporal periodicity,

since an intensification of sexual libido may equally be produced by accidentally exciting impressions and by spontaneous periodic processes of development.

However, in 1920, in answer to the problem of recurring nightmares and anxiety dreams, Freud put forward another suggestion that offers more than a spark of hope for the sufferer but which has failed to attract as much attention as his wish-fulfilment theory. From studying neurotic symptoms, the repetitive play of children, and the recurring fearful dream, Freud drew the conclusion that these are attempts to master events that could not be dealt with originally.

Sigmund Freud did so much to illumine the dark workings of the mind that it is hardly just to blame him for not coming up with all the answers to dreams and nightmares. He never claimed to understand the whole truth. What he did was to pioneer a path that no one had cared to admit existed, a path for others to explore.

Freud's biographer, Ernest Jones, was a whole-hearted devotee of Freudian concepts and on these he based his work *On the Nightmare*. This was mostly written in 1909 and 1910 and was therefore not governed by the idea of 'mastering a stimulus retrospectively'. The book contains, to use John Bond's phrase, 'the origins of many old epithets and quaint names', a multitude of beliefs surrounding the nightmare and an analysis of how they are linked to the folklore and mythology of the vampire, witch, devil, incubus, and werewolf. One section is devoted to the etymology of the words 'mare' and 'mara', demonstrating—at least from a psychoanalytical standpoint—how the horse and the night fiend could be melded together and interchanged.

As a seeker after a rational explanation for the nightmare, the eighteenth-century Dr Bond would have been perplexed by Dr Jones' claim as to its true significance, which sounds more as if it had issued from the lips of a witchcraft-bedazzled medieval theologian than a twentieth-century medical man involved in psychoanalysis. In the preface Jones assured the learned professions and the general public that from his intensive research he had concluded that the nightmare was caused by the weight of guilt and terror everyone inherits in the unconscious, and that religion was one of the best ways of helping human beings to cope with the burden. A sceptic might add: 'That surely depends on how much the religion had contributed to instilling guilt in the first place.'

If the nightmare is taken as a neurotic symptom, then we are all born tainted by its causes, from the view of Jones and his kind, rather like those who believe that we are marked with original sin from birth. It is an interesting topic to debate, but I think less than helpful for the parent who gets up at night to comfort a child screaming in the aftermath of a nightmare.

Stripped of all its fascinating historical and legendary references and conjectures about meanings, Jones' book aimed to demonstrate that 'the malady known as Nightmare is always an expression of intense mental conflict centring about some form of repressed sexual desire'; and, indeed, for many of those medieval instances of incubus, the nightmare as the dark and poisoned fruit of the tree of repressed sexuality seems a peculiarly apt explanation. However, Jones proceeded to locate the greatest dread in the area of maximum repression and this he unhesitatingly associated with incestuous desires. The same explanation held good for all fear dreams, the degree of terror aroused corresponding to the guilt over the repressed incestuous wishes striving for satisfaction in fantasy form. If such a wish were not suppressed there would be no terror and instead of a nightmare the sleeper would simply experience an erotic dream.

Jones was wholly convinced that the monsters and similar aggressive creatures that prowl the nightmare are caused by repression transforming the highly desirable, but taboo, into something utterly repellent. That this transposition occurs in mythology and fairy tales as well as in dreams suggests a deeply embedded conflict between desire and inhibition within the human psyche. Since Jones regarded many children as possessed of a sadistic view of sexual functions, he interpreted nightmare nasties as really parents in disguise.

Even now it is easy to see why Jones' contemporaries must have been shocked by such theories. There are plenty who would still feel uneasy when confronted with them. The nightmare in itself is disturbing enough without Jones' explanation.

An amusing example of how one person at least reacted to Jones' opinions occurred in 1909 when Jones wrote: '... the association in general between the sexual instinct and the emotions of fear and dread is a very *intimate* one ...' The aghast printer altered 'intimate' to 'distant' and, although the author corrected this at the proof stage, 'distant' was the word to appear on publication.

For Ernest Jones, and those of similar Freudian outlook, his thesis was supported by the facts produced from psychoanalysis. By 1914 doctors and psychologists outside Freud's own group of founder psychoanalysts had reluctantly begun to accept his approach to the problems affecting the human mind; but it was also around this time that the rift occurred between Freud and his closest collaborators, springing from private and professional differences.

Those who differed from Freudian theories of psychoanalysis, not surprisingly, reached other conclusions about the reasons for and importance of dreams and nightmares. They did not disagree with Freud's basic premise that the dream, pleasant or horrific, was a significant psychic event, but they were less convinced by the meanings he ascribed to dreams and his methods of interpretation. The wish-fulfilment theory, and the emphasis on erotic desires pervading the unconscious, did not satisfy them, nor could they view dream dramas as purely neurotic symptoms mirroring those early recollections and experiences that an individual could neither surmount nor integrate into the adult character.

Freud undoubtedly suffered personally when the brilliant men he respected and trusted to uphold and develop his ideas began rejecting them to follow their own divergent paths. It must have been particularly painful when Carl Gustav Jung, whom he had come to regard as the heir-apparent to his kingdom of ideas, broke away to found a separate school of therapeutic psychology.

This can be seen as a rather fortunate parting of the ways because Jung's ideas were to lend balance to Freud's, and add another dimension to the world of dreams. With their insistence on the original causes being the meaning behind a dream, Freud's theories might, quite unintentionally, lead people to despair for they look back at factors which cannot be altered, and so irredeemably seem to jeopardize the future. Jung, however, took the view that dreams—including the nightmare and the anxiety dream—are ways of leading us towards a richer, more complete existence.

In *Civilization in Transition* he described the dream as

> a little hidden door in the innermost and most secret recesses of the psyche, opening into that cosmic night which was psyche long before there was any ego consciousness, and which will remain psyche no matter how far our ego consciousness may extend ... All consciousness separates; but in dreams we put on the likeness of that more universal, truer, more eternal man dwelling in the darkness of primordial night. There he is still the whole, and the whole is in him, indistinguishable from nature and bare of all egohood. Out of these all-uniting depths arises the dream, be it never so infantile, never so grotesque, never so immoral.

Perhaps these beautiful imaginative phrases show why Freud criticized Jung's dream interpretation methods as 'unscientific' and overdependent on intuitive understanding. For Freud the dream demonstrates how we are shackled to our physical natures; for Jung the dream is essentially spiritual and encompasses all the known and unknown regions of the human psyche. Dreaming is the means by which we try to discover the reason for being—a restatement of all past unresolved problems—and the meeting-point between past and future. Since the dream is the product of the individual's psyche, Jung believed that if we could really comprehend it we should know more about the entire psychic process, and consequently become better integrated as individuals.

As he regarded dreaming to be a vital factor in human existence, Jung could not allow that it and its interpretations are only to be associated with neuroses. Pointing out that many people had been spurred on to great ambitions and deeds by their dreams, making them dissatisfied with life as it was, he argued against the dream being merely the fulfilment of a wish. Like those of us who have woken suddenly from an anxiety dream or nightmare, Jung wondered how the dream can be the guardian of sleep when it is often instrumental in disturbing it.

He could not accept the dream as some cunning device to trick the dreamer out of understanding what the unconscious is saying —and, if the censorship mechanism is so important, why can it be circumvented? Nor would Jung accept the manifest as a façade disguising the true meaning because it is difficult to comprehend. That would be like saying that a page of Chinese writing makes no sense and is therefore obscuring its meaning. The actuality would be that we do not know how to read Chinese. If we want to understand the page, then we had better start learning the language.

Jung noticed that one dream often seems to interpret a previous one, as if the unconscious tries to find terms with which to make itself understood. Therefore, an important Jungian concept is that no one dream can be interpreted on its own merit. Only by examining a series can it be seen whether certain factors recur or are always absent.

Because he believed that each dream was unique to the individual, any mechanical or arbitrary method of interpretation through symbols could scarcely reveal the meaning for that individual. This system is viable only in the case of certain universal symbols, which mean the same thing to all people of all centuries. When it came to that extensive list of Freudian sex symbols, Jung wondered how many of the objects—each with an utterly different function—could represent the same thing. He considered it more valuable to discover what the objects in a dream meant to the dreamer, whom he encouraged to talk about them. This is known as 'amplification' and certainly does not always reduce a gun, a knife, or a cigarette to meaning a penis, or a stove, a vase, or a ship to meaning a vagina or womb. Unlike free-association, amplification requires the subject to concentrate on the object under discussion in order to perceive exactly what it does mean to the self.

Jung also argued against some things in dreams being regarded as symbols while others were interpreted at their face-value. How could the truth be approached if the interpreter decides which are symbols and which are not? Perhaps most significantly from the practical point of view, Jung thought it essential that the psychoanalyst should undergo analysis—something Freud had never experienced. Only through this could a doctor become aware of the motives and causes behind his or her own approach and reaction to a patient's problems and dreams.

Freud deciphered many of his patients' dream symbols in sexual terms because this produced a helpful solution to their neuroses as well as *his* own undoubted problems. While Jung never rejected Freud's important discoveries about sexuality, he could not accept sexual desire as the be-all-and-end-all of dreams: ambition, religion, patriotism, maternal love, altruism, hate, and fear can be just as powerful impulses.

Jung's concept of the unconscious was far more mystic and complex than Freud's. He believed that it not only derived its material from repressed conscious experiences but also from universal archaic structures in the brain, and racial and familial memories. Like some fantastic kind of computer the unconscious is able to create infinite permutations and from this source emerge more dream images and thought associations than could ever be created through conscious concentration. Just as the body contains a physical self-regulating system so, according to Jung, does the unconscious attempt to balance the personality through the compensatory role of dreams. Unlike the wish-fulfilment theory this compensation process is related to the present rather than all those unrealized childhood aspirations.

Jung believed dreams could help because they represent what

is repressed in the personality and tell us not just what we *desire* but what we *need* to be complete. Thus the dominant person will dream of being submissive, the excessively tidy of being disorganized; the rake will experience guilt, the brave will be cowardly, the timid will be brave, the unnoticed will be recognized and the meek will dominate ... No wonder, then, that quite innocuous-seeming dreams make us anxious and frightened for we find ourselves in situations we would normally shun.

For Jung the dream was the provider of the equilibrium that life requires to follow a proper course: love and hate, youth and age, birth and death, joy and sadness, safety and risk. These are not merely opposing concepts. Together they offer a totality. We cannot experience one without knowing the other. Jung also saw the dream as containing everything the conscious mind rejects and forgets and, through its compensatory role, possibly indicating factors that have been overlooked in waking life. Thus the dream helps to solve problems over which one has wracked one's brains all the previous day. In this way Jung felt that dreams might be predictive (as the ancients had believed) for, by revealing a potential that circumstances had forced the dreamer to abandon, they might serve as signposts towards maturity.

However, this is not the totality of the Jungian unconscious: he believed the individual also possessed a 'collective unconscious', containing the universal ancestral experiences that appear in 'primordial images'. He explained that through the collective unconscious human beings house not only all the truly beautiful and great thoughts, feelings, and impulses conceived by humanity, but also every deed of shame and abomination ever perpetrated. From this source sprang the meaning of existence and those fundamental preoccupations that have always conditioned humankind: birth, life, death, love, bravery, beauty, evil, religious inspiration, and the conflicts inherent in development and maturing.

It was from the collective unconscious that Jung believed the truly meaningful dreams arose—powerful, beautiful, and sometimes terrifying. Such 'big' dreams may apply to a group—as with religious prophecies and visions—or they can be directed to the individual and occur during significant phases of life which are accompanied by profound psychological changes.

Just as our bodies still carry traces of our primeval aquatic ancestry so our minds inherit the potentials of human imagination. Jung described the form in which these 'primordial images' manifest during conscious life as 'archetypal images', and their potentials as 'archetypes'—the pattern of thought found in religion, religious rituals, myths, fairy tales, dreams, and nightmares.

Jung never claimed that the archetypes themselves were inherited; only that the structures creating them were repeated in each of us. It is a theory difficult to prove or refute since, by the time an infant can report its sleep adventures, how can we gauge for certain whether or not particular dream shapes have been fashioned from environment, upbringing, or nursery stories? However, the similarity in imagery, portraying universal longings, terrors, emotions, and difficulties, emerges again and again in basic religious and secular tales, irrespective of continent or century, and discernible despite the variations in language and customs. Indeed, since so many dream symbols are to be found in world mythology Jung often used myths to help interpret a particular dream.

The earliest personal dream that Jung could recall is related in *Memories, Dreams, Reflections*. It was both strange and meaningful since it haunted his thoughts for the rest of his life; for Jung it was a clear example of content arising from the collective rather than the personal unconscious. How else could such primitive symbolism invade a little boy's dreams? It was also what we would describe as a nightmare since the child awoke sweating and terrified, and fearful of sleep on subsequent nights in case the dream returned. Jung was between three and four years old when he dreamed of entering a large, underground chamber of stone. Enthroned on a platform was a huge upright object made of flesh, with a single eye at its head, gazing upwards. Although this fleshy pillar did not stir, the child was frozen with horror, sensing that at any moment it must creep from the golden throne towards him. Then he heard his mother's voice somewhere outside and above, calling: '... That is the man-eater!'

Only much later did Jung begin to interpret this dream that seemed to talk of matters far beyond his comprehension. For him this was no Freudian penis or castration-fear dream; he was convinced he had been shown the 'ritual phallus'—a subterranean god 'not to be named'. Jung believed that his intellectual life took its unconscious beginnings from this early dream, which introduced him into the mysteries of the earth and illuminated the kingdom of darkness.

Not all Jung's childhood nightmares took such sophisticated form. Like so many children, he suffered bad dreams when his parents' relationship was in crisis—the charged atmosphere invading the child's psyche rather than being seen or understood at any conscious level. Jung's vivid anxiety dreams had to do with small things becoming large and overpowering—of a tiny ball approaching from afar until it swelled into a huge and overwhelming object, of birds perched upon telegraph wires which grew thicker and thicker until the sensation of fear shattered sleep ...

At this time in his life, night was laden with fearful and incomprehensible events. His parents were sleeping apart. He shared his father's room but a strange power seemed to emanate from his mother's. She, too, was a mysterious nocturnal being. One night Jung believed he saw a vague, semi-luminous shape emerge from her door; the head separated from the body and floated before 'like a little moon'; hydra-like, another head immediately grew; it, too, detached itself. The macabre scene was played out some six or seven times.

It is worth noting here that one of the best known archetypes is the Great Mother, the perfectly good woman, goddess, virgin, or saint, who intercedes and saves. The reverse of this archetype is the Terrible Mother, who frequently figures in fairy tales and myths. She is the angry goddess, the wicked witch, the cruel step-mother, and the 'Night-mare LIFE-IN-DEATH' of Coleridge.

Can this apparently archetypal maternal duality account for the fact that the nightmare is so often categorized as female?

Frequently in dreams children reflect these two aspects of the mother: when she is a kind, loving, and approachable sanctuary, and those inexplicable, terrifying occasions when, for the child, her anger is unintelligible and dreadful—as if the familiar figure had been demoniacally transformed into a malign and retribution-seeking being.

Those nightmares of monsters, ogres, and vampires, or those in which we crawl about dark caverns or wander beneath the sea, hark back to primeval existence, Jung believed. The images represent the darker emotions: lust, power, cruelty, guilt, and punishment. To Jung these bad dreams, however much they may make us fear sleep, might be usefully absorbed into the personality so long as they are correctly interpreted.

Once dream and nightmare became legitimate subjects for psychiatrist and psychoanalyst to pursue, fresh theories began to emerge, and existing ones were modified, expanded, or even fused together. No one disputed that the unconscious might reveal vital clues about the individual's mental state during sleep. Not everyone, however, can agree on the exact significance of the nightmare images: the 'collective unconscious' is no more a totally acceptable hypothesis than repressed infantile sexual desire.

Most tend to regard nightmares as fundamentally a childhood problem so even where it occurs in adulthood the subject's infancy is examined for clues as to the proper meaning.

The small child's perception of its helplessness when confronted by its own internal feelings and the vast and terrifying external world, as expressed in early nightmares, seems to be revived whenever older dreamers feel themselves threatened by parallel overwhelming forces. Obviously, as imagination and experience develop, dreams become more complex but ego-regression probably accounts for the similarity of nightmare shapes among dreamers of widely differing ages. In one study of 'combat nightmares', some soldiers' bad dreams began to alter from reliving specific battle-scenes to being menaced by the monsters of childhood. We are not so much delving into cosmic night as reverting to our own infancy and this may well contribute to the inordinate panic and vulnerability felt by otherwise 'controlled grown-ups' during a nightmare attack; it also explains why, on waking, the adult's terror and confusion resemble that displayed by a child in similar circumstances.

There are theories that the vampire, spider, crab, and octopus which menace and disgust us, mainly in the bad dreams of childhood, are the result of the individual's 'objectification of physiological sensations'—their ubiquity based more on shared physiology than any primitive racial memory. Feelings that frighten a baby can stick in the memory as sensations which could overpower. Stomachache may make the child feel as if some terrible crab were grasping its vitals. Because children, animals, and primitive minds locate blame outside themselves for things they cannot control, their troubles seem to be inflicted by some invisible, external creature. So it is not 'I have a pain'. Rather it is 'this pain is not my doing', transforming 'it' (the pain) into a vile being which is 'doing a bad thing to me'. In much the same way, the child's experience of orgasm, which leaves it feeling weak and overpowered, becomes a vampire that has sucked its strength. Naturally these fears can be aggravated by parental threats and rebukes so it is hardly surprising that such shapes intrude in our darkest dreams.

The conflict that stems from fear of the consequences of yielding to our own deepest impulses is widely regarded as one of the chief keys that open the door to let in the nightmare. Sex, aggression, and fear itself are projected outside the self and represented as 'ravening' beasts or terrible figures that pursue and annihilate. Ogres, witches, and similar horrors may symbolize retribution from parents, teachers, or guardians for having flouted authority, if not in reality then by secretly containing the self-will towards the forbidden thing.

Psychologists warn parents that the use of excessive threats as deterrents for quite trivial activities, and the imposition of too rigid a code on a very small child, will cause not only nightmares but also neuroses. The sense of approaching catastrophe that characterizes many nightmares may well be the result of some undetected moral conflict. From an early age we are instilled with a very black-and-white sense of right and wrong on which our whole personal worth seems to hinge so we are bound to fear that any transgression (in thought as well as in deed) may forfeit the affection, attention, and even presence of those on whom we depend completely. No wonder, then, that the nightmare, which contains our miseries and anxieties, is associated with the most vulnerable, impressionable, and exploratory stage of life.

As if they are reactions to perils which we have to surmount in the course of our development, anxiety dreams and nightmares frequently occur at critical phases in childhood and adult life, starting out with our terror of abandonment, of strangers, and of physical hurt and culminating with our dread of failure, impotence, and death. In the case of healthy human beings these apprehensions are not usually apparent during waking hours.

One explanation as to why a nightmare erupts each time we are faced with some fresh task or situation is that we feel defenceless and anxious until we have conquered it. This may well echo that earlier greater vulnerability when the baby feels unable to control the movements of the 'love object' on which it totally relies. How can it be sure that the mother will not desert it or that it will not be 'gobbled up' by some 'thing'? Another explanation is that, in order to progress, the individual has to assert the self; in the very young this is associated with destructive wishes against those who seem to impede it, whom it views as 'aggressors'.

This pitting of the self against the adult world naturally brings the child into conflict with its own impulses. Murderous rage against those it loves and depends on for reassurance and everything else (or is supposed to love, such as brothers and sisters) may erupt in nightmare as wolf, tiger, or unidentifiable monster; but the victim, more often than not, is the dreamer and not the target of its fury, as if the dream is demonstrating that the result of giving way to the primitive urge must be the destruction of the self. Sometimes the nightmare monster goads the child to carry out a terrible deed but then the dreamer is suddenly transformed into the object of its own violent, secret wishes.

You will often see a child projecting unacceptable behaviour onto a toy or a long-suffering pet. If you scold your small daughter she may well punish a doll for 'doing' whatever was 'nasty', 'forbidden', or 'rude'. In that way she identifies with you, the 'aggressor', sheds some of her own shame and fear of your displeasure, vents her own anger at having been thwarted, and perhaps continues the banned activity through an inanimate medium. When a child has been the victim of some kind of violent attack, a similar defence mechanism may appear in its nightmares: the dreamer allies with the attacker in an attempt to evade the danger of another's hostility by 'internalizing' those threatening attributes. Yet, once again, angry sounds or monsters materialize to imperil the dreamer as its ego reacts.

The borderline between desire and deed is hair-thin in a very young mind so if it wanted someone 'hurt' or 'dead', and a dream was full of disaster, it may seem as if the act of violence has somehow taken place, and the consequences must be borne—consequences that mean retaliation, or desertion and rejection, by those the child depends on, which is why the dreamer *has* to be the victim in its own nightmares. The confusion a child experiences on waking from a dreadful dream alone in a dark room is largely due to this inability to distinguish between reality and fantasy. Not only does it take time for this skill to be mastered, it is one of the important steps in the successful development of the individual's ego, and requires parental sympathy and support.

It is necessary, therefore, that a child who wakes in screaming, bewildered terror is given love and reassurance so that it can come to grips with reality and not feel rejected or punished. In this way it gradually learns what is dream and what is not, and begins to apply objectivity during sleep, employing the calm and reasonable qualities displayed by its parents who have gently insisted that the nasty things are not real. Bad dreams still frighten the child as much as they do more experienced adults but at least a part of the mind can then argue: 'This is only a dream.' And that is a very big step.

Children from violent and deprived backgrounds seem particularly predisposed to sleep disorders and their ability to discriminate between the events of real life and nightmare is visibly impaired. The terror in their dreams is merely another aspect of the existence they encounter by day. Adult figures on whom they have to rely do not appear as aggressors only in nightmare but are so in reality. Perhaps no one comes to comfort them or they are punished for crying out by parents who feel helpless to deal with the infantile terror which is often an echo of their own. Or perhaps—and this is even worse—the adult treats the child's grotesque fantasies as 'real' for his own purposes and threatens that the nightmare assailant—ghost, monster, or nasty person—'will get you if you're bad'. There are those, too, who use the child's nightmares to hide their own guilt and say about something harmful that has actually occurred: 'It's not true, you dreamed it.' Such treatment can scar the child's mind, retard its ability to hold on to reality, and may later make it more prone to psychosis.

'We are such stuff as dreams are made on', and we ignore that at our peril.

Any sufferer will agree that the most distressing kind of nightmare is the one that returns again and again. You go to bed not just with the apprehension that you will have a bad dream but also the foreknowledge of the form that the dream will take. It seems a punishment handed out by the darker gods.

While Robert Louis Stevenson was studying law at Edinburgh, and in conflict with the narrow Presbyterian standards set by the city's professional classes, he was the victim of a particularly depressing repetitive nightmare.

> ... in his dream-life, he passed a long day in the surgical theatre, his heart in his mouth, his teeth on edge, seeing

monsterous malformations and the abhorred dexterity of surgeons. In a heavy, rainy, foggy evening he came forth into the South Bridge, turned up the High Street, and entered the door of a tall land, at the top of which he supposed himself to lodge. All night long, in his wet clothes, he climbed the stairs ... and at every second flight a flaring lamp with a reflector. All night long, he brushed by single persons passing downward —beggarly women of the street, great, weary, muddy labourers, poor scarecrows of men, pale parodies of women—but all drowsy and weary like himself, and all single, and all brushing against him as they passed. In the end, out of a northern window, he would see day beginning to whiten over the Firth, give up the ascent, turn to descend, and in a breath be back again upon the streets, in his wet clothes, in the wet, haggard dawn, trudging to another day of monstrosities and operations. Time went quicker in the life of dreams ... and it went, besides, more intensely, so that the gloom of these fancied experiences clouded the day, and he had shaken off their shadow ere it was time to lie down and to renew them ...

Precisely how long Stevenson put up with this nightmare is not certain but it was 'long enough to leave a great black blot upon his memory, long enough to send him, trembling for his reason, to the doors of a certain doctor; whereupon with a simple draught he was restored to the common lot of man ....'.

Stevenson was fortunate. Most people's recurring nightmares reappear years after the original stressful happening. They usually stem directly from an objective experience in adult life as well as infancy. The best-known example is the soldier or civilian who has undergone a mental and/or physical shock during war. But equally traumatic circumstances include: going into hospital, accidents of any kind, surgery, assault (especially by a parent figure), and the loss of someone on whom you depend. In the nightmare these events may be perfectly recognizable, just like a filmed record, or they may be distorted by condensation and symbolization, like the patient who had been treated for cardiac arrest but could only recall a nightmare about huge giants stamping on the chests of tiny people!

Some authorities contend that the repetitive anxiety dream and nightmare, as a symptom of neurosis, does not necessarily result from the *obvious* objective experience. Rather it is linked with something in early life where the ego felt itself similarly threatened by annihilation. Those who have treated cases of war neurosis (whether resulting from World War I or the American action in Vietnam) show that many patients had unhappy relationships and childhood backgrounds marked by nightmares, fear, and insecurity. So the man who suffers a persistent suffocation nightmare apparently as a result of a tunnel caving-in during a prisoner-of-war escape attempt, may in fact be reliving the experience of a difficult birth.

Birth, near-suffocation, and abrupt separation from the mother in the first hours or days of life may bruise the unconscious but, as long as no similar incident occurs, and the child feels secure as it develops, those earliest of objective experiences are usually insufficient to breed nightmares. However, when the original fears are confirmed by a later event, or the child continues to live with insecurity, the dread that spawns the nightmare may remain.

It should be emphasized that the 'objective experience' which triggers off a bad dream need not be unpleasant. That depends on how much a harmless event seems to substantiate a current underlying anxiety or stirs memories of something disturbing from the past. The small girl who has dreadful nightmares when her parents are away for a weekend is not necessarily reacting so much to the present as to her previous apprehension that some past act of naughtiness and rebellion would result in parental rejection. Present facts seem to justify her original fears.

Those who propose that our sleeping adventures are the products of unresolved problems see the ordinary dream as working towards an answer so that sleep may continue untroubled; but they are compelled to define the nightmare as a 'failed dream', since it insists on stating the anxiety without offering any solution, until the sleeper is woken by intolerable emotional strain. Yet if we are prepared to accept the nightmare not merely as a symptom of our problems but as trying to help us come to terms with something from the past, we might, rather grudgingly, look on it as an instrument of adaptation.

Not a very efficient one, you may counter, when it destroys sleep and frays nerves.

In return, a theory is offered that the nightmare may be attempting to save us from something worse. The fear provoked by the causal traumatic event is at least confined within the sleep boundary so it does not fill consciousness and overwhelm the ego as it must initially have done to produce the trauma. If it did, the result would be psychosis.

Some evidence exists to support the idea of the nightmare as container of anxiety. When patients suffering from depression and paranoia not unnaturally forced themselves to stay awake to avoid nightmares, the daytime psychotic symptoms worsened. However, when they were treated for insomnia the nightmares did return *but* there was also a lessening in those daytime symptoms. Where people begin to recover from psychosis it has been recorded that often they experience more nightmares; but if the improvement is maintained the quality of the dreams becomes less and less disturbing, until perhaps we could reverse that famous phrase into 'a madness, a nightmare, a dream'.

One thing is common to all nightmares and many anxiety dreams—an exaggerated response to an internal danger which we are compelled to treat as if it existed externally, so that we wake and try to get the comfort of another person. This hints that the process might have something to do with safety and protection. Recent neurophysiological sleep studies tend to support the idea of the nightmare as a biological alarm system. The phases associated with dreaming appear to maintain an almost constant psychic awareness during sleep so that the body can be alerted to potential external hazard. The nightmare may therefore be a residual primeval mechanism which made the sleeping organism immediately aware of danger and so helped towards the survival of the human species.

Those who pursue the shadows in the mind have yet to prove a definitive cause of and role for the nightmare but existing theories are not to be disregarded simply because they cannot be upheld by clear-cut scientific experiment. Perhaps it would be more sensible to conclude that our nightmares are explained by an amalgam of several different ideas which are concerned not only with the individual's development but also with that of the human race.

# The Pitiless Muse

*So two nights passed: the night's dismay*
*Saddened and stunned the coming day.*
*Sleep, the wide blessing, seemed to me*
*Distemper's worst calamity.*
*The third night, when my own loud scream*
*Had waked me from the fiendish dream,*
*O'ercome with sufferings strange and wild,*
*I wept as I had been a child;*
*And having thus by tears subdued*
*My anguish to a milder mood,*
*Such punishments, I said, were due*
*To natures deepliest stained with sin,—*
*For aye entempesting anew*
*The unfathomable hell within,*
*The horror of their deeds to view,*
*To know and loathe, yet wish and do!*
*Such griefs with such men well agree,*
*But wherefore, wherefore fall on me?*
*To be beloved is all I need,*
*And whom I love, I love indeed.*
                        The Pains of Sleep  S. T. COLERIDGE

Few people in any one generation possess the talent to transmute dream and nightmare into an art form. Alas for Samuel Taylor Coleridge, the muse that inspired him to compose 'The Pains of Sleep' was not one to be courted, exploited, and put aside until needed again. The agonies so vividly described were born from his own experience. By 1803 the opium that had once brought the creator of 'The Ancient Mariner' his magnificent, 'streamy' half-consciousness had transformed his sleep into a nightmare-ridden hell. The beguiling opium dreams had been purchased at the highest price: the cost of a brilliant and original intellect and the metamorphosis of its owner into what we, of this half of the twentieth century, know as a junkie.

To his close friend, Tom Wedgewood, also a drug addict, Coleridge wrote on 16 September 1803:

> But the Night is my Hell, sleep my tormenting Angel. Three nights out of four I fall asleep, struggling to lie awake—and my frequent Night-screams have almost made me a nuisance in my own House. Dreams with me are no Shadows, but the very Substances and foot thick Calamities of my Life.

This letter is not merely an exaggerated form of sympathy-seeking. Others could testify all too grimly to Coleridge's 'tormenting Angel'. While he was staying at Dove Cottage, Grasmere, with the Wordsworths, Dorothy and Mary were compelled to take turns at sitting up with him while he slept. At the very first intimation of any approaching nightmare the women would rouse him. This was the only escape route that Coleridge could find to evade the fiend's embraces.

His poem evokes the agonized emotions of the nightmare rather than precise details of its contents; Coleridge's private notebooks are much more revealing. Descriptions of several nightmares show recurrent incidents of violent sexual aggression with Coleridge as the hapless, unwilling victim: lickerish females laid hands on his penis and importuning boys grabbed at his scrotum. The homosexual elements in Coleridge's nightmare fantasies may well echo some forced initiation into homosexuality during his school-days at Christ's Hospital; but the poet was undoubtedly a heterosexual, although his upbringing had clearly so imbued him with a terrible guilt about his own natural appetites that he longed to divorce spiritual love from physical love, with the resulting conflict tinting his nightmares.

Other terrors to parade through his sleep included: maiming and distorting images, being spied upon in particularly intimate circumstances, and the sensations of being lost or abandoned. Perhaps most telling for the man whose great talent was never to be fully realized were those bleak dreams in which he seemed to near some splendid, half-glimpsed destination that was never ultimately attained.

Inserted in the 1817 version of 'The Rime of the Ancient Mariner' is one of the most evocative nightmare word pictures in the English language:

> *The Night-mare* LIFE-IN-DEATH *was she,*
> *Who thicks man's blood with cold.*

The fiend that had been unchained by the deadly poppy was to stalk Coleridge's sleep in dark and terrible splendour until his death; the sleeper was its toy to be tossed into hell whenever an occasion arose.

Yet he could view nightmares with cool objectivity as long as they were not his own. Like other educated and intelligent people of his day, Coleridge took an enlightened standpoint. The nightmare was the result of a circulatory or digestive disturbance, and the mind

> by aid of the imaginative faculty, converts its judgement respecting the cause into a personal image as being the cause—the mind ... attributes the painful sensation received to a corresponding agent: an assassin, for instance, stabbing at the side, or a goblin sitting on the breast.

Scarcely belonging in the same literary stable as Coleridge, although admired by him, was Mrs Ann Radcliffe who saw the nightmare as inspiration. With the possible exception of *The Mysteries of Udolpho* her 'Gothick' works are not much read or appreciated nowadays. However, contemporary readers were not deterred by the stilted style nor by the way in which the wildest mysteries always had at their conclusion a disappointingly prosaic explanation: popular taste at that time tended towards the macabre, the frenzied, and the taboo; murder, gore, ghosts, incest, and rape were some of the choice ingredients for the artistic creations of the Romantic Movement's darker nightmarish aspect.

Ann Radcliffe's attitude to the nightmare was quite different from that of Coleridge. The fiend was billed as her commercial collaborator and she claimed to eat specially indigestible food just before retiring in order to procure the nightmare's visit so that its substance, where suitable, could be incorporated into her tales.

Anyone familiar with the feverish goings-on in her novels will probably not be too surprised by this admission. You cannot avoid sensing that Ann Radcliffe's grotesque muse was the commonplace offspring of toasted cheese or some such plausible parent that sat heavily on the digestive tract rather than of the soul. Her nightmare pangs provided no more than a delicious skin-deep *frisson* of horror whereas Coleridge's anguish arose from a psyche tortured by the malign and eternal fiend that had terrorized humankind from its outset.

That delightful story-teller Robert Louis Stevenson was another creative genius who put the dream and nightmare to work. How pleasant to learn that he was freed from the childhood bondage of the 'night hag' and in adulthood made himself master of the powers which had first sent her to him. For Stevenson the brain during sleep was a tiny, lighted theatre. While the body lay dormant intricate dramas were performed nightly upon this stage. Those who created these plays for Stevenson's entertainment he called his 'Brownies' or 'little people'. He educated them in the commercial requirements of the exacting market-place, they shared his financial worries and his training, and showed him how to build up emotion and plot to suit his stories best. Stevenson was prepared to attribute at least fifty per cent of his success to these manikins.

The 'Brownies' who 'have not a rudiment of what we call conscience' evidently liked their stories to be 'somewhat fantastic ... hot, full of passion and the picturesque ... and they have no prejudice against the supernatural'. No wonder they provided Stevenson with scenes for that never-failing spine-chiller *The Strange Case of Dr Jekyll and Mr Hyde*.

Of course, in true muse-fashion, the 'little people' were not always to be relied upon. Sometimes Stevenson would waken too soon, believing he had a complete tale. His excitement would give way to vexation as he discovered the performance was unfinished. At other times, when he slept too deeply, the Brownies seemed to perform their roles aimlessly and drowsily so that on waking the play had to be recognized as nothing but a 'tissue of absurdities'. Still, if we consider the rich variety of Stevenson's work, we must accept his tribute to the 'little people'; more often than not they were of honest service to him.

It has been mooted that creativity and insanity are two likely reactions to those fundamental conflicts which may give rise to a severe nightmare attack. Unhappily these conditions are sometimes indivisible and, while more phlegmatic mortals may be amused by the antics of the 'mad artistic genius', an individual so burdened is unlikely to derive much hilarity from the state. In certain people creative endeavour has achieved a great deal in counteracting mental instability by integrating painful memories and unbearable experiences. By mastering the nightmare, instead of succumbing to its dominion, the sufferer may save the self from madness.

At sixty Mark Twain received the kind of blow which must threaten the sanity of any parent. A cable arrived to tell him that his favourite child, Suzie, had died suddenly of meningitis. Twain later recorded that it seemed almost impossible that he could have undergone a 'thunder-stroke like that and live'. The shock and grief inspired him with guilt and rage. Overwhelmed by these unmanageable emotions, he turned in on himself to dwell among dreams and fantasies.

As the details of his nightmares grew more terrifying so his grasp on the reality of waking life began to wane. In these dreams the unprincipled and uncontrollable other self for whom Twain

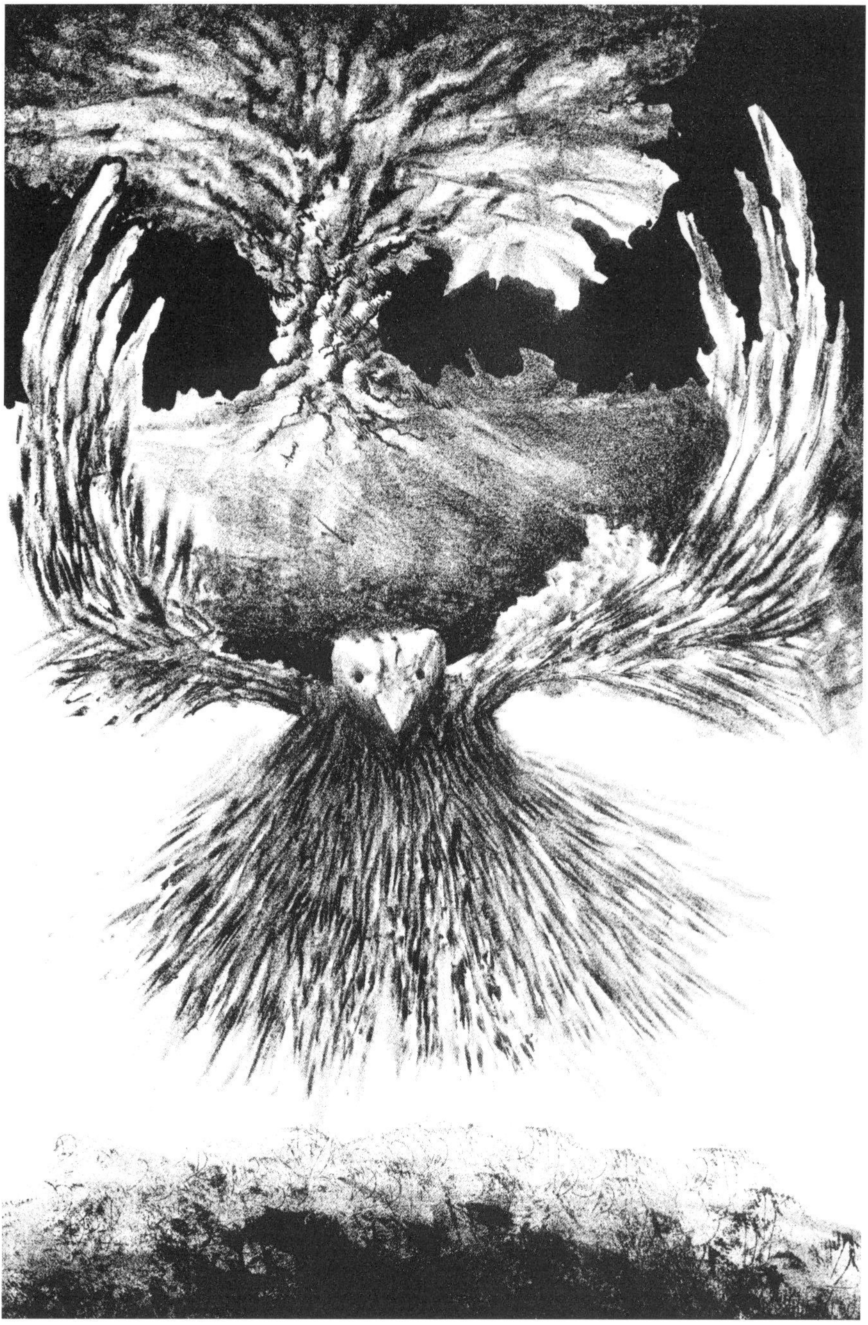

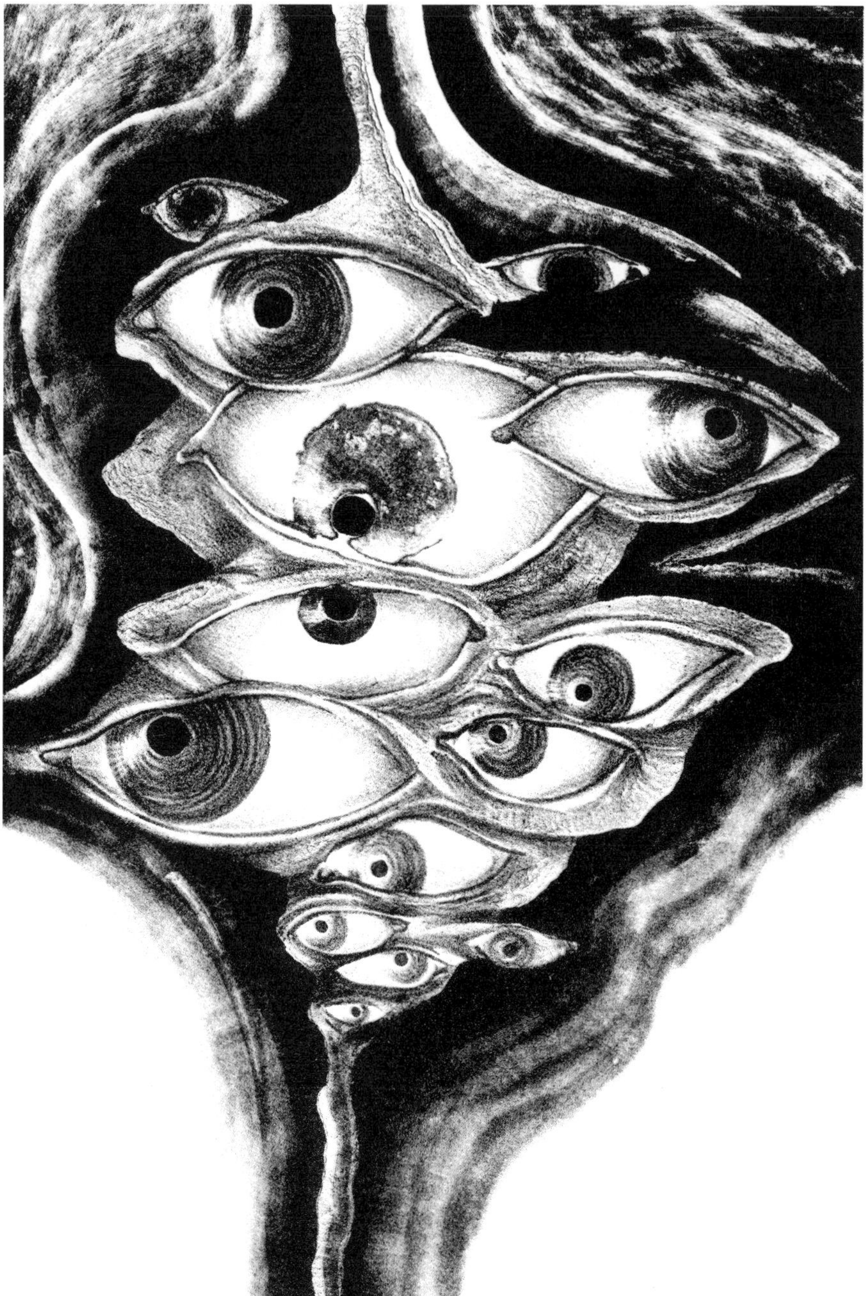

refused to take responsibility would go to places and do things which were inconceivable to him in waking life. This 'creature' indulged in forbidden sexual practices and wandered lost in caves and through the corridors of 'monstrous hotels'. His mind was engulfed with visions of fire and destruction. Twain managed to invest all these harrowing images and emotions in his literary output. Although he worked as if driven by the demons of perdition the effort enabled him to retain control on his sanity but the irony and bitterness that personal tragedy had brought him were increasingly reflected in his later works. He used his own battle to separate dream from reality as the foundation for tales where the characters' dreams become actuality.

The nightmare is a harsh and demanding muse that refuses to be ignored and its painful influence may go on festering for years because of the dream's 'failure', being unable to resolve those conflicts arising from some overwhelming and intolerable event or memory which gave shape to the dream.

When he was in his sixties Henry James wrote *The Jolly Corner* based on 'the most appalling yet admirable nightmare of my life' —one that had occurred when he was thirteen. Both the dream and the story are about the terrifying struggle between a man and a supernatural entity which threatens to destroy him. The ghost is possessed by aspects of the personality that the man could have had if he had had less fear. Naturally the tale is much more complex than the original nightmare but, while it mirrors and elaborates the dilemmas contained in the dream, it cannot resolve or diminish them.

There are so many writers whose works are based on dreamed experiences that it would be beyond the scope of this chapter to list them. Left to our own devices most of us would probably come up with some author whom we felt certain had based a plot on a personal nightmare. If you are familiar with the works of Edgar Allan Poe, I think you may agree that the tales contain so many of the elements associated with dream and nightmare it is difficult to doubt that their creator sometimes drew from his own dream experiences.

Occasionally the nightmare muse that takes possession of the mind seems to inhabit some limbo between complete sleep and proper consciousness. It was in such a state that the theme for the book which was to immortalize her came to the nineteen-year-old Mary Godwin (later Mary Shelley). While staying beside Lake Geneva, Mary Godwin, Shelley, Byron, and the extremely neurotic Dr Polidori, inspired by the current craze for supernatural tales, each declared they would compose a ghost story. The three men all made a start but Mary had to admit herself defeated. Then, after an evening listening to Byron and Shelley discuss 'the nature and principle of life', Mary retired very late, ostensibly to sleep.

> When I placed my head upon the pillow, I did not sleep, nor could I be said to think. My imagination, unbidden, possessed and guided me, gifting the successive images that arose in my mind with a vividness far beyond the usual bounds of reverie. I saw with shut eyes, but acute mental vision—I saw the pale student of unhallowed arts kneeling beside the thing he had put together—I saw the hideous phantasm of a man stretched out, and then, on the working of some powerful engine, show signs of life, and stir with an uneasy, half vital motion . . .
>
> I opened my eyes in terror. The idea so possessed my mind that a thrill of fear ran though me, and I wished to exchange the ghastly image of my fancy for the realities around . . . I could not so easily get rid of my hideous phantom; still it haunted me. I must try to think of something else. I recurred to my ghastly story . . .
>
> Swift as light and as cheering was the idea that broke in upon me. 'I have found it! What terrified me will terrify others; and I need only describe the spectre which had haunted my midnight pillow.' On the morrow I announced that I had thought of a story.

Indeed she had: *Frankenstein: or the Modern Prometheus*. Not only was it a remarkable work for so young a girl but its curious originality has earned it a special position in horror literature and acclaim as the first true science-fiction novel. Of course it was Mary's skill and application that fashioned the novel but the spark which brought *Frankenstein* into being had definitely fallen from the nightmare's brand as it hovered in that twilight zone.

A very tenuous thread links Mary's mother, Mary Wollstonecraft, with what is probably the most famous pictorial study of the nightmare. Before she married William Godwin, Mary had been infatuated with the Swiss painter, Henry Fuseli. Indeed, she had rather unwisely and naively confided to his wife, Sophia: 'I find that I cannot live without the satisfaction of seeing him and conversing with him daily.' Not surprisingly, Mrs Fuseli promptly barred her from their house. Fortunately Mary's friends persuaded her to go to Paris in 1792 to get over this rather juvenile attack of adoration.

It is hard to imagine Fuseli having much sympathy with the opinions she expressed in her *Vindication of the Rights of Women*. His later works were overtly erotic and near-pornographic, sometimes depicting two women satisfying the lust of one man, and his own attitude to the female sex was distinctly ambivalent, which seems to emerge in the painting 'The Nightmare'. Woman was either the cruel, demanding virago-courtesan or the innocent submissive victim of man's most voluptuous desires. Perhaps a key to Fuseli's basic character can be found in Leigh Hunt's words: 'He painted horrible pictures, as children tell horrible stories; and was frightened by his own lay figures ...' The brooding, powerful horror and unambiguous lubricity of 'The Nightmare' probably compensated him for not feeling as potent or as commanding as he would have wished to be.

Although one nineteenth-century writer declared that Fuseli 'had supped off raw pork chops that he might dream his picture', this would have been too hit-and-miss an approach for the artist who conceived and executed his painting with the clear ambition of being noticed and fêted at the Royal Academy Spring Exhibition. Its appearance in 1782 scandalized, excited, and delighted those who saw it, and Fuseli's reputation was established.

Of course artists had been painting dreams and dreamers for centuries. The Bible and classical legends had more than enough raw material to prompt them. Yet Fuseli's work, although there was nothing revolutionary in the style of painting, was a new departure. Something about 'The Nightmare' disturbed onlookers whether or not they were willing to be so affected: Fuseli had attempted and—to judge by the results—largely succeeded in conveying the *sensations* associated with the true nightmare. As a highly educated man the artist's own explanation as to the true causes of such a dream would have been based on current scientific reasoning, but for his painting Fuseli had nonetheless borrowed from the age-old traditions of folklore, mythology, and religion pertaining to the nightmare. He had linked even the most sceptical observer with the dark mind of the past.

Examine a copy of that painting today and you will find yourself feeling vaguely uneasy. We are not to be frightened by pictures of hobgoblins any more but we are still disturbed by any power that we cannot fully comprehend.

The figure of the sleeping girl with her head thrown back is clearly in the embrace of some sexual attacker from whom she is powerless to break free. It is obvious, too, that she cannot see her tormenter and the sensations she is experiencing are represented by the two other beings on the canvas. The malevolent demon squatting on her belly, stifling movement and breath, is that incubus which pagans and Christians once blamed for the nightmare's sensual symptoms. The staring-eyed steed conveys force, menace, and sexuality as well as being one of those traditional forms of transport used by the nightmare.

While the educated no longer accepted the nightmare as a demonic visitation they were currently steeping themselves in all the supernatural material they could lay their hands on, so Fuseli's painting had a fashionable as well as a much more deep-rooted appeal. Horace Walpole—no mean creator of macabre fiction himself—pronounced Fuseli's painting to be 'shocking'. It was probably the artist's break with tradition that inspired this shock. All very well to depict sex, horror, and violence in some historic setting, made romantic by its distance, but Fuseli had pictured the nightmare in a contemporary bedroom and its immediacy could hardly be glossed over. The spectator was personally involved and perhaps made uncomfortable by his or her private reactions and imaginings to the message contained within the painting. (Popular attitudes do not change much over the centuries: think of all those readers who avidly accept the violence and sexual excesses in historical novels but are disgusted when a similar plot is played out against a familiar, modern background.)

Fuseli's composition was to have a rather curious influence on the linguistic roots of the English word 'nightmare'. So many writers made the mistake of regarding the *horse* as the nightmare instead of the actual incubus that it is rather a pity that we cannot tell whether Fuseli intended the animal to be a mare or a stallion. That a confusion over the word's meaning did not obtain too widely in England before Fuseli's painting seems clear from Dr Johnson's definition:

> NIGHTMARE (night and according to Temple, *mara*, a spirit that, in the northern mythology, was related to torment or suffocate sleepers). A morbid oppression in the night, resembling the pressure of weight upon the breast.

The physician, scientist, and didactic poet Erasmus Darwin was a friend and admirer of Henry Fuseli and he may have been among the first to create the impression that the nightmare was actually a female horse. In his long poem 'The Loves of the Plants' Darwin goes to elaborate lengths to describe the painting, and from that it seems evident he was labouring under a partial misapprehension. Compared with the painting's extraordinary magnetism Darwin's verses are, to say the least, heavy-handed.

*So on his* NIGHTMARE *through the evening fog*
*Flits the squab fiend o'er fen, and lake and bog;*
*Seeks some love-wildered Maid with sleep oppress'd,*
*Alights, and grinning sits upon her breast.*
. . . . . . . . . . . . . . . . . . . . . . . . . . . . . . . . . . . . . . .
*Back o'er her pillow sinks her blushing head,*
*Her snow-white limbs hang helpless from the bed;*
*While with quick sighs, and suffocative breath,*
*Her interrupted heart-pulse swims in death.*
*—Then shrieks of captur'd towns and widow's tears,*
*Pale lovers stretch'd upon their blood-stain'd biers,*
*The headlong precipice that thwarts her flight,*
*The trackless desert, the cold starless night,*
*And stern-eyed Murderer with his knife behind,*
*In dread succession agonise her mind.*
*O'er fair limbs convulsive tremors fleet;*
*Start in her hands and struggle in her feet;*
*In vain to scream with quivering lips she tries,*
*And strains in palsy'd lids her tremulous eyes;*
*In vain she wills to run, fly, swim, walk, creep;*
*The* WILL *presides not in the bower of* SLEEP.
*—On her fair bosom sits the Demon-Ape,*
*Erect, and balances his bloated shape;*
*Rolls in their marble orbs his Gorgon-eyes*
*And drinks with leathern ears her tender cries.*

The first four lines appeared on a print of the painting in 1783 and the rest of the poem was published some six years later. It has been suggested, although not proved, that Fuseli's original sketch did not contain a horse but that he painted it in at Darwin's prompting. Whatever the truth, one thing is certain: the painting was a runaway success. Engravings of it spread through Europe and excited great admiration. The erotic undertones were undoubtedly a strong attraction. Seeing a copy at the Leipzig fair in 1783, Goethe's patron, Duke Carl August of Weimar, wrote: 'I have not seen anything for a long time that has intrigued me so much.' No doubt, working for commission, Fuseli himself painted several different versions of the original; and other artists and book illustrators were swift to borrow his theme and present it in a form where its source could scarcely be contested.

To show just how familiar 'The Nightmare' became to the English public at large, caricaturists such as Cruikshank, Rowlandson, and Seymour took it as the basis from which to satirize famous persons and political events. Napoleon, William Pitt, Charles Fox, Lady Hamilton, and even Nelson, hero of the Nile, all took turns on the nightmare couch to be transformed into figures of ridicule, either as the sleeping victim or the crouching demon. Today, some ingenious advertiser could take such a ubiquitous painting and plaster it all over hoardings in order to promote a particular brand of beer, detergent, or soup.

Through its very popularity 'The Nightmare' became debased and hackneyed. Yet it managed somehow to retain something of its original dramatic impact, which suggests that it contains more than the cheap thrill associated with the mass of Gothic horror tales.

There is one more curious little enigma about this painting. Despite a particular interest in dream paintings, Sigmund Freud made no mention of Fuseli's 'The Nightmare' in any of his works. What makes its absence the more remarkable was that Freud apparently had a copy of it in his flat in Vienna. Although his biographer and adherent, Ernest Jones, used a version of 'The Nightmare' as the frontispiece to his work *On the Nightmare* he, too, made no real reference to it; and Jung, who was after all a fellow countryman of Fuseli, also failed to refer to this painting.

Was there something about its composition that defied the giants of psychology? Certainly Fuseli's 'The Nightmare' scarcely fits in with Freud's theory that the dream is the fulfilment of a wish in diguise. In fact, as we have already seen, Freud was singularly reticent on the whole subject of nightmares, suggesting to a later sceptical generation that this kind of dream challenged his interpretation.

Perhaps the answer to the riddle is really quite simple: Freud and Jung were concerned with understanding the workings of the individual's mind. What Fuseli had achieved was a representation of the horror and helplessness associated with nightmares *in general*.

Coleridge who, as we know, was no stranger to nightmares or the delights of poetry and fiction with a diabolical flavour, dubbed Fuseli as 'a Brusher-up of Convulsia and Tetanus upon innocent Canvas'.

Such scathing comments cannot apply to those works of Francisco Goya which were inspired by his own tortures at the hands of the nightmare. Besides Goya's 'Caprichos' and 'pintas negras' (black paintings), Fuseli's 'The Nightmare' does seem a mere theatrical contrivance—a polite drawing-room piece to frighten and titillate polite impressionable ladies and gentlemen. Goya's studies are something quite different. Their horror is scarcely a pretty conceit to catch the eye. They strip bare the universal soul and make each of us shudder, not just at the artist's inner visions but at the horror he depicted as an indisputable fact—a potential in all humankind. We of the twentieth century are too familiar with words like Buchenwald, Hiroshima, and napalm to infer that Goya's dreams have validity only in the realm of madness. We cannot pretend human beings are not possessed of a darker side—a side that, if we are fortunate, shows itself only in nightmares.

At forty-six—and again at seventy-three—this artist of unparalleled vision and talent was stricken with a severe malady which affected his central nervous system; the first attack also brought him the additional curse of deafness. During these bouts Goya encountered the nightmare fiend in all its terrible grandeur, and never again was his view of the world and its people quite the same. The nightmare had drawn open a curtain to show that demonic madness and bestial passion were not just the 'stuff of dreams'.

In these nightmares the rule of Satan seemed absolute. All the traditional values were turned upside down and distorted so that the terrors were at once familiar and strange. The tales of witchcraft and superstition fed to him in childhood arose again with even more compelling force. Violence, obscene cruelty, and cannibalism were scattered on his pillows by the remorseless night hag.

The cruelties of warfare that Goya recorded in his 'Disasters of War' mirrored not only the actual horrors of the French invasion but those which he had observed in his nightmares. Real life gave truth to fantasies. It is significant to note that his representation of a nightmare figure as a squat and bewhiskered male bears a close resemblance to a French soldier in one of his savage studies of the rape of Spanish women.

The 'black paintings' with which Goya decorated the walls of his home, 'the House of the Deaf', are successful attempts to liberate himself of all the fiend had taught him; they are the manifest keys by which the painter had escaped the shackledom of madness. Yet Goya never merely recorded his nightmares. Instead he translated his own horror and suffering into terms that could be immediately understood by all human beings. By externalizing private terror and disgust he was denouncing humankind's ruthlessness. His pictures are indictments against inhumanity, credulity, and ignorance: a protest that loses none of its meaning because it was originally voiced in another century.

For me the 'Capricho' that sums up the overpowering and undermining sensation of the nightmare experience is the famous number forty-three—the one that Goya intended as the introductory plate to the collection. It shows the figure of the artist sprawled asleep at his work bench, his head buried in his arms. A great cat seems to be gazing at him with huge, unwinking eyes which cast a spell. An 'infernal cohort' of large-eyed screech-owls and bats swarm down towards the sleeper. Their gaze hypnotizes the observer. You can almost hear the insistent beating of their wings and the horrible, triumphant screams. Although these creatures are outside the man you cannot escape the knowledge that they have actually risen from his mind to tyrannize him. Goya's caption to this 'Capricho' is: 'The Sleep of Reason

Produces Monsters.' Later he added this comment to explain that which scarcely requires explanation: 'Imagination abandoned by reason begets impossible monsters; united with it, it is the mother of the arts and brings forth marvels.'

What more need be said about the shapes the nightmare conjures into existence to oppress both creative and non-creative sleepers?

Occasionally a writer will grant us a glimpse of the raw material sent by the nightmare muse and even from that higgledy-piggledy, unrefined stage we get a graphic preview of the eventual completed work. In his *Book of Dreams* Jack Kerouac, the doyen of the Beat Generation, recorded his dreams and nightmares, writing them down while he was still barely awake, so that reading them gives one the vivid impression of entering the dream world, where events change from pleasant to nonsensical to horrific in what seems like less than the twinkling of an eye.

Anyone who has read Kerouac will immediately recognize his dreams as an underlying part of his books. Many of the characters he meets in sleep are to be found in *On the Road*, *The Subterraneans*, and *Dharma Bums*; according to Kerouac's introductory words, they do 'further strange things for no particular reason than that the mind goes on'. His bad dreams bear the official nightmare hallmark. They portray misery, war, feelings and memories of shame, guilt and punishment, and situations where the dreamer is running away or hiding . . .

Of course the nightmare scenes in a book or play need not arise from the author's first-hand encounter with the pitiless muse. Using the horrific dream as a vehicle, the writer can convey a character's conflict and guilt, murderous intentions, and unacceptable sexual impulses. To the audience a nightmare can demonstrate the inability of the character to cope with the forces threatening from within and without.

The most familiar dramatic nightmares must be those written by Shakespeare and yet they lose none of their impact because we know them so well. Remember the sleep-walking scene in

*Macbeth*. Self-loathing and guilt have replaced Lady Macbeth's first adamantine resolve to remove all that stood between her husband and kingship. Only her nightmares tell of the true effects that those bloody deeds had on her unconscious. For 'the thick-coming fancies' which disturbed her sleep the doctor could offer no anodyne; he told Macbeth that this was an instance where 'the patient must minister to himself'.

In *Richard III* the Duke of Clarence suffers a nightmare that not only foretells his murder but also displays his unquiet conscience at having deserted his father-in-law, Warwick, which led to his death and the murder of Prince Edward. To the Lieutenant of the Tower, Sir Robert Brakenbury, Clarence confided the content of his nightmare:

> *I have pass'd a miserable night,*
> *So full of fearful dreams, of ugly sights,*
> *That, as I am a Christian faithful man,*
> *I would not spend another such a night,*
> *Though 'twere to buy a world of happy days,*
> *So full of dismal terror was the time!*
> . . . . . . . . . . . . . . . . . . . . . . . . . . . . . . . . . . . . . . .
> *Methought that Gloster stumbled; and, in falling,*
> *Struck me, that thought to stay him, overboard*
> *Into the tumbling billows of the main.*
> . . . . . . . . . . . . . . . . . . . . . . . . . . . . . . . . . . . . . . .
> *The first that there did greet my stranger soul,*
> *Was my great father-in-law, renowned Warwick;*
> *Who cried aloud, 'What scourge for perjury*
> *Can this dark monarchy afford false Clarence?'*
> *And so he vanish'd: then came wandering by*
> *A shadow like an angel, with bright hair*
> *Dabbled in blood; and he shriek'd out aloud,*
> *'Clarence is come; false, fleeting, perjur'd*
> *Clarence . . .'*

We have already seen that his brother's nightmare on the eve of

Bosworth Field was an historical fact but Shakespeare points out the complex psychological reasons behind such a grim example of an anxiety dream, and how the character of the king—at least in this drama—is beginning to disintegrate. Rather than trepidation at the morrow's battle, or his massing enemies, it is the internal strife arising from all the crimes he had to commit to gain the crown that brought Richard his nightmare.

> *Have mercy, Jesu!—Soft! I did but dream.*
> *O coward conscience, how dost thou afflict me!*
> .........................................
> *What do I fear? myself? there's none else by:*
> *Richard loves Richard; that is, I am I.*
> *Is there a murderer here? No;—yes, I am:*
> *Then fly. What, from myself? Great reason why:*
> *Lest I revenge. What, myself upon myself?*
> *Alack, I love myself. Wherefor? for any good*
> *That I myself have done myself?*
> *O, no! alas, I rather hate myself*
> *For hateful deeds committed by myself!*
> *I am a villain: yet I lie, I am not . . .*

How many kings and commoners in fact and fiction have had their sleep wrecked by the fiend that insists on bringing them face to face with a memory or deed that the conscious mind chose to obliterate, forcing them to recognize, however briefly, the several sides of personality that all possess?

Art teaches nothing new about bad dreams but it emphasizes their essential features much more convincingly than any text book. The Russian novelist Fyodor Dostoevsky frequently employed nightmares to highlight a character's inner struggles. In *Crime and Punishment* he explained:

> . . . dreams often have singular actuality, vividness and the extraordinary semblance of reality. At times monstrous images are created, but the setting and the whole picture are so truth-

like and filled with details . . . that the dreamer . . . could never have invented them in the waking state. Such sick dreams always remain long in the memory and make a powerful impression on the overwrought and deranged nervous system.

All who borrow the nightmare's shape in works of fiction take pains to demonstrate its thorough-going semblance of reality, no matter how bizarre the situation. Having survived the earthquake, Robinson Crusoe dreamed of a man descending from a great black cloud, surrounded by a flame so bright that the castaway could scarcely bear to look at him. In a terrible voice the nightmare figure proclaimed: 'Seeing all these things have not brought thee to repentance, now thou shalt die.' Then he raised a great spear to kill poor Crusoe who mercifully woke up. Daniel Defoe made his character declare:

> No one that shall ever read this account will expect that I should be able to describe the horrors of my soul at this terrible vision; I mean, that even while it was a dream, I even dreamed of those horrors; nor is it any more possible to describe the impression that remain'd upon my mind when I awak'd and found it was but a dream.

It is not always necessary to depict a scene to communicate the power of the nightmare. Often the word used figuratively is sufficient to supply a verbal image that cannot be ignored, as when Thackeray wrote in 1860: 'For weeks past this nightmare of war has been riding us.' Nowadays nightmare is an overworked adjective, so frequently found in headlines to underline anything from a battle field to a holiday traffic jam, that we might be excused for ignoring the magnitude of horror it is intended to express.

How writers of another age used the word provides us with an excellent clue as to what contemporary popular opinion held the nightmare to be. Both Shakespeare and his contemporary, Michael Drayton, present a cheerfully bawdy image of the nightmare's sexual behaviour. In *Romeo and Juliet* Mercutio says:

> *This is the hag, when maids lie on their backs,*
> *That presses them, and learns them first to bear,*
> *Making them women of good carriage . . .*

Drayton points to the same widespread belief that the nightmare chiefly attacks those lying on their backs, especially if they are young and lusty:

> *Mab, his merry queen, by night,*
> *Bestrides young folk that lie upright,*
> *In elder times the mare that hight,*
> *Which plagues them out of measure.*

The popular superstition that the nightmare flew like a bird or rode horses to do its devilish work is supported by the antiquary, John Aubrey—'It is to prevent the Night-Mare, the Hag from riding their Horses . . .'—and the 'marvellous Boy', Thomas Chatterton—'The death-owl doth sing to the night-mares as they go . . .'

Perhaps the most effective use of the nightmare in fiction is to establish the correct atmosphere for a tale of the supernatural. Many ghost stories may be compared with waking from a nightmare, when you cannot be sure whether you are awake or still dreaming. Eerie literature, hinging on the nightmare, is so preponderant in many languages that anyone who is a devotee of this genre must have a personal favourite, so I am going to cite only the ones I prefer as examples.

In *Lost Hearts*, M. R. James, that exponent of the weird short story, related how the small boy, Stephen Elliott, went to stay at his cousin's house where he had a very strange dream. He found himself looking through the glazed panels of a disused bathroom in the same corridor as his own bedroom. The moonlight showed a figure lying in the bath: 'A figure inexpressibly thin and pathetic, of a dusty leaden colour, enveloped in a shroud-like garment, the thin lips crooked into a faint and dreadful smile, the hands pressed tightly over the region of the heart.' As Stephen watched, the being started to move and groan. Horror woke the boy who found himself standing in the moonlit corridor. Courageously he managed to look into the bathroom. The bath was empty. Yet the terror of the nightmare only heralded worse to come in real life for Stephen's cousin intended the boy's heart to be the last of the three which would give him the secret of eternal life.

In Sheridan Le Fanu's best-known tale, *Uncle Silas*, Maud Ruthyn dreams of a French governess leading her secretly to an old oak cabinet in the library.

> There was a key in the door, which I experienced a guilty horror of turning, she whispering in the same unintelligible way, all the time, at my ear. I *did* turn it; the door opened quite softly, and within stood my father, his face white and malignant, and glaring close to mine. He cried in a terrible voice, 'Death!' Out went Madame's candle, and at the same moment, with a scream, I waked in the dark—still fancying myself in the library; and for an hour after I continued in a hysterical state ...

One of the most gripping novels in the English language is Emily Brontë's *Wuthering Heights* and the claustrophobic power it exercises over the reader is intensified by Mr Lockwood's nightmare, which occurs almost as an introduction to the tragic tale. Forced to stay at Heathcliff's house, he dreamed that a waif-like child, called Catherine Linton, was trying to get in through his window. Although he savagely rubbed the creature's wrist against the broken window until the blood soaked the bedclothes still she would not release him.

> 'Begone!' I shouted, 'I'll never let you in, not if you beg for twenty years.'
> 
> 'It is twenty years,' mourned the voice; 'twenty years. I've been a waif for twenty years!'
> 
> Thereat began a feeble scratching outside, and the pile of

books moved as if thrust forward. I tried to jump up; but could not stir a limb; and so yelled aloud, in a frenzy of fright.

His cry brought his host who, poor wretch, would have borne with such a nightmare if it gave him his beloved Catherine's company.

Accounts of the nightmare are not confined to serious literature. Occasionally one or more of its characteristics are introduced into a popular, light-hearted work to highlight a character's secret wishes or dilemma. For instance, in the musical *Fiddler on the Roof* Tevye pretends to have a nightmare in order to convince his wife, Golde, that their daughter, Tzeitel, should marry the tailor she loves rather than the well-to-do widower butcher with whom they have already arranged a match. When Golde wakes him from the feigned nightmare, Tevye relates his dream which is translated into a lively musical scene.

The 'nightmare' shows what looks like a wedding celebration. Golde's grandmother, also named Tzeitel and long since dead, arrives and is delighted to find that her great-granddaughter is going to marry the *tailor*. Golde tells her 'No, the bridegroom is to be the *butcher*', whereupon the old lady flies into a rage and into the air, and yells furiously. The family dispute becomes even more heated when the butcher's late wife materializes, extremely put out by this arranged marriage. She vows that three weeks after any wedding she will appear in the night and take the bride by the throat. Laughing demoniacally, she demonstrates her intention on Tevye.

Her husband's nightmare—especially because of her grandmother's role in it—convinces Golde that Tzeitel should wed the tailor. The butcher's wife, she decides, is an evil spirit called up by the butcher. And so the 'bad dream' is instrumental in making everyone happy.

Nor do nightmare sequences appear only in adult entertainments. Stories, plays, and puppet shows presenting monsters, punishment, conflicts, and terror are tremendously popular with small children and give them the opportunity of identifying with

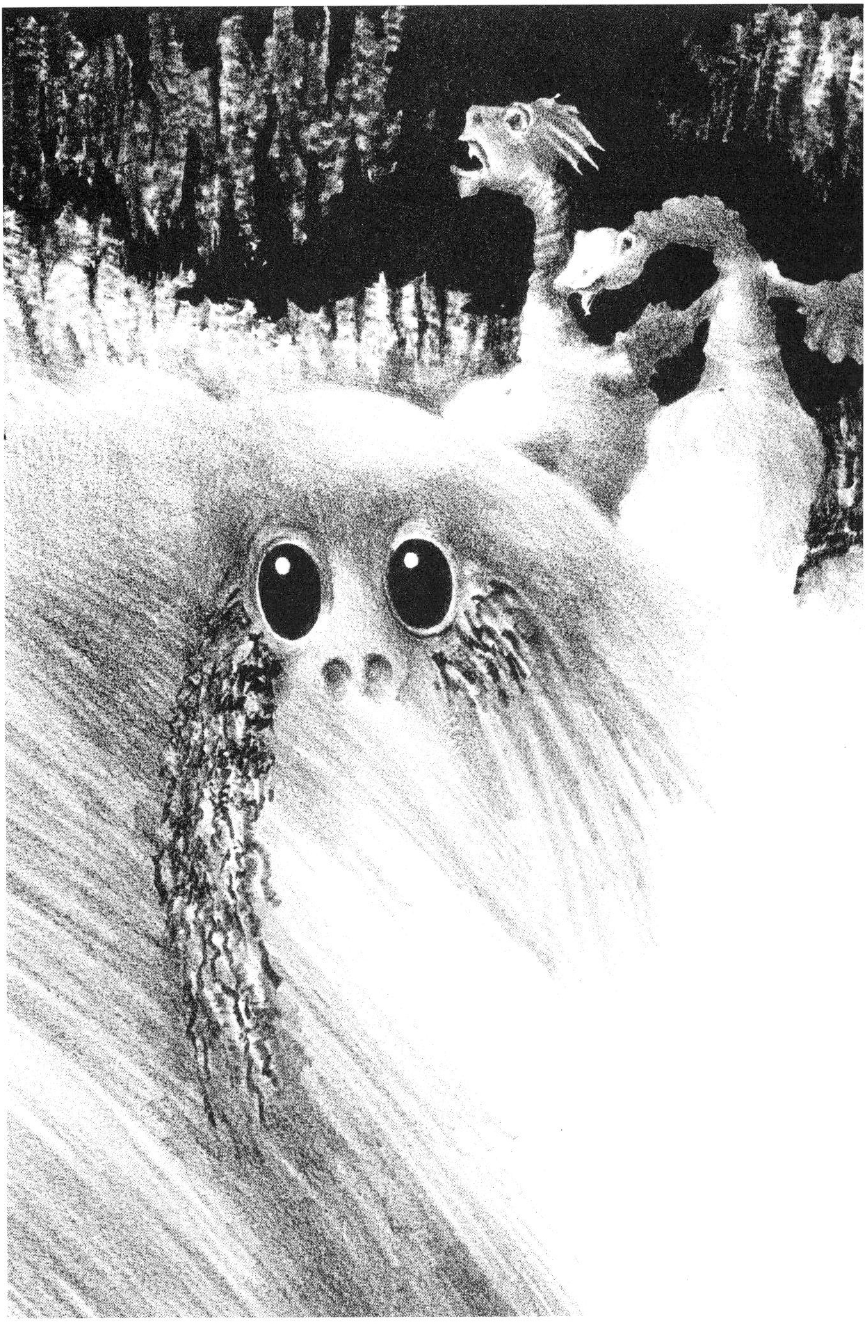

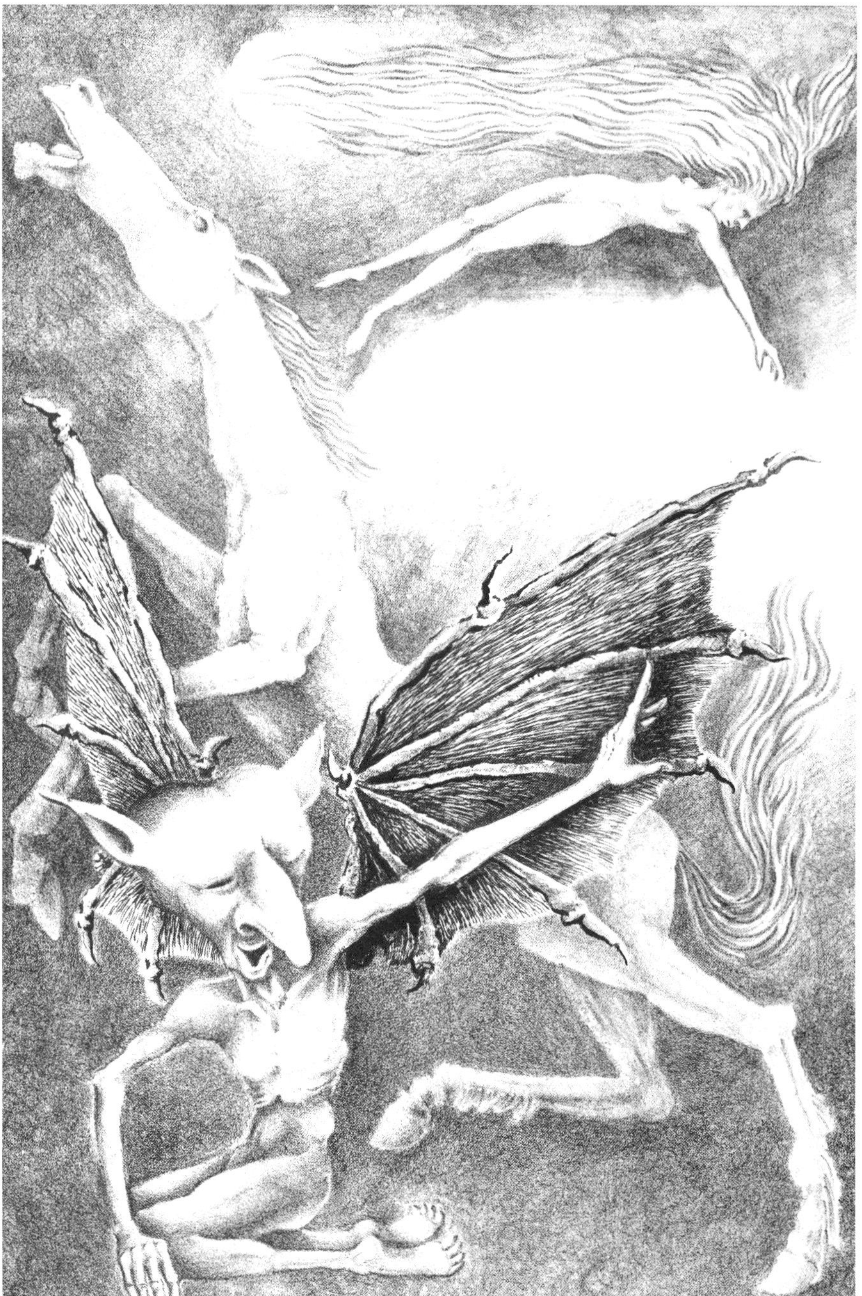

either the wicked or the one that brings retribution. Such shared experiences of horror and aggression, as seen in the typical 'Punch and Judy' performance, allow the child to learn to control fear and to understand that this personal emotion is actually shared by others.

Despite, or probably because of, its frightening illustrations, Maurice Sendak's delightful tale *Where the Wild Things Are* has enormous appeal for youngsters. It recounts the adventures of one naughty little boy and contains many of the elements that are common in childhood nightmares, so that any child suffering from bad dreams has the chance of identifying with Max—the wildest of the Wild Things, and the one able to tame the others.

In the story Max puts on his wolf suit and behaves, according to his mother, like a 'wild thing'. When she tells him off he threatens to 'eat her up' and consequently is deprived of dinner and sent to bed.

In his dream Max voyages to a strange jungle full of terrible Wild Things. The illustrations support their ferocious and nightmarish reputation—the monsters look like those found in children's drawings of their own bad dreams. Because he is the wildest of them all the Wild Things make Max their king and he commands that they have a 'rumpus'. At last he tells them to stop and *sends them to bed without their dinners*. Missing familiar warmth and love Max decides to go home but the Wild Things beg him to stay and say they will eat him up—because they love him so much. Undeterred by their gnashings and roarings Max departs, to find himself back in his room, and his dinner still hot.

Here is a tidy little example of the dreamer dealing with the unacceptable and uncivilized facets of his personality that rear their heads in nightmares—by projecting them onto monsters. Comforting to the reader is the knowledge that the hero is stronger than, and therefore able to control and escape from, the wildest impulses.

Therapists treating children suffering from bad nightmares have found that a child will often take the dream's horrid contents, and whatever significant event triggered it off, to weave into a story. The more detailed and elaborate the tale becomes the less the child will remain in the role of the victim. The helplessness experienced in nightmare is gradually replaced by a situation directed by the child.

The conversion of the pitiless muse into a form of creative activity by children and adults may not resolve basic problems but it can relieve the terror. The private fear becomes a shared and communicable theme so the individual is able to contain traumatic experiences without their inflicting greater psychological damage.

We have examined the nightmare as a creative force and now we must look at its fundamental themes—those dream experiences shared by different centuries and cultures which, however tricked out in idiosyncratic detail, remain universal.

# Fearful Patterns

> ... Dreams and visions are infused into men for their advantage and instruction ...
> ARTEMIDORUS OF DALDUS, SECOND CENTURY AD

It makes little difference to the nightmare whether you are tiny and helpless or mature and sophisticated: still its most cunning ruse is to isolate its victim. Even when you wake to a reassuring face, a kind voice, and the blissful reality of your own familiar bedroom, your confused feelings of dread, disgust, or defeat cut you off from the lot of normal human beings. It is hard to communicate what you have been through since merely by being worthy of the fiend's attention you alone seem to stand convicted of some monstrous evil.

Yet the nightmare makes us all—young and old—brothers and sisters in fear under the skin. Just as the agony columns in newspapers and magazines help by showing us that our worst personal problems are not unique, one can take some comfort from knowing that one's skirmishes with the nightmare are not so different from those of our early ancestors—or those that will overtake the sleeping citizens of the twenty-first century. 'Advantage and instruction' may be had even from the nastiest dream experience once it can be understood.

Demonologists, anthropologists, and psychoanalysts have already introduced us to those formidable but ubiquitous monsters, ogres, ghosts, witches, and incubi that seem to be particular cronies of the nightmare; modern manuals of psychology and ancient books of interpretation show that there are certain other dream patterns which appear again and again, regardless of time, place, age, or culture. In the land of sleep you may learn to recognize these other universal shapes even if you cannot always elude them. Whether or not they turn into fully fledged nightmares will depend on the amount of terror and anxiety induced, and that, like the task of unravelling their meaning, relates to the individual's memories, experiences, problems, and conditioning.

If we turn to Artemidorus' *Oneirocritica* we see not only familiar basic dreams but also how interpretative techniques do not necessarily alter with civilization or technological progress. This definitive work influenced all subsequent centuries of European dream books and linked them to Assyrian, Babylonian, and Egyptian beliefs. Artemidorus made the first real attempt to bring reason and evidence to oneirology instead of relying upon a mass of quasi-religious beliefs or philosophical arguments.

Both Freud and Jung paid tribute to the painstaking researches of this Roman savant who covered every aspect of dreaming and who thought it ridiculous to apply arbitrary interpretations to such an individual process. Although he warned all would-be oneirocritics against being too facile and logical in explaining a dream, he believed that interpretation depended upon the effect dream images produced in the conscious mind of the *interpreter*! (It is curious to note here that ancient Indian and Chinese theories of interpretation, unlike contemporary near-Eastern and European counterparts, shared our modern view that deciphering the dream depends on the associations aroused in the *dreamer's* mind.)

Obviously some of Artemidorus' writings sound naive and limited by today's standards but many of his interpretations of the major dream symbols closely resemble those found in psychoanalysis. Even more intriguing: some of his meanings have much in common with those described by anthropologists working among African tribes as yet unmarked by Western concepts. This presents a fascinating example of how not only dreams and nightmares, but also their interpretations, can link people of totally disparate centuries, continents, and religious teachings.

For Artemidorus the mouth represented a house and the teeth its inhabitants, so the classic dream of losing teeth expressed a fear of, or wish for, the removal of someone close to the dreamer. For an African a similar dream symbolizes the loss of a wife or child. According to both Artemidorus and the African tribesman, floods predict misfortunes in legal matters and bad-tempered employers. For the Roman a fire in the sky foretold war; for the African a bush fire signifies much the same thing.

In assessing dreams Artemidorus divided them into two categories. The first was fairly simple, and related to those which were the fruits of conditions present in the dreamer's body and mind: a thirsty man would dream of drink, and someone in love of the beloved. The second type was far more complex, and its interpretation rested upon the oneirocritic's skill: these were dreams referring to the future. They were often beyond the dreamer's understanding and contained symbols that might yield verbal or visual puns to complicate their meaning further. Anyone accustomed to wrestling with cryptic crossword clues will have some idea of the difficulties involved.

To dream of having a barber cut your hair was considered a good omen for, as Artemidorous explained, the Greek word for 'being barbered' was very similar to the word for 'joy'. He also quoted Aristander on a dream of Alexander the Great, who was besieging Tyre. The king dreamed of a satyr dancing on his shield; Aristander encouraged him to take the city, explaining that the dream meant *sa Tyros*—'Tyre is thine'.

Puns usually lose their meaning in another language, as anyone who has tried to tell a typical English joke in German or French will appreciate. This may explain why some of those glib interpretations in modern dream books appear nonsensical—especially if they are updated versions of far earlier manuals, which in turn had garnered their interpretations from poor and mangled translations of Greek and Latin. However, this concept of word play has not been discarded by modern analysts, who see it as one fascinating method by which the unconscious cloaks its secrets.

These dream puns come in various forms: *visual*—showing an abstract situation or expression in picture form; or *verbal*—including a play on proper names, colloquialisms, the rearrangement of relevant words, and the cunning replacement of a like-sounding word with one of an entirely different meaning and spelling.

You might try examining a particular dream in those terms. See it as a cartoon that needs a snappy, accurate caption and even your worst nightmare might provoke a belly laugh. Say you had an unpleasant dream about blundering lost in a dense, pathless forest. It might, of course, spring from memory of an actual experience. There again, the trees could symbolize problems among which, in waking life, you seem to wander, unable to find a way out. After all, we do have that useful phrase which succinctly sums up a like situation: 'I couldn't see the wood for the trees.'

In interpreting his second category of dream, Artemidorus advised the oneirocritic to consider all factors known about the dreamer: name, nature, occupation, and character and whether any particular dream occurred regularly. We can see why he considered it so important to consider all these details just by examining one seemingly horrific dream in *Oneirocritica*.

> To see oneself crucified is a good portent for those who navigate and for men short of money; those, on the other hand, who have plenty of money, will have afflictions and disappointments from this dream; bachelors will see in it a promise of marriage, serfs a promise of liberty. To see oneself crucified in a public establishment or monument is a sign that one will be in charge of, or hold the office inherent in, this establishment or monument...

You may protest that a dream with a cross in it must have a religious connotation but, remember, a crucifix does not usually have such significance for someone of non-Christian faith. Instead, it might symbolize an underlying awareness that the dreamer has reached some tricky crossroad in life or it could be one of those puns—meaning that you are cross with something or someone!

By now I trust you have seen enough of the mental and physical acrobatics of the nightmare to take Artemidorus' advice and avoid applying any mechanical system of interpretation, however profound, simply because similar dream patterns do repeatedly arise. That is likely to lead the individual into a quagmire of nonsense. If half a dozen people sit down to a late-night indigestible snack not all of them will suffer nightmares any more than all will have identically shaped dreams or dreams with a common meaning. One person's flying dream may be a delicious free-wheeling experience to be courted into returning; for another it is a harrowing nightmare that spells downfall.

Artemidorus considered flying dreams to be fortunate as long as the dreamer landed easily and woke immediately; it was less favourable to dream of flying head downwards! The Assyrians warned that repeated dreams of flying not far above the ground meant loss of possessions. A modern interpretation also sees such dreams as heralds of disaster. Freud connected flying and floating dreams with infantile sexual sensations (aroused in romping games). Others interpret them as memories of pre-birth existence. Some go back even further, claiming they are an archaic echo from the time when our aquatic ancestors floated in a vast sea. Another view is that the flying dream represents a wish to overcome the difficulties in life, or the method by which the unconscious compensates the individual for waking feelings of inferiority. It may also symbolize a longing to escape from a particular situation or life style . . .

If it has been your misfortune to experience any of these typical nightmares, choose what explanations you will from sexual repression, archetypal imagery, conflict over desire and basic impulse, traumatic childhood or adult memory, or external or physiological stimulus. Accept the sensations and images for what they seem to be, or take them as symbolic and larded with puns, or follow Gestalt therapy and regard each dream image (however horrible) as an aspect of the self that requires unifying to produce a positive whole person. But, unless you know as much as possible about what these patterns mean in terms of your life, you may as well pick an interpretation off a list with a pin, or decide to believe it is all the work of a ghost, a god, or a demon.

*Being chased and rooted to the spot* Widely differing explanations as to causes do not radically alter the universal fearful patterns any more than does the age of the dreamer. Even in those areas where witchcraft is blamed for procuring the nightmare, the most typical kind is still of being chased by an aggressor (animal, human, or supernatural) yet being unable to flee or cry out. From recent research into the physiology of sleep it now seems that this dream does reflect at least one actuality: it occurs at that stage when the body's motor activity *is* temporarily paralyzed. However, as most REM phases do not erupt in this nightmare, we must search for more clues in the psyche.

The inability to move may reflect an actual impasse in your daily life caused by the conscience blocking an ambition or impulse. However, those who see sex behind human problems need look no further. For them the sensations are those associated with the mounting sexual excitement and immobility that precedes orgasm, and the terror will probably signify a struggle between desire and fear that fulfilment means total annihilation as the penalty for surrendering to something you have been conditioned against. 'Chased' may be a pun on 'chaste' so if a woman has this nightmare it could be deciphered as a sort of 'cave-man' fantasy: a secret longing to be carried off which robs her of personal choice or responsibility, accompanied by an inherent fear of losing her virtue. As many liberationists will agree, it is more likely that her apprehension is of losing her freedom!

Even if conflict over sexual desire does exist, the terror may echo a far earlier occasion. Think of the tiny baby lying in its crib, virtually a prisoner, and terrified of practically everything. It cannot explain its fears and far worse, it cannot run from them. If regression accounts for some of the horror contained in nightmares then paralysis dreams stand a good chance of being interpreted in terms of infantile experiences. Freud even theorized that the witches and ogres in children's bad dreams represent parents—their nasty, feared, and threatening aspects appearing in unambiguously ugly terms. He also believed that nightmare robbers and intruders refer to memories of grown-ups creeping around a child's room at night to ensure it was asleep or not doing anything prohibited.

Frozen, silent helplessness in the face of danger is not just the stuff of nightmares or childhood. It happens in the real life of grown-ups and the first of our species must have known all about such terror when being hunted down by whatever was then the predator. This nightmare pattern could also be one of those atavistic traces stemming from our racial infancy.

We are not always paralyzed in these dreams of pursuers and attackers. Sometimes we keep on running, the distance between us and danger ever decreasing. Many regard this, and other typical nightmare shapes, as punishment dreams. These are the consequences of the dreamer disobeying the conscience by some daytime thought, action, or inaction. That conscience may still be speaking with a parental tongue as you strive, albeit unwittingly, to be all those things that would make you your parents' good little boy or girl! Paradoxically, and naturally dependent upon the dreamer's character, the nightmare threatening some awful fate may be the result of stifling large emotions by day—in order to preserve a cool, calm, and collected exterior—which attempt to burst through in wild abandon during sleep.

In Jungian terms the attacker may be your 'shadow'—that archetype within the personality which contains all that we do not wish to acknowledge about the self. It is in direct contrast to that other archetype, the persona—the mask or character we present to the world. The expression 'lose face' signifies just what we fear will happen to us in front of others if they get a glimpse behind the mask. The more perfect we try to be by day (which means denying our baser self), the more the ugly shadow seeks to catch up in sleep. It is trying not so much to swamp our best motives as to integrate the self. Seen in this light, it does not seem surprising that the early aesthetes were so plagued by what they termed incubus. They had denied too much of the personality to be balanced human beings.

Gestaltists employ the terms 'topdog' and 'underdog' in interpreting many nightmares. The 'topdog' is a dictator telling all the other dream images (aspects of the self) just what to do. The 'underdog' is meek, defensive, and apologetic and endures its bossy counterpart. In Gestalt therapy you are advised to decide which dog is the nightmare attacker. If it is the 'underdog'—because it feels it has been 'put down' all day and not allowed any say—you should, as with the Jungian shadow, yield to its will, accepting it into your personality. But if it is the 'topdog' that is hounding you, you are warned to ignore all its cunning tricks for, like all dictators, it wants complete submission by day and by night: the more psychic territorial demands you yield to the more it will want . . .

*Falling* 'I was drifting off to sleep—in fact, I probably was asleep—when suddenly I felt myself falling, falling; there was no ground beneath. I awoke abruptly with my heart in my mouth, and my breath shallow and laboured . . .' Here is a sensation many will recognize—and there is an old wives' tale that if you land in your dream you will die. This is negated by all those who have 'fallen to earth' in their dreams; usually they discover that the dream is showing them that the 'fall' they dreaded in real life did not have such unpleasant consequences.

There may be a perfectly adequate physiological explanation for this type of dream, such as the actual lowering of blood pressure when we 'drop off' to sleep. There again, it may be caused by some traumatic memory of an accident where the nightmare forces the individual to confront moments consciously repressed. Your subconscious could even be trying to draw your attention to some unsafe piece of household equipment which might precipitate a fall if not dealt with.

Less provable, but worth considering, is the theory that we are experiencing a primordial fear from the time when humankind's ancestors lived in trees, and falling would have involved some disastrous results.

However, as not everyone suffers this weird falling dream, the collective unconscious need not be its source. Such nightmares may hark back to the individual's infantile experiences of a particularly frightening fall, or of being dropped by an adult, or of the time when uncertain small legs kept tumbling their owner to the ground. Perhaps there is an unconscious dread of returning to a state where we had no control over ourselves and therefore no rights or status.

Some prefer to interpret the falling nightmare in symbolic terms, such as the fear of falling below other people's expectations of our worth, or of a moral lapse. (We talk of a 'fallen woman' or 'a fall from grace'.) It may be the dread of failure—being toppled from some proud summit of achievement and prestige. Indeed, it can be argued that those who find themselves compelled to climb ever higher in business or profession may really be trying to erect a wall against some sort of objective childhood terror; but no matter how far they rise there remains an underlying anxiety that some 'fall' will hurl the individual into the original cause of fear.

If sexual interpretation is still your preference then the falling sensation can be associated with the dizzy feelings surrounding orgasm. Freud, who admitted he had never experienced one of these falling dreams, rejected contemporary physiological explanations and plumped instead for infantile memories of romping, see-saws, swings, and so on, where pleasure is accompanied by fear and giddiness and the child may feel for the first time a degree of sexual stimulus to the genitals. This explanation satisfied Freud since it tied in with many of his patients' neuroses.

*Water* The setting is a river, sea, or lake and the dreamer or someone familiar is in danger of being overwhelmed by the element.

I can recall a particularly vivid water nightmare that recurred regularly when I was small. I was sitting in the back of a car which my father was driving through suburban streets that led into the countryside. Suddenly the road ended as if severed by a knife. In its place was blinding blue water. There was never time to brake and we always hurtled soundlessly into those icy deeps. I would wake, struggling for air, believing myself trapped within the car plunging beneath the waves . . .

Whatever this dream meant I have no idea, but it was 'broken' quite recently by a trivial incident when, for the first time, I attempted to visit Holy Island off the Northumberland coast. Unfortunately I had not checked the crossing timetable and the tide was high, so that the road leading from the mainland across the causeway ended abruptly in a vast expanse of glittering sea with no sign to show that at low tide it continued safely on to the island. As soon as I saw the road leading straight into the water I experienced total recall of the childhood nightmare long since forgotten. This was just how the scene had looked in my dreams. Needless to say, the real life visit ended harmlessly.

In this I was luckier than the nightmare-plagued poet, Shelley. In 1822 he and Mary were staying with Jane and Edward Williams at a villa near Lerici. One June night Mary was woken by Shelley's appalling screams. He rushed into her room, evidently fast asleep. Although she tried to rouse him he continued screaming. The frightened Mary ran to Jane Williams while Edward went to help Shelley who had now woken. The poet insisted that he had never been asleep and that what had terrified him was no nightmare but a waking vision. However, as he had no recollection of crying out, the others were convinced he must have been dreaming.

In this nightmare Shelley was lying in bed when Edward, supported by Jane, came to him. Both were in a dreadful state, torn and bleeding and scarcely able to walk. 'Get up, Shelley,' Edward urged, 'the sea is flooding the house, and it is all coming down.' Shelley looked out of the window and saw the sea rushing in towards the terrace. Then the dream changed. He saw himself strangling his beloved Mary, which was what had brought him into her room, yet he had not approached the bed for fear of scaring her. It was Mary jumping up that had woken him or, as Shelley preferred it, 'had caused his vision to vanish'.

This watery dream, however frightening, is too imprecise to be taken as a proper omen of the tragedy that was shortly to occur.

On 8 July, having visited Byron at Leghorn, Shelley and Williams were sailing back to Lerici in the *Don Juan*. They never arrived. Their yacht foundered, or was perhaps run down by pirates who believed a rich English 'milord' (Byron, in fact) was aboard. As the sea claimed them, did either recall Shelley's 'vision'?

Some water nightmares may actually stem from burning thirst. For instance, after a serious operation, as you lie in that drifting twilight zone, you might dream of drowning in cold oceans: this could be a somewhat overdramatic attempt on the part of your unconscious to compensate you for the few careful drops of iced water the nurse actually allowed to wet your lips.

As with any bad dream your water nightmare may refer to some objective experience: an adult sailing accident or a terrifying swimming lesson in childhood when the choking, deafening waters closed over your small head for what seemed an eternity.

Like that other typical frightening dream of crawling through underground caverns or tunnels, the source of water nightmares may belong to the individual's lost memories of pre-birth—of floating in the uterine waters. Negatively such dreams may be interpreted as a desire to return to the pleasurable state before birth, which some insist is the first trauma; more positively the nightmare could be read as the individual's wish to be reborn, to slough off old habits and acquire a new life style. Naturally anxiety attends any such step into the unknown.

Turn to the mythology of most cultures and you will discover examples of characters having to plunge into the deep seas or hazardous underworld situations that symbolize the unconscious and the darker impulses, in order to gain sufficient insight to overcome whatever their obstacle is and be reborn in happiness and enlightenment. Others contend that these swimming, drowning, floating, and similar watery sleeping fantasies are faint echoes from that primeval age when life began and was nurtured in the seas. After all, we still possess the Eustachian tubes linking mouth and ears, so why should we not also enshrine the concomitant vestigial memories?

Perhaps you have dreamed of struggling in the sea, caught up by some impossible tidal wave, with the shore and safety always beyond your reach. This might be deciphered as a battle to master your primitive unconscious drives or, more optimistically, it could be your unconscious urging you to fight to attain a particular goal in waking life, no matter how much the present 'tide' appears to be against you.

There again, the waters may symbolize punishment for daring to think or do something that the 'topdog' prohibits. The element may also represent your own emotions which you have reined in too tightly for your own real good.

In interpreting this, or any other dream or nightmare, so much depends on whether the individual's needs are best served by regarding the dream's events and symbols as purposive—pointing towards a possible future, stating a present predicament, or recalling something that happened long ago.

*Nudity* At one time or other most of us must have had some sort of nudity dream. You are walking down a main thoroughfare, surrounded by people who either ignore you or point disapproving fingers and snigger when suddenly you realize you are stark naked or only scantily dressed. Although you feel extremely worried by the situation there seems no escape. You awake hot and flustered . . . sometimes amused as well as dismayed.

Thomas Hardy confessed to a perennial dream of this type. He was being chased but managed to evade his pursuers by rising heavenward like an angel. Unlike an angel, however, he became agitated and embarrassed on realizing he lacked underclothes!

Freudians think that these 'exhibitionist' dreams relate to the time when a baby is displayed naked for the admiration of all and allowed to run about in its birthday suit as if this were the most normal habit in the world. Then comes that extremely puzzling moment in any child's existence when it has to unlearn a behaviour pattern. What was acceptable and amusing yesterday suddenly becomes rude, silly, or naughty. If this point is emphasized with a good deal of scolding, so that the child feels 'loss of face', it may well grow up shy and self-conscious. The adult exhibitionist nightmare could be an example of the unconscious striving to attain that early carefree state where nudity was not equated with shame, while the guilt and anxiety are induced by the censor stepping in to curtail any surrender to such 'dangerous' impulses.

Most interpretations will treat this dream as symbolic. Perhaps the individual fears making an 'exhibition' of him or herself in terms either of sexual prowess or of some professional activity. There may be a desire to release repressed longings—to be absolutely honest and open—but the dreamer dreads that showing the true self to the world will result in criticism, ridicule, or disapproval.

*Falling Teeth* The actress Sarah Siddons once dreamed that all her teeth fell out while she was on stage. The dubious comfort offered her in real life by Mrs Piozzi, Dr Johnson's friend, was that she would be acting long after she had lost all her teeth. If you've ever had this falling-teeth nightmare you will agree that it can be a most unnerving experience. The feeling is sometimes so real that on waking you even examine your teeth just to make sure they are in the same condition as they were on going to bed.

Dreams about teeth have a particular significance in all societies, and today's 'pop' interpreters often explain falling, decayed, or stained teeth as a prelude to future unhappiness.

A perfectly simple physiological explanation may lie behind this dream. Minimal discomfort of the teeth or gums might be overdramatized into total decay and toothlessness by the 'Grand Guignol' author of dreams; or your subconscious may be aware that all is not well in your mouth. The dream could reflect anxiety about a forthcoming dental appointment or refer to a traumatic one in the past. I must warn you against panicking if last night you had a nightmare about your teeth. This universal dream is so common that the likelihood of these interpretations being a correct diagnosis is too slight to be taken seriously on every occasion.

If the dream is viewed symbolically we arrive at far more

complex interpretations. Freud's ideas hinged on his theories that, in the dream, symbolization allowed one part of the body to represent another more erogenous one—so making interpretation of our dreams even more complicated. He thought that for men falling-teeth dreams signified an emission of semen or a fear of castration, and also wrote that Jung believed that when a woman had such a dream it was usually associated with childbirth.

Another possibility is that this kind of dream is about growing up, since the loss of milk teeth is a significant stage in any child's development. However disturbing, the nightmare may be trying to force its victims to realize they are already mature, or else warning them that it is high time they started behaving in a more adult fashion.

Although most children have few anxieties about shedding their milk teeth, even encouraging 'looseness' where adults promise financial reward, many a small and insecure being must be alarmed on discovering that something previously fixed in its mouth has become wobbly and then falls out. This may go further towards explaining the degree of anxiety in the adult's falling-tooth nightmare than more contemporaneous reasons.

There again, this dream might reflect a feeling that during the day you have somehow damaged your image—or a certain situation makes you feel powerless—that is, 'toothless'!

*Examination* Anyone who has ever had to face any sort of examination or initiation test will recognize this universal dream, which can become a crushing nightmare; not only does the dream depict you making a perfect idiot of yourself and failing (often the questions are too unintelligible to be answered!), but you are forced to go through the training course again with all that that entails in loss of face, time, and opportunity. Not very difficult to interpret to be sure—it springs from the natural apprehension of failure.

But what about those occasions when the dream manifests itself and yet you have long since qualified? Some will interpret this in erotic terms: the problem or need to gain sexual experience

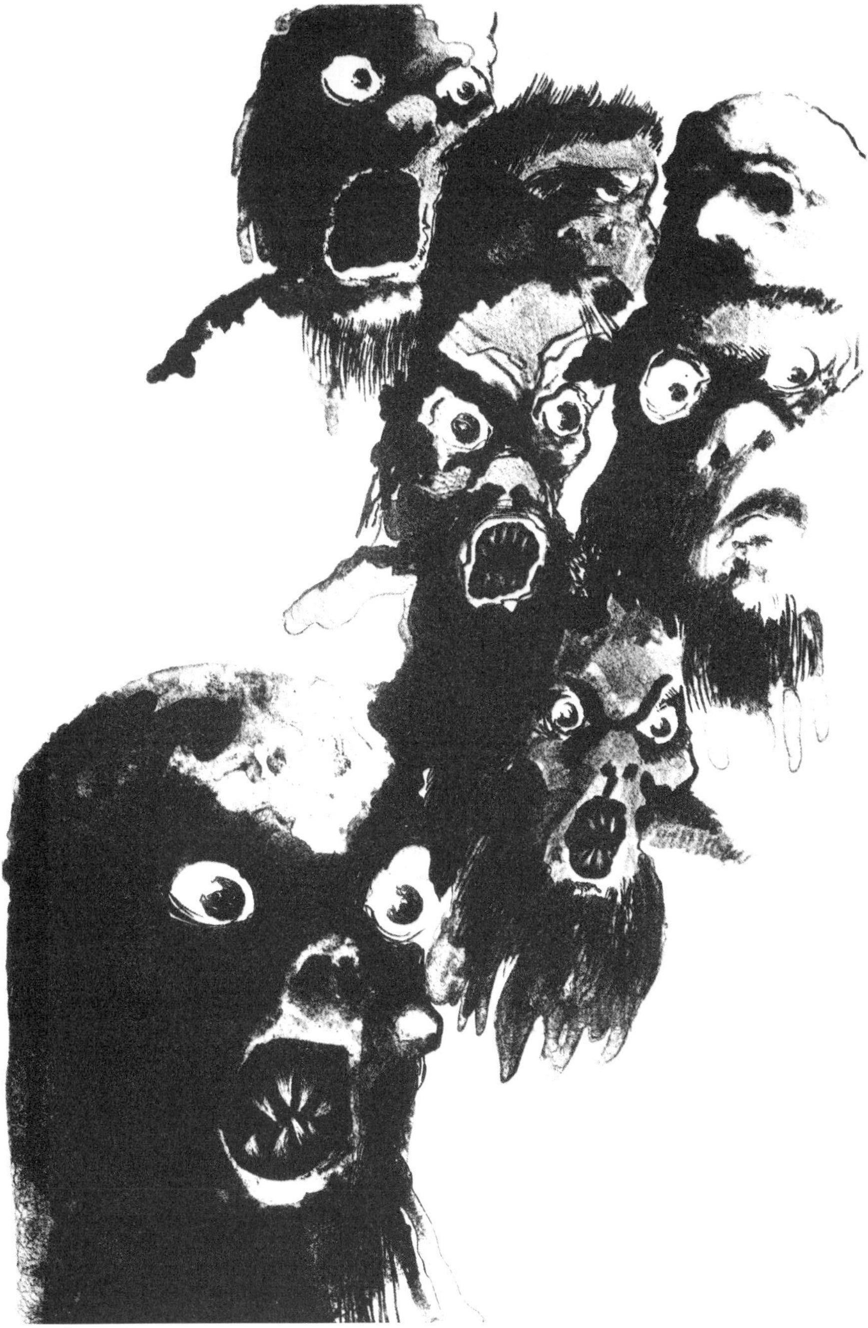

and maturity. Of course this may be true for anyone who has an underlying apprehension about his or her performance in the bedroom. However, at a much wider level it has been recognized that the examination dream frequently arises before the individual has to tackle some unexceptional but anxiety-provoking task. It is as if the unconscious is telegraphing a message meant to reassure rather than disturb by pointing out how much you needlessly worried in the past. 'Remember this old bogey-man', it seems to be saying. You wake, relieved that it was only a bad dream; the present proves just how groundless were those early worries. George Bernard Shaw, among others, demonstrated another version of the examination dream: finding himself on stage without knowing a word of his role. He concluded that such dreams must spring from overwork.

Depending of course upon the individual's circumstances, the dream may be reminding you how far you have progressed and how much effort was involved, so that your present waking lifestyle should be more appropriate to your achievement.

There is a popular belief that examination dreams symbolize an individual's ill-preparedness for death, and religious people may well be reflecting a feeling of 'spiritual failure' in such dreams. Others point out that this dream occurs when we feel 'tested' by some specific situation in daily life. The problem is to discover just what that is in order to find a solution.

*Climbing* Climbing dreams can induce a horrid sense of insecurity and anxiety. You climb higher and higher—up stairways, mountains, or even the sheer faces of buildings—and still seem to get nowhere. Robert Louis Stevenson's recurring Edinburgh nightmare can be taken as a particularly evocative example (see pages 111-12).

Freudians use sexual terms to decipher these climbing dreams and suggest that anxiety over achieving penile erection and orgasm is their basic cause. Quite possibly it is so in some instances but, once again, we must look to the individual. A more symbolic approach to this sort of dream yields richer reward. It might then reveal a desire for promotion, or to realize some personal or professional ambition, but these longings are punctuated by a fear of failure. Or, like the swimming dream, it might represent the unconscious urging you to rise in life despite a natural timidity. You are not so much being shown an endless problem as being encouraged to go forward and conquer it.

*Missing Trains, Buses, and Ships*   'I ran along an endless platform forever bumping into people and luggage trolleys, but the train started to move. I ran harder but I couldn't catch it. Everything seemed set to prevent me; I saw the train disappearing from sight, and felt terribly anxious and miserable . . .' And sometimes, when you do manage to catch the train, it is the wrong one, or the journey is so ghastly you wish you'd never started out . . .

For Sir Oliver Lodge and many others recurring travel difficulties were the most frequent and unpleasant nightmares. This is another universal theme; but before someone smartly points out that it can hardly be found in the dream lore of ancient and primitive peoples, may I suggest, as an extension of the category, dreams about delay in setting out on an important journey, muddle over travel arrangements, or difficulty in reaching the final destination.

Rather curiously Freud suggested that 'missing the train' dreams were about dying—which is, at least, a change from sex. The train symbolizes death. Failure to climb aboard would express an unconscious desire to comfort yourself that dying is not your immediate fate. Many have pointed out the inconsistency in this interpretation by citing a similar dream where we *manage to catch the train* and feel relieved and happy; then the drama can scarcely be termed a nightmare or anxiety dream. Does this mean that we are in fact hoping to be assured of an imminent demise?

A more suitable explanation is that the journey, be it by train, boat, plane, horse, or on foot, represents our process through life. When we fail to get transport we may be indicating a fear that we are not progressing as we would wish—after all, we use colloquialisms like 'missed the boat' or 'took the wrong turning' to describe opportunities that miscarried. The dream may also be read purposively, not just as a statement of a present problem but as a demonstration that our attitudes need altering if we are to make that train or complete the journey in order to achieve the desired progress. If you feel your 'train' nightmare is one that may be read in 'topdog' versus 'underdog' terms, you have to decide which one is complicating your journey and why. Perhaps 'topdog' is saying you *ought* to stay home and conform, so thwarting the 'underdog's' wish to travel, pursue a career, or generally enjoy more freedom of thought and activity than your original conditioning permitted.

*Death* As we have witnessed from accounts by its victims, the nightmare takes particular delight in disturbing sleep with images associated with death and funerals. Unless you are aware that someone is sick, such dreams are rarely predictive. It is always important if you dream of your own death: sometimes this is translated as a wish to return to the maternal womb but, much more significantly, it usually implies a desire for resurrection and a fresh start.

The typical death nightmare involves a relative—a marital partner, a parent, brother, sister, or child—and is accompanied by overpowering feelings of anguish, guilt, and fear. Tears may even flow during sleep. Clearly these nightmares may be interpreted quite simply as an apprehension of the time when a particular person dies, or reflect how the dreamer feels if such an event has already taken place. The death dream may be trying to force the individual to come to terms with the fact that something is irrevocably over, and he or she must learn to go on living.

Sometimes this dream shows that we feel a person is 'moving away' from us in real life. The people in our death dreams—including strangers—may represent aspects of the self we wish or fear to 'lose', or they demonstrate that our feelings for someone or something are 'dead'. When parents dream that a child is dead, lost, or hurt it may mirror a very natural anxiety but it might also be a subtle punishment dream. Gestaltists would suggest that the 'topdog' is nagging you to conform to your parents' standards; perhaps during the day you let your child do or say things that your own parents would disapprove of and the dream is trying to force you into a traditional mould.

A death nightmare can also express a deeply disguised and ambivalent wish: a parent, especially a father, may feel thoroughly displaced by all the attention shown to a child which his unconscious wishes would 'go away'.

Freud believed that most death dreams sprang from the dreamer's repressed desire for the death of a particular person, not at the time of dreaming, but left over from some occasion in childhood. The death wishes of children are not always as cruel or absolute as they sometimes appear. Usually they are incapable of understanding the consequences of their own immediate desires or actions. By 'dead' they mean 'gone away', or not being a nuisance and 'preventing me from doing or getting what I want'.

Such situations are repeated in adulthood; there are always those for whom society expects us to love and care, who perhaps stand between us and a loved person or object, or our freedom, and the inadmissible infantile hatred may well up in dreams accompanied by feelings of grief and guilt in order to evade the censor. Our nightmares need not be connected with the death of that current 'problem' person but associated with someone who provoked similar emotions long ago.

The nightmare that shows us usurping or killing an illustrious figure, accompanied by feelings of dread and followed by terrible retribution, can be translated in Freudian terms as that old infantile wish to overthrow a parent sneaking past the censor. However, it can be interpreted in a much more productive manner: it may represent a *need* to break away from authority, be it a restrictive family background, a job, an emotional situation, or a philosophy. It may be urging the dreamer to shake off old shackles, assert individuality, and take responsibility for making personal decisions. A too rigid conscience may be limiting our potential and this internal authoritarian, rather than any external one, needs to be rebelled against. The punishment is your conditioning (the 'topdog') trying to force you to stay in the old pattern. Here is a nightmare of violence or death that is trying to demonstrate symbolically the individual's needs.

One or more of these fearful patterns will have rung a tocsin in your memory. From the universality of the themes it is clear that the nightmare and the anxiety dream are not manifestations designed merely to give the sleeper a harrowing night. Frequently they arise at important stages in the life of child and adult—stages that may be unpleasant and difficult but which one has no chance of circumventing. Either we continue, bruised and buffeted but matured by the experience, or get jammed and regress, so that the insurmountable stage remains a mental or physical burden and barrier.

There are two different ways of reacting to our worst dreams, however we choose to interpret them: we may succumb to their terror, shutting our ears, eyes, and memories in the desperate hope that they will eventually leave us in peace; or, comforted by the awareness that others have reached this point in fear too, we may—as the advertisement has it—'learn something to our advantage'. Even the darkest nightmare contains a message to the self; it may be very painful when deciphered but it can offer the individual a chance to deal with a past or current predicament and may present an opportunity to progress emotionally; that is, if we dare look into and decipher its meaning.

# The Dark Prophet

From the visions of drunkards and madmen, one might doubtless deduce innumerable consequences by conjecture which might seem to presage future events. For what person who aims at a mark all day will not hit it? We sleep every night, and there are few on which we do not dream; can we wonder then that what we dream sometimes comes to pass?

*De Divinatione* CICERO

How ironic that Cicero, having 'excellently discoursed on the vanity of dreams was as yet undone by the flatterie of his own', demonstrating that not even the most disbelieving is immune from seeing a particular dream as something out of the ordinary.

The dream in question depicted Julius Caesar's nephew, Octavian, gaining control of Rome. The orator allied himself to this cause and, when it proved successful, naturally hoped for political preferment. However, the dream had failed to show him the eventual nightmare 'pay-off': that Mark Anthony would succeed with his plea to Octavian that Cicero and his brother be destroyed.

In the Roman world, where many were seriously involved in various forms of divination, Cicero's scepticism was refreshing—but must largely have fallen on deaf ears. Today it would earn him the approbation of inflexible rationalists who limit the mystery of human potential and the universe to what may be explained according to proven facts. Anything that cannot be so encompassed must be superstition, a misunderstanding, coincidence, scientific heresy, or fraud. This attitude entails closing the eyes to a number of extraordinary events because as yet they have no explanation. Fortunately, extreme examples of late nineteenth-century pragmatism are being replaced by a more open-minded approach, in scientific circles as well as generally.

That a glimpse of some future event may be had in sleep must be one of humankind's oldest universal beliefs, and one that has not been eliminated by space-age technology. The dream and the nightmare are the nearest that most of us get to a 'paranormal' experience for they ignore the laws governing time and space, and transport us into past and future, allowing us to see things never beheld during waking life. So it is not surprising that people continue to accept that certain dreams do come true. Nor is this just an eye-catching gimmick to boost the circulation of sensational newspapers and paperbacks; scientists, doctors, and philosophers allow that precognition and telepathy do occur in sleep. Yet how the phenomenon can be explained is as difficult for the specialist as the layperson; traditional establishment views of time, space, and causality have been elbowed out of the way by quantum physicists who make some very esoteric claims about the probabilities relating to time, which permit that occasionally an event may precede the cause. The fact that the barriers between the conscious and unconscious areas of the mind are weaker in sleep may be the reason why those precognitive experiences arise more often at night.

You may be wondering what the predictive dream is doing with a chapter of its own in a book on the nightmare. The reason is quite simple: few such dreams ever show pleasant forthcoming events. Approximately half relate to death, disaster, and injury (in that order) overtaking someone close to the dreamer. The contents of the balance of these predictive visions reveal a curiosity: they are trivial to be sure but, unlike our normal sleeping dramas, usually fail to reflect day-to-day interests, aspirations, or problems about family, sex, or, as you could reasonably expect, work. In fact, the precognitive nightmare, even at its most mundane, is the rogue of the species!

You might argue that it is not a prophetic dream but simply an example of our old foe, the typical nightmare, made significant by a subsequent but coincidental event. Why, therefore, should it not be interpreted symbolically or according to one or other of the schools of psychoanalysis to reveal the dreamer's difficulties rather than linked with the unwritten future? That is a perfectly rational standpoint *except* that this particular kind of dream refuses to lend itself to normal treatment.

Those who do have precognitive dreams, either on a regular or a one-off basis—and twice as many women as men seem to experience them—claim that they are quite unlike the usual run-of-the-monster-and-pursuer nightmare. For one thing, instead of being the centre of the stage, the dreamer is frequently an onlooker.

Ten days before the Hon J. Cannon Middleton, an English businessman, was due to set sail on the *Titanic*, he dreamed of the great ship floating upside down with the passengers and crew swimming around her. This unnerving experience was repeated the next night but, as he reported to friends, in the dream he seemed to hover above the wreck. Although the nightmare's details did not agree exactly with what later occurred it was fortuitous for Mr Middleton that his trip was cancelled for business reasons since, according to his wife, he was not the sort of person to postpone a journey on the strength of a scaring dream.

The precognitive dream tends to be more colourful, vivid, and memorable. It may be repeated not just on consecutive nights but also several times in one night. Sometimes its details will not fade over a few days, as if the subject is being forced to bear them in mind. Above all, the nightmare presents such a sense of reality that the victim is made more than normally uncomfortable and depressed.

Since dreams have never been easy to decode there has always been a problem as to just how much notice should be taken of their predictions. Where a prophecy is pleasant it does not much matter. However, where a nightmare foretells catastrophe there was, and is, a need to know if its message is genuine or merely a rather nasty fantasy.

In the *Odyssey* Homer suggested that false dreams come through an ivory gate but the ones that really inform the dreamer about the future 'issue from the gate of burnished horn'. This hardly simplifies the situation. Like Cicero we are left wondering if last night's ostensible precognitive bad dream slipped in through an ivory or horn gate. 'Wait and see' is not particularly helpful advice when yours is a disaster nightmare. However, let me assure you that if you had a gruesome dream last night the odds are heavily against it coming true. For all the precognitive nightmares reported only a handful do come true. Some must be accepted as genuine examples of foreknowledge or telepathy which cannot be argued out of court simply because we cannot explain how; but a proportion are pure coincidence, or the dreamer, guided by hindsight, unconsciously rearranges memory of the dream's precise contents, to 'be wise after the event'.

How many of us have met the over-anxious parent who, on hearing about an accident to a child, cries: 'I knew this would happen. I saw it in my dream.' Parents have lots of dreams enshrining fears for an offspring's health and safety, especially when it learns a new skill or embarks on a fresh stage of life. Usually when the facts of such premonitory dreams are examined dispassionately they are rarely an exact or adequate description of what subsequently happened. We've all at some time experienced that *déjà vu*—the 'I've been here before' feeling—probably arising when an actual event, place, or nuance echoes something from a forgotten dream. If we are to be absolutely objective can we be sure that no more than a familiar chord has been struck rather than the playback of a whole concerto? Occasionally, when a particular real life situation does occur, someone will recall having dreamed it—but that is no foundation on which to base the case for precognition.

Critics have tended to dismiss the evidence for predictive dreams as too anecdotal; with purely personal matters it is impossible to decide how much any subject was subconsciously aware of circumstances that would have a definite bearing on the future. All investigation has had to depend on someone reporting a dream, and then waiting on events to prove it veridical. However, the discovery of REM and NREM sleep has meant that much more complex experiments on dreams can be attempted under laboratory conditions. From the 1960s onwards Doctors Ullman and Krippner have been testing telepathy and precognition during sleep at the Maimonides Dream Laboratory, New York.

Two experiments using Malcolm Bessant, an English psychic, who had earlier, spontaneously and apparently correctly, predicted the death of de Gaulle and the wreck of a Greek oil tanker connected with Aristotle Onassis, produced a startling fourteen out of sixteen instances of precognition. It would have seemed a promising deal to bet against this possibility: the odds were calculated as five thousand to one in the first series and two thousand to one in the second. Some will see this as substantiating what they have always believed: that ESP (extrasensory perception) occurs in sleep. Others of Cicero's kidney will admit it is curious, but inconclusive, and argue for more experimentation.

Disappointingly, the laboratory does not seem to provide an atmosphere conducive to those dramatic disaster dreams so we are no nearer to setting up a human radar station—an advance warning system based on the visions of 'reliable' dreamers in a controlled setting. The real difficulty with laboratory-tested samples of precognition is judging whether or not the subject might have picked up material telepathically from those carrying out the experiments. Too many examples of dream telepathy exist for its likelihood to be entirely denied—however much of a doubting Thomas you are.

The bullet has replaced antique dagger or arrow as the assassin's weapon but now, as in the past, quite a few messages delivered by the 'Dark Prophet' concern the death of someone important. The leader, or hero, who goes almost knowingly and willingly to destruction, is an archetype found throughout history and religion so it is scarcely surprising that this image is repeated in the nightmare—the leading actor borrowed from the world's headlines. However, investigators of precognition feel that dreams about famous people are too commonplace to provide definitive proof of prophecy since there is always more than an even chance that real life will mirror the worst assassination nightmare.

In his book *Patterns of Prophecy*, the psychic and author Alan Vaughan described how he had a dramatic nightmare about Robert Kennedy's murder prior to that event. He sent details of the dream to the Society for Psychical Research in London, and also to Dr Stanley Krippner at the Maimonides Dream Laboratory. Unfortunately the warning did not reach Kennedy on time, although Mr Vaughan doubted that the senator would have paid any more attention to it than his brother John had done when various clairvoyants had stated that his life was in jeopardy. Real life was so like this dream that it must send a shiver along even an unimpressionable spine.

Television has brought the faces of the great into everyone's living-room. Yet long before its invention people were experiencing uncanny premonitory dreams about personalities with whom they could not have developed even the tenuous relationship supplied by the evening news programmes.

On 2 or 3 May 1812, a West-country businessman, John Williams, had a curiously detailed nightmare showing the murder of Spencer Perceval in the lobby of the House of Commons. He awoke and told his wife, who dubbed it an empty dream. Twice more he tried to sleep but on each occasion had the identical dream. Understandably he grew alarmed and felt it his duty to go to London and communicate the vision. His friends, fearing he might expose himself to ridicule, dissuaded him from going. Williams said no more but watched the newspapers every evening with more than normal apprehension.

On the evening of 13 May his son showed him a paper. The dream had come true. Mr Perceval, the Prime Minister, had indeed been shot dead in the House of Commons' lobby on 11 May. But now we come to more uncanny facts. Later, when Mr Williams went to London on business, he bought a print depicting the murder only to discover that all its details, including the colours of the clothes, right down to the buttons on the assassin's coat, conformed exactly with his nightmare. Prediction or coincidence?

We can only speculate how the course of history might have been altered if just one warning dream had been heeded. On 28 June 1914, Monseigneur Joseph de Lanyi, Bishop of Grosswarden, had a nightmare of a black-bordered letter decorated with the arms of his one-time pupil, the Archduke Franz Ferdinand. Then he saw the Archduke and his wife in their limousine. A man stepped from the milling crowds and fired two bullets into the car. Across the scene the dreamer read: 'Dear Dr Lanyi, my wife and I have been victims of a political crime at Sarajevo, June 28th 1914, 4 am.'

Horrified, Lanyi awoke to find the time at 4.30 a.m. Not only did he write down this incident but also drew a sketch of it. When he failed to make others believe his dream must come true, he celebrated an early Mass for the Archduke. Ten hours after the nightmare the murder took place—the spark that ignited the holocaust known as World War I. That the dream letter was apparently penned half an hour before Lanyi awoke is bizarre.

As with all examples of the apparently precognitive nightmare we are supplied with more questions than answers.

The earliest recorded assassination nightmare took place in Cicero's lifetime. Most of us are fairly familiar with it from Shakespeare's *Julius Caesar*:

> Calpurnia here, my wife, stays me at home:
> She dream'd tonight she saw my statua,
> Which, like a fountain with an hundred spouts,
> Did run pure blood; and many lusty Romans
> Came smiling, and did bathe their hands in it . . .

Shakespeare based his account on Plutarch, who related how on the night before the murder Calpurnia in a troubled sleep dreamed of holding her husband's stabbed body in her arms and weeping over it. Next day she begged him to postpone the meeting with the senate. Since Calpurnia was not given to 'womanish superstition' Caesar did not shrug off the dream or her distress. All the same, fate, or his enemies' determination proved too strong to be side-stepped.

Calpurnia's nightmare quite likely sprang from the apprehension which must dog the families of all important figures, fuelled by gossip of the extraordinary omens currently manifesting in the Eternal City.

A problem with historic dreams is that we can never be quite certain if a chronicler 'improved' on the details to make a better tale or to score a point for or against the subject. William Rufus was heartily disliked by the Church so it is less than miraculous that a number of priests foresaw his death in their dreams. Not surprisingly William greeted their prophecies with derision. On the night before Tyrrel accidentally shot that fatal arrow the king had a dream to which perhaps he should have paid attention: of a cold wind passing through his side.

Under close scrutiny certain nightmares that have been accepted as proof of precognition may be explained in other terms. A few days before his death, Abraham Lincoln dreamed that a body on a catafalque was lying in state in the White House, surrounded by weeping people and a guard-of-honour. When he asked a soldier who was dead, back came the answer: 'The President. He was killed by an assassin.'

If, subsequently, Lincoln had not been assassinated, this dream would have less impact and only serve to highlight the president's apprehensions about his enemies from the South.

Other ostensible precognitive nightmares may arise from a dreamer's subliminal knowledge churned into consciousness during sleep. The notorious 'Red Barn' affair seems to fit this. Maria Marten had not been seen by her family for almost a year when on three consecutive nights in 1828 her mother dreamed she had been murdered and buried in the Red Barn. At her insistence the floor was dug up—and Maria's mutilated remains were discovered. That August, Maria's lover William Corder was hanged for this murder.

Most ineptly, he had pretended that he and Maria were married but his contradictory behaviour, anxiety about the barn, and the fact that one of Maria's brothers had seen him near there on the afternoon he and Maria were presumed to have eloped, must have fed Mrs Marten's fears. There again, it is quite possible that she picked up telepathically Corder's guilty thoughts and memories.

Prodromic nightmares—those that seem to give advance intimation of some ailment before any symptom shows—often sound incontestable and, while they must not be ignored, cannot be used safely as a sole method of diagnosis since many perfectly healthy people experience similar frightening dreams. Those that do come true may well be explained as an unconscious awareness of the disorder, or they may be triggered off by the minutest physical manifestation. Before tuberculosis was diagnosed a young girl regularly dreamed of being buried alive. She could even feel the cold heaviness of damp earth pressing on her body, and awoke sweating with terror. As night sweats are a feature of respiratory illness, this may have been an instance of the diabolical dream-maker producing a drama to include such a stimulus.

Some patients, for several weeks before they had had their complaints diagnosed, dreamed of knives cutting into their intestines and being knocked on the head. Prediction—or apprehension of what might possibly lie in store? Others, who were eventually operated on for cerebral tumours, reported that for a year or so before any sign of the disease appeared they had nightmares in which they were wounded in the head, invariably in the identical spot as the tumour.

One woman had a scary dream of sitting on the lavatory wearing a pink nightdress when suddenly blood spurted from her mouth and nose. Not long afterwards reality copied the dream. Those studying the case concluded that it was more likely that her unconscious had known of the peptic ulcer which caused the bleeding than that this was an instance of precognition. That the doctor found her in the bathroom, wearing a pink nightie, may be seen as coincidence based on details borrowed from her everyday life. The same subject dreamed of being in hospital, having had an operation. Later she did go to hospital for surgery.

Instead of being a prophecy her dream is a neat example of Freud's wish-fulfilment theory—her unconscious, aware that she needed treatment for an old complaint, managed to get the whole unpleasant business over and done with in a bad dream!

Therapists who employ the dream to tap the individual's unconscious are not adverse to recognizing it as a potential vehicle for extrasensory perception. Indeed, some admit it is quite weird how patients often dream details of their own (the doctors') lives, which they must be picking up telepathically. Certain psychiatrists have attempted to influence patients towards therapeutic dream symbols and situations via telepathy!

Freud was among the first to allow that telepathy might occur during a dream although this did not alter his methods of interpretation. Given how much he had already risked with his revolutionary approach we must admire him for going even further out on a limb by cautiously suggesting that the original method of communication might have been telepathy which was superseded by a more efficient means, and that archaic traces of it remain to manifest under favourable conditions such as sleep.

Certain prophetic nightmares seem to be clear examples of telepathic communication: those who have dreamed of a friend committing suicide have frequently been shocked to discover this dream has come true. Somehow the suicide's intention reached them in sleep, making the dreamers feel there should have been some way of intervening.

Several people may simultaneously appear to dream of the identical horrific event with more or less similar details. Whether all are prompted by the actuality or whether some are just tuning in to others' nightmares is impossible to ascertain. There are even weird accounts of three dreamers having the same nightmare *without* any external inspirations: so Tom may dream of trying to murder Dick, and Dick may dream of Tom trying to kill him, while Harry dreams of witnessing the bloodthirsty spectacle. The fantasy may require three quite different interpretations for Tom, Dick, and Harry but what counts is that on one night the same nightmare spectre crossed three separate paths through sleep.

While telepathy between people in fraught circumstances is widely accepted if not explained, less familiar is the apparent bond between the animal and the human world. In *The Times* of 21 July 1904 there appeared an account of H. Rider Haggard's remarkable experience, authenticated by several reputable witnesses.

On the night of Saturday 9 July the author had a most vivid and unpleasant nightmare. His cries of distress—sounding more like an animal's than a human's—roused his wife who woke him. As he struggled back to consciousness the dream changed. At first he had felt horribly oppressed as if drowning. Then, suddenly, he saw his favourite black retriever, Bob, lying on its side in rough undergrowth beside water. The animal seemed to be trying to transmit that it was dying. Somehow Mr Haggard felt his own personality rising from the dog's body.

At breakfast next morning husband and wife discussed this dream. Neither took it seriously for Bob had been seen the previous evening. Later the dog was nowhere to be found. Eventually its body was discovered in the river against a weir. It had been killed by several blows to the head and its front legs were broken. Further investigation revealed that Bob had been hit by a train on the Saturday night. Its body had been carried some way along the track until it toppled among the reeds beside the river. Obviously the nightmare could have been one of those curious coincidences but its intensity suggested something else.

Mr Haggard, and many others, concluded that either the dog was trying to communicate with its owner in its death-throes or, if it had been killed outright, some three hours before the nightmare, then its spirit (or whatever you choose to term it) was contacting its master before it passed into whatever you believe follows death. A stranger-than-fiction tale without any easy explanation.

The *Titanic* is renowned not only as one of the worst sea tragedies ever but also for its association with a large number of paranormal experiences—eight out of every ten precognitive cases

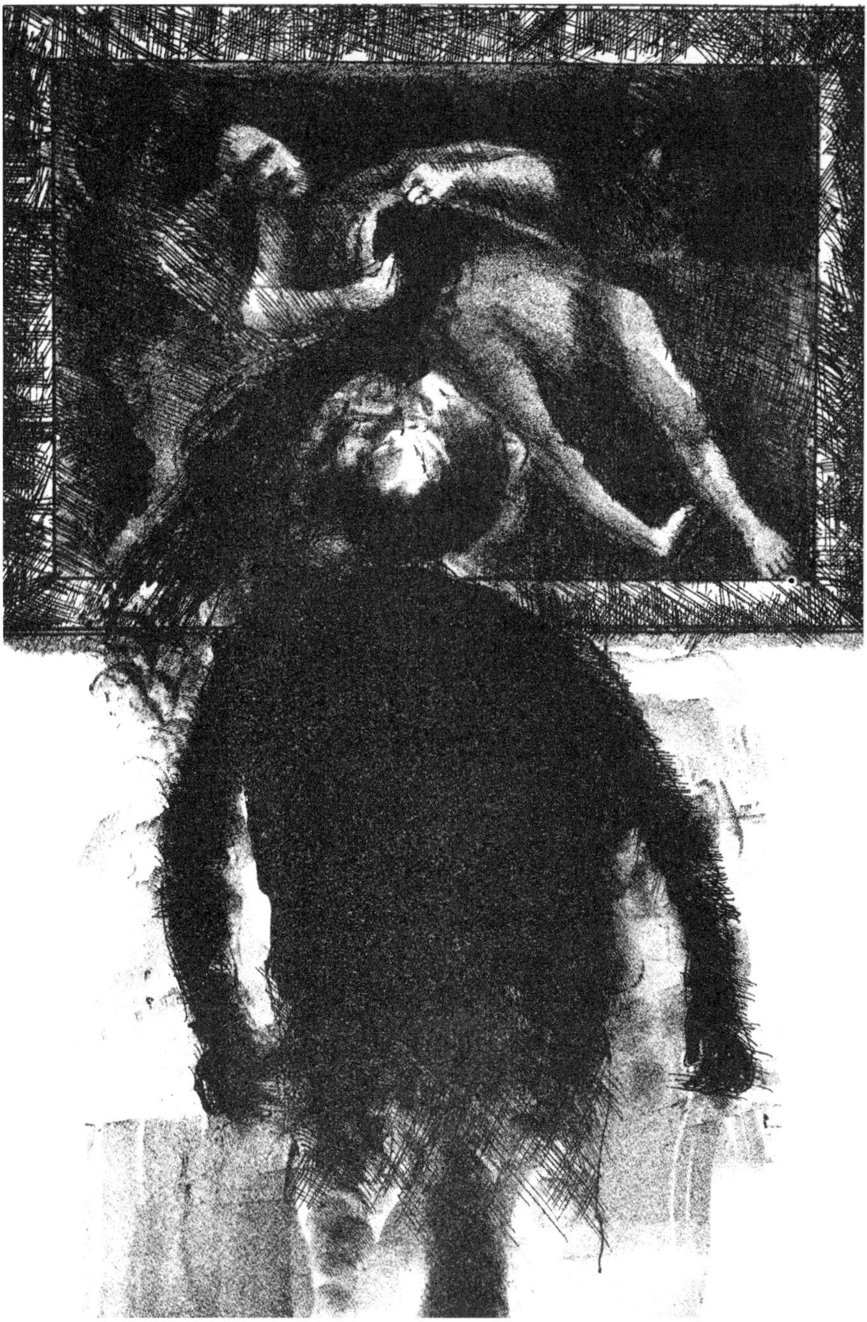

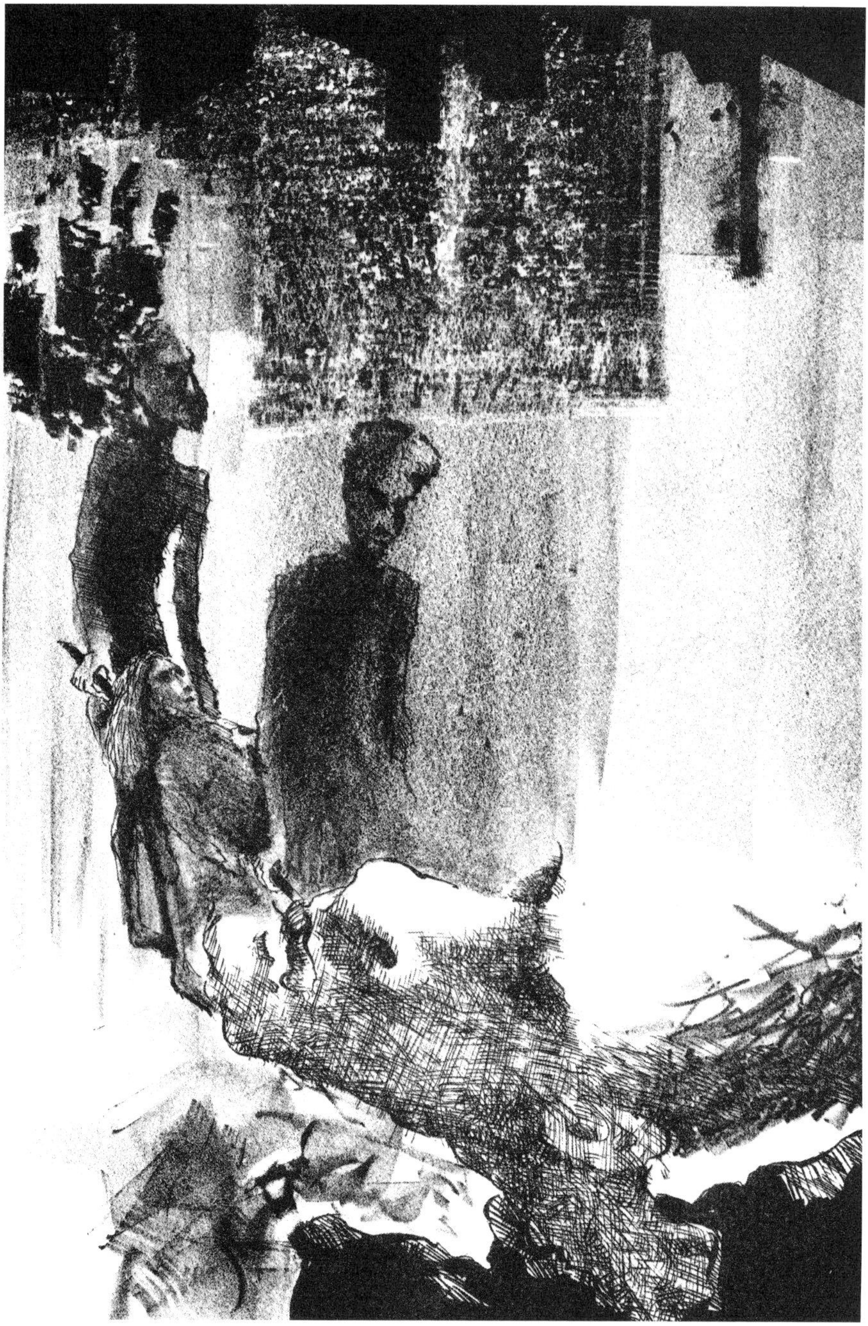

involved a nightmare. How curious that a ship with the reputation for being so unsinkable that it had insufficient lifeboats should give rise to more catastrophe premonitions than any other similar marine disaster.

On the night that the ship hit the iceberg several people had extremely accurate nightmares portraying the scene. One lady in New York dreamed that her mother was in a crowded lifeboat rocking perilously in the open sea. Much distressed, she woke her husband. (Marital partners seem the first to hear the predictive nightmare and, torn from sleep, are not always the most sympathetic listeners!) He scoffed at her for being upset by a dream, especially as they both knew that her mother was safe and sound on dry land in England.

Next day the *Titanic's* fate was blazoned across the world headlines. The lady read her mother's name on the passenger list—fortunately as a survivor. She had planned the trip to surprise her daughter. At about the same time as the dream occurred she had been in an overcrowded lifeboat, convinced it must capsize, and thinking of the daughter she would never see again.

Nightmares signposting the *Titanic's* sinking were experienced by a variety of people holding different views on the likelihood of precognition. A teenage girl, whose uncle was a crew member and died in the disaster, had the most unforgettable dream of her life. Two nights before the accident she dreamed of walking along a local road and suddenly seeing a large ship, which began to sink at one end. She heard a fearful scream and woke in a disturbed state. When she returned to sleep the dream reappeared.

Among the many to perish was the Spiritualist, editor, and journalist W. T. Stead. One psychic had warned him against travelling by water in the middle of April 1912; and another had a terrifying dream, which he associated with Stead and not himself, of people screaming and struggling in the sea around a great black ship. Stead dubbed him a 'gloomy prophet' and went to his death—without the excuse of being a sceptic!

Of course the *Titanic* made news before ever it set sail and so could conceivably appear in dreams. Many insist that the fabric of the dream cannot be woven from totally unknown threads but this is demonstrably untrue—especially in the instance of the precognitive dream. When the wife of General Toutschkoff had three nightmares of her husband being killed at a place called Borodino she had never heard of such a village; nor could it be found on any map, being too small to be included. Then Napoleon's Grand Army marched into Russia and the Battle of Borodino became part of history. When the General's wife was informed of her husband's death the details corresponded with those in her dream.

In the 1920s, as a result of J. W. Dunne's *An Experiment with Time*, many intelligent folk started keeping pads and pencils by their beds to record dreams and check them against subsequent events. It was this aeronautical engineer who demonstrated that the existing concepts of time were in need of rethinking to accommodate the inexplicable—apparent examples of precognition. His own attempt at an explanation was extremely complicated and related to 'serial' time—an infinite amount of 'times' all flowing at different rates.

Although his time theories have now been displaced by those of the quantum physicists, Dunne's book still provides absorbing and challenging reading. In it he recorded samples of his own predictive dreams. The most famous is a nightmare that occurred in the autumn of 1913 in which he saw a train falling over the embankment to the north of the Firth of Forth Bridge. He had a vague presentiment that such an accident would occur in the following spring and related the dream to his sister. Both of them, half jokingly, warned friends against travelling north in the spring. Then, on 14 April 1914 the Flying Scotsman was derailed. It crashed down an embankment north of the Forth Bridge.

Dunne also highlighted the curious fact that sometimes the prophetic nightmare is not of the disaster itself but represents a newspaper account of it. Just as headlines, in the first flush of any catastrophe, mistake the number of casualties or extent of disaster, so will the dream's contents tally with this error.

Foreknowledge of newspaper reportage occurred long before Dunne remarked on it. On 29 November 1874 the ship *La Plata* foundered off the Bay of Biscay. On the night of 2 December a lady dreamed of a ship sinking with sixty people drowned, which she confided to her husband. The next day he brought home the papers with the story of *La Plata's* fate and the loss of sixty lives. Eventually it was learned that only fifty-eight people had died so it seemed that the dreamer had received her advance information from the press. Nowadays the ubiquity of television means that the 'Dark Prophet' has another extremely vivid source to tap, which may frighten and mislead as well as inform.

Occasionally dreamers have witnessed the completion of their nightmares in real life when they had absolutely no power to influence the situation. The following dream can hardly be explained in terms other than premonition—unless you have a preference for complete coincidence, in which case you could be stretching the bounds of that possibility further than somebody who accepts the idea of precognition.

Mark Twain and his brother, Henry Clemens, worked on Mississippi river boats. One night, in their sister's house at St Louis, Mark Twain dreamed of his brother's body lying in a metallic coffin, supported on two chairs in the sitting-room. On Henry's breast rested a bouquet with a single red flower at its centre. Mark Twain told their sister this dream which so affected him that on waking he believed Henry to be dead.

A few weeks later, by chance, the brothers were returning to St Louis on separate boats. On the boat on which Henry was travelling the boiler exploded. As a result he and others were killed. All the casualties, apart from Henry Clemens, were put in wooden coffins but the ladies of Memphis moved by the tragedy that had overtaken such a young man, collected money for a metal coffin. When Mark Twain went to see his brother's remains the scene was as in the dream, except that the sitting-room was in Memphis and not St Louis. Only the flowers were absent. As he stood beside that metal coffin a lady entered to place on Henry's breast a bouquet of white flowers with a red rose at their heart.

That Mark Twain was granted a paranormal glimpse of his brother after death could not have deflected Henry's fate for it had not shown how he would meet his end. Sometimes, however, where a disaster affects many people, and is heralded by a significant number of precognitive experiences, we are forced to wonder if the 'Dark Prophet' might not be trying to encourage us to take evasive action.

On 21 October 1966, at 9.15 am, a coal tip slid down on a small Welsh village and killed 144 people. The name Aberfan was forever engraved onto the world's roll of tragedies that might have been prevented.

Dr Barker, the consultant psychiatrist at Shelton Hospital, Shrewsbury, visited the village the following day and wrote in the *Journal of the Society for Psychical Research* (December 1967) of being:

> appalled by the devastation and suffering I saw everywhere. It occurred to me there might have been people ... throughout Britain, who had experienced some warning of this disaster, possibly in the form of a strong premonition. Since the Aberfan disaster was such an unusual one, I considered that it provided an excellent opportunity to investigate precognition.

Later he contacted Peter Fairley, then science correspondent of the London *Evening Standard*, who launched a nationwide appeal for persons claiming foreknowledge of Aberfan to report their experiences. Within two weeks seventy-six replies reached Dr Barker. At about the same time the Psychophysical Research Unit at Oxford also asked for cases of precognition relating to the same calamity. Altogether some 200 persons alleged that they had experienced premonitions in the guise of dreams or visions or an overpowering sense of distress on or before the day of the disaster.

Thirty-six of Dr Barker's letters came from dreamers, the majority of whom were female. Their ages ranged from ten to seventy-three and the dreams varied from a vague impression to a fairly accurate picture of a terrible catastrophe. Many of these dreamers related their nightmare to friends or relatives *before* the disaster occurred, which rules out accusations of hysterical afterthoughts. The time elapsing between dream and event was anything from six weeks to two hours. Most of the dreamers had no association whatsoever with Aberfan and in many instances no previous claim to any similar kind of dream. Dr Barker acknowledged that:

> The similarity between the various experiences is striking and appears to be much more marked than the dissimilarity between them. Analysis of all the incoming material certainly suggested the possibility of a disaster occurring at Aberfan itself, namely children, Wales, a Welsh miner, Welsh national costume, mountains, valleys, black pitch and shale, digging, the name Aberfan, screams, horror, avalanche, buried houses, burial, school . . .

Particularly moving was the case of ten-year-old Eryl Mai Jones, who lived in Aberfan and was a pupil at the Pantglas Junior School. On 20 October she had a dream which she told to her mother '. . . of going to school. There was no school there. Something black had come down all over it.' Eryl Mai was one of the 128 children who died.

Other dreams included 'screaming children buried by an avalanche of coal in mining village', 'screaming children and creeping black slimy substance', 'crowds of people on hillside. Mud everywhere; man holding lamp with little boy beside him', 'children standing by building below black mountain; hundreds of black horses then thunder down hillside dragging hearses', 'screaming child in telephone box; followed child to house enshrouded in black stream', 'a cross-shaped communal grave at bottom of hill', 'falling debris and crowds of men digging', 'being smothered in deep blackness', 'blackness, hearing voices and pressure of people', and 'people running, crying and holding their heads; house tipping up' . . .

Some of these dream images are so remarkable as to be unnerving. It would perhaps have been more remarkable still if, on the strength of random reports, the authorities had evacuated Aberfan to prevent disaster (or the White Star Line had cancelled the *Titanic's* maiden voyage or supplied sufficient lifeboats) just because some people had had premonitions. Even something as untoward as seeing the future must be organized before officialdom might be persuaded to sit up and take notice.

As a result of the Aberfan investigations, Dr Barker and Mr Fairley set up the British Premonitions Bureau in January 1967 (afterwards run single-handed by Mrs Jennifer Preston of Southeast London). In 1968, after Dr Barker's address to the American Society for Psychical Research, a Central Premonitions Registry was established in New York, and another one in Canada.

The role of any such organization is to collect premonitions of natural disasters, air crashes, political events, and assassinations—anything, in fact, that could affect the lives of a number of people. Until the inception of these 'watchdogs', most predictions were based on dreams but only a small amount of material that reached the British Premonitions Bureau arose from sleep. This seems to substantiate the theory that most precognitive nightmares have a horizon delineating a personal rather than a group fate.

The other aim of these institutions is to discover sufficient individuals possessed of a proven degree of precognition. Their independent forecasts could be cross-checked and, if found reliable, would form the foundation for an 'early warning' system, which would mean that society could really take a safe step into the future.

Such a system would have to offer a very clear picture of the time, place, and type of catastrophe otherwise the public could be subjected to widespread needless panic. An abortive alarm might mean that a genuine one would be treated in much the same way as was the boy who cried 'wolf' once too often. However cynical it sounds, we must face reality: would those in power really make major changes in political, national, or mercantile arrangements on the strength of any 'reliable' disaster premonition?

A somewhat macabre and short-lived version of a premonitions bureau was instituted in Mexico in the sixteenth century not long before the arrival of the Spanish conqueror Hernàn Cortés. The Aztecs had what can only be regarded as a 'death wish'—a highly pessimistic view of the future—so perhaps it was not odd that so many of them dreamed that the empire was about to come to an end. Montezuma, doomed to go down in history as the last Aztec emperor, summoned these melancholy dreamers to his palace. Thousands obeyed and were massacred for their pains because not one of them proffered a fortunate omen. From that day nightmares were not spoken aloud. This did not stop the dreams or alter fate: it merely prevented people from talking!

The problem of the precognitive nightmare remains. Just how much notice should we take? Let's face it: if everyone paid attention to all the dire sleeping and waking predictions that were made an awful lot of journeys would never be undertaken, the famous would remain safely at home and, if we bear in mind Edgar Cayce's trance prophecies, the inhabitants of Los Angeles and San Francisco should have left town long ago and not contemplate returning until after 2001. It may be some comfort to Californians that 1969 was a bumper year for earthquake predictions. Remember what happened? Nothing.

As we know, dreams have a tantalizing habit of fading during the day leaving behind a chimerical impression. Even when you recall how unpleasant the nightmare was, its precise details usually begin to blur as time passes, unless committed to paper or tape recorder. How many people claim their memory is good, or that they never exaggerate, and then proceed to relate a 'true', but undocumented, prophetic dream they had ten years ago which has suddenly and precisely come true? It is not a question of deliberate falsehood but we are all human, and therefore fallible and suggestible.

In 1965, in the *Journal of the Society for Psychical Research*, G. W. Lambert recommended five points for establishing a link between dream and future event:

1 The dream must be reported to a reliable witness *before* any event takes place.
2 The time between dream and event should be quite short.
3 At the time of dreaming the circumstances should be improbable.
4 The dream's contents must be literally rather than symbolically portrayed.
5 Details of dream and event must correspond.

Dreams of Californian earthquakes hardly fulfil the third requirement since that state lies in the earthquake zone; so it is quite natural for people to have subconscious fears of such a disaster. However, if a lot of us dream that London was going to be demolished in an earthquake—something very remote indeed—then I for one would advise immediate evasive action. As a rider to the fourth requirement symbolism is acceptable where the dreamer can interpret the meaning before the event.

We can add to the list a further requirement that it should be beyond the power of dreamers to influence any happening directly, subconsciously, or through other people by telepathic suggestion . . . just as dreamers must not have been able to come by knowledge telepathically which could lead them unconsciously to make a presumption about the future.

A nightmare told by a young woman teacher to the analyst treating her for mild depression seems to fit these reliability requirements. In her dream she was dining with three men, two of whom she knew; the third, although she could recall his stature and voice, remained unidentified. All stayed overnight in this man's house. She slept but awoke feeling frightened and then went back to sleep. Again she woke, sensing that the unknown host was going to kill himself. She got up to find an incomplete suicide note. The stranger came into her room so she hid the note. He gave her a twenty-dollar bill. The scene changed. Now she was in this man's room. He demanded a rope which she could not give him. When she asked why he was going to do this terrible thing, he replied: 'Because it hurts too much'. Then the teacher really did wake up, thought of a friend, M, and went back to sleep.

What happened subsequently was supported by a newspaper report as well as her own testimony. Almost a week later she was with M (who had the same figure as the unknown dream man) plus the two others from her dream. M asked her to get something for him and gave her a twenty-dollar bill to cover the purchase. There was nothing unusual about his demeanour, nor did the teacher mention her dream to any of them. Next day—exactly a week from the dream, and at the same time as she had woken and thought of him—M jumped to his death. Neither the dreamer nor any of his friends had the faintest inkling that he would kill himself. As for the teacher no similar dream had ever before disturbed her sleep.

Like Mark Twain's nightmare, the details in real life do not tally precisely, but the events were completely beyond the dreamer's control. It was Jung who pointed out that a dream might contain 'an anticipatory combination of probabilities which may coincide with the actual behaviour of things but need not necessarily agree in every detail'. However, he also warned against overvaluing this prospective role in case it lead to a negation of freewill and an unquestioning acceptance of the dream as a guide to living.

That the future may occasionally be witnessed in dreams may make some despair that there is no freedom of choice—fate is already signed and sealed and there is nothing that can be done to avert catastrophe. Here Jung offered practical comfort for he believed that our freedom could only become doubtful when everything can be foreseen—and that is something nobody is proposing.

Apparently we can supply real-life situations, previously seen in a nightmare, with quite a different ending: that is, if the dream is recalled in time, when circumstances may be altered by the individual's intervention. A child has been prevented from drowning, a car crash avoided, and a coachman saved from a bad accident by dreamers recalling the fatal climax of their precognitive nightmares. Here we are presented with another riddle. Was disaster averted or were the original dreams, by not coming true, merely frightening and misleading fantasies?

There are hundreds of instances of the ostensibly precognitive nightmare. Citing them does not bring us nearer to explaining how they manifest. If you happen to believe that your astral body can separate itself from your physical body during sleep, and voyage back and forth in time, then you are probably not seeking an answer. However, if you do not accept this belief—held not only among primitive societies—then you are forced to examine what we imply by time. Humankind has arbitrarily imposed a system for its own convenience. The concept is simple: a straight line along which we progress. We cannot go back, except in memory, and we cannot travel forward any faster than clock or calendar allows. We are caught in the present. Yet precognition makes nonsense of this idea. Like the White Queen in *Alice Through the Looking Glass*, who screamed and bled *before* the pin pricked her finger, the events in a nightmare may precede their cause.

Although the rarified realm of new physics discusses the probability of all time being in the present, or even a two-dimensional time, nobody is offering a definitive answer. There are no easy explanations but this does not mean that true premonition cannot occur.

Technology has subtly hinted that the world can be simplified but what becomes abundantly clear is that the universe is a great deal more complicated than anyone imagined. Each new discovery reveals fresh questions and shows just how complex is the scheme of things—a scheme we may not have begun to appreciate in the midst of our clever mediocrity. The more we find inexplicable the wider is the horizon. Only when we insist on fitting everything into the limits of known rules do we dwarf our potential. By recognizing an unknown we accept a challenge that the human race has much more going for it than sometimes seems the case.

Such an every-night occurrence as our journey into sleep, even peopled with the darkest shapes, suggests there are forces within waiting to be exploited. Another age may regard us as uncivilized for failing to make use of our powers of precognition just as we term 'primitives' the human beings who lived before the invention of the wheel.

# The Pains of Sleep

But now farewell—a long farewell to happiness—winter or summer! farewell to smiles and laughter! farewell to peace of mind! farewell to hope and to tranquil dreams, and to the blessed consolations of sleep!
*Thomas de Quincey* CONFESSIONS OF AN ENGLISH OPIUM-EATER

The infant explores its world by tasting everything within reach—sometimes with detrimental results. In its racial infancy humankind sampled the vegetation of the environment and discovered that while some substances were good to eat others caused particular sensations: ecstasy, terror, the alleviation of pain, hunger, misery, and fatigue, the induction of sleep, the evocation of dream and nightmare. Depending on the society, such plants were viewed as sacred, assimilated into religious, healing, social, and even fighting customs—or outlawed. Thus psychoactive substances have been with us ever since we learned to apply the results of our innate curiosity.

Botanists, explorers, scientists, and anthropologists rediscovered these plants and took them into the laboratory in order to penetrate their mysteries. Further wonders and terrors were revealed. Modern techniques permit the stabilization and production of drugs by chemical means, which makes them widely accessible. The positive aspect allows improved treatment of mental and physical disorders but the shadow side is dependency on substances that may make the voyage into the land of sleep a veritable hell—and even worse when they are withheld.

Lest you are feeling complacent that the facts in this chapter hardly apply to you, let me say at once that the individual who takes a nightmare trip need not be a 'junkie', an 'acid head', or a 'speed freak'. Perfectly respectable citizens who obtain their medicine through a doctor may be disturbing the fundamental sleep pattern, which could give rise to anxiety dreams or extremely nasty nightmares. And, even if you never swallow a pill, please do not imagine yourself immune. Your diet might well contain the fatal seeds that summon up the fiend.

Next in popularity to the supernatural agency as a cause of dream and nightmare is a gastro-intestinal disturbance. Eating particular foods was long thought to promote special dreams. Quaint ideas like putting a sliver of wedding cake beneath your pillow to dream of your future partner must largely be based on sympathetic magic but diabolical or dramatic visions called for more substantial nourishment. Fuseli was reputed to eat raw meat to induce brilliant dreams. How much 'The Nightmare' owes to munching uncooked beefsteak at dead of night is a matter of speculation; but it makes a pleasing theatrical touch which is probably just as the artist intended.

A recent report showed how many housewives still cling to the belief that eating cheese at bedtime causes nightmares. It is easy to scoff at such ideas as ignorant superstition, fit only for a pre-scientific age, but now science has demonstrated that the 'raw-head-and-bloody-bones nightmare' rumoured to be the offspring of toasted cheese, raw meat, or pancakes is not such an old wives' tale after all.

Foods that are rich in protein, such as eggs, meat, and cheese contain the amino-acid tryptophan. Giving a subject a large dose of this chemical not only brings on the first REM period early— in less than forty-five minutes from the onset of sleep in most instances—but this phase is characterized by exaggerated eye movements, indicating very lively dreams, or nightmares. In one experiment the subject began to shout during this first REM period —which is unusual in itself—and woke to recount a horrible saga of being tortured!

Exactly how likely you are to suffer nightmares as a result of your evening eating habits will depend on: how late and how much you eat, whether you have a tendency towards nightmares normally, or whether there is some underlying anxiety which may take the opportunity to parade through sleep on the strength of a wedge of Gorgonzola. Even when beckoned with tryptophan-bearing agents the nightmare cannot always be relied on to put in an appearance. Consider all those who do indulge in weird nocturnal snacks and then go straight off to sleep without the slightest murmur from the fiend.

The techniques of the sleep laboratory have at last permitted doctors to study how psychoactive agents can alter sleep patterns so they no longer have to rely solely on reports from individuals that are naturally subjective and often unintentionally unreliable. Think of all those people who claim they never had a wink of sleep last night. Clinical investigations usually demonstrate that they do sleep—restlessly—but instead of recalling how often they awoke, they forget altogether the periods of sleep between times.

It is more than a pity that so many doctors, who would not think of trusting patients' own diagnoses of most ailments, continue to accept claims of sleeplessness and dole out prescriptions for hypnotics and tranquillizers which do help initially but if continued over a long term may aggravate the condition. Most medicaments that do us good can have side-effects on sleep, the intensity relating to the amount and frequency of dosage. Antibiotics and penicillin, for example, although not prescribed for anything to do with sleep, will still increase the length of the first two REM periods of the night. That is not to imply that these invaluable treatments can give you nightmares—they do not—but they merely demonstrate how fragile is our continent of sleep and how easy it is to disrupt its structure.

After thalidomide nobody in the civilized world should need reminding that apparently harmless medications can have quite unlooked-for powers, but in the past people had no idea of this unless they found out the hard way—through personal experience. How many herbal concoctions must have been responsible for summoning up the nightmare, either while the medicine was taken on a regular basis or when it was discontinued, purely because some substance inhibited or increased the amount of REM time in sleep?

The constituents of the legendary witches' flying ointment were chiefly deliriants that produce delusions and excitation followed by deep sleep, their alkaloids repressing REM activity at different rates. Usually the would-be witches rubbed the unguent on their bodies, and then flew off to consort with the devil and pursue other spectacular achievements—or, at least, so they believed. Meanwhile eye-witnesses saw them asleep in their own beds. The drugs probably entered the bloodstream via cuts, scratches, and the mucous membranes.

Fairly recently a German professor experimented with a paste of belladonna, henbane and thornapple as recommended by an ancient recipe. He and his colleagues applied it to their foreheads and underarms, and fell into a prolonged sleep filled with nightmarish dreams of taking wild rides, performing crazed dances, and being involved in some really strange goings-on, reminiscent of those witchcraft confessions, which may tell us something about the powers of auto-suggestion as well as ancient simples.

Similar mixtures were also taken orally for medicinal as well as magical purposes. Sustained use might well have whistled up the nightmare, but even more likely was its visitation once the drugs were suspended. Since its shape would be fashioned by whatever was in the subject's mind it is likely that the dreams resembled those that occurred when witchcraft was intended. But how much more terrifying it must have been when similar images manifested without any preliminary preparations. Remember, such folk would usually be treating whatever happened in the nightmare as the real thing.

Because heroin is so often associated with the addict and international drug connections, we are inclined to forget that its provenance—opium—was once a thoroughly respectable preparation, more widely employed than our pervasive sleeping-pills and tranquillizers. Since earliest times the opium poppy has been recognized as an invaluable source of pleasure and medication. It serves as analgesic, bringer of sleep, and dispeller of anxiety. But this miraculous anodyne has too costly a debit side: once physical dependence is established it will summon up the nightmare in all its dreaded splendour; if the victim tries to break free the most appalling withdrawal symptoms result which can only be counteracted by the drug. Indeed, there is no freedom in most instances: to lead a more-or-less normal existence an addict needs to take carefully monitored doses to maintain stability in much the same way as a diabetic has to use insulin.

During the nineteenth century the English employed opium so freely that in 1840 the average intake is estimated to have been around a quarter of an ounce (480 grains) per individual. That is nothing compared to the amount taken at the peak of his addiction by one of the most famous of English opium-eaters, Thomas de Quincey. He claimed a daily intake of 8,000 drops of laudanum (tincture of opium), the equivalent of some 300 or more grains . . . but this was long before the days of drug standardization so it is impossible to judge just how much real opium anybody was taking. (The drug also turns the habitual user into a less than reliable truth-teller!)

Opium was the basic ingredient in many cheap patent remedies which were sold openly in local chemists and widely advertised. These were not only an asset to quack practitioners but also to the medical profession at large. Opium and its derivatives were prescribed for hysteria, ulcers, 'flu, travel sickness, coughs, rheumatism, hangovers, stomach disorders such as colic and dysentery, and every conceivable ache and pain. Try to imagine a raging toothache before the invention of our 'safe' proprietary painkillers: you had no recourse other than to opium. The treatment was effective and relatively harmless, unless you found the side-effects too pleasant (and that must depend on untried areas of your character) and began to resort to it on a regular basis. Self-medication contributed enormously to addiction, particularly among women, because opium-based mixtures were so often taken to mitigate menstrual pains.

So many famous nineteenth-century literary figures were prescribed opium for chronic ill-health that it is little wonder we have been left graphic accounts of their nightmares. Just how many unfortunate children were plagued by the fiend as a direct result of becoming habituated to an opium-based mixture is hard to say; but as nursemiads were prone to the dubious practice of dosing their small charges with laudanum, particularly on Saturday nights when they wanted to be free to enjoy themselves, it sounds as if the nightmare must have been putting in overtime!

Some of that century's foremost citizens were addicted, which did not impair their mental capacity or reputation. William Wilberforce took opium daily for forty-five years and Clive of India for twenty years until an overdose killed him. The problem with opium is that the physical symptoms it cures are in fact those it procures as soon as you try to stop taking it; furthermore, where someone is using it for pleasure, it becomes necessary, as with any other drug, to keep increasing the dose to elicit the old magic.

Because opium was perfectly legal it was possible for anyone to become its casualty, so the attitude to the addict then was quite different from that of today: a mixture of pity and disapproval rather than detestation for the 'junkie' as a criminal or 'drop-out'. Indeed, opium addiction was regarded as preferable to drunkenness since alcohol was thought to inflame the passions whereas opium was believed to subdue them. Nevertheless, there was little understanding of the addict's inability to break the habit simply by employing will-power.

Society only deplored those who clearly used the drug hedonistically; opium-smoking—a habit first associated with the underworld but later to attract the 'decadent Bohemian' middle-class element—could not be excused on the grounds of ill-health; nor was there much sympathy for the plight of cotton mill workers who celebrated Saturday night's brief freedom from drudgery with opium pills or a few coppers' worth of laudanum to blur the harshness of their existence—the drug being cheaper than beer or spirits.

In the literary circles of the Romantic Age there existed a naive admiration for the concept of the opium-inspired work of art, as if the substance had somehow created it autonomously, using an artist as its mouthpiece. A similar credulous attitude was common among many impressionable people in the 1960s who saw 'tuning in' to some drug as a short-cut to Nirvana and artistic expression, only to discover that the road lead in less pleasant directions if the journey continued too long. Flirtation with drugs is all very well, as long as it does not lead to addiction. That may be compared to the difference between dream and nightmare.

The honeymoon period of blissful reverie and dreams, directed at a semiconscious level by the user, disintegrates once dependence is established. What remains is an indissoluble union with a monstrous partner. The self is the slave and the drug directs the mind where it dreads to go. Images can no longer be controlled. In sleep the nightmare erupts in its worst guise to remind the prey of all that would normally be repressed.

A drug user has to be happy, guilt-free, and willing to go wherever the drug leads in order to avoid the 'nightmare trip'. But which human being, who has become an addict, can fulfil those requirements? Addiction means that duties are neglected, beloved and respected people are let down and, where there is great intellectual ability, as possessed by Coleridge and de Quincey, there is also the awareness that this is being dissipated if not utterly destroyed. In such circumstances dreams can only become nightmares.

Remember 'The Pains of Sleep': it is all there—the unspeakable agony and guilt. Before he died, Coleridge wrote: 'After my death I earnestly entreat that a full and unqualified narrative of my wretchedness, and of its guilty cause, may be made public, that at least some little good may be effected by the direful example.' You have only to read the nightmares that Coleridge confided in his notebooks and you will meet the fiend in all its unambiguous nastiness without any attempt to clothe it in high-flown literary language—then you cannot fail to understand what an excess of opium does to the body and soul.

Coleridge had originally turned to the drug for reasons of ill-health (probably the chronic results of childhood rheumatic fever) but then stayed with it for pleasure. At first, as for many, opium was Coleridge's boon companion, then it became his master. Opiates—and the alcohol he resorted to when the drug's effects became intolerable—both depress the central nervous system, and alter the patterns that we now know compose sleep. They also summon up the nightmare when used in excess.

You might argue that not all of Coleridge's opium dreams could have been too intolerable, for that enchanted fragment 'Kubla Khan' is reputed to be the child of one such dream. The story of its creation, as fostered by the poet himself, is that in 1797 he had taken two grains of opium to check a bout of dysentery and had fallen asleep for about three hours while reading Purchas' *His Pilgrimage*:

> In Xanadu did Cublai Can build a stately palace, encompassing sixteene miles of plaine ground with a wall, wherein are fertile Meddowes, pleasant Springs, delightful Streames, and all sorts of beasts of chase and game, and in the middest thereof a sumptuous house of pleasure, which may be removed from place to place.

During the time that he slept Coleridge alleged that some 200 to 300 lines of perfect poetry were 'given' him by the opium. He awoke, recalling them clearly, and instantly began to write 'Kubla Khan'. After fifty-one magical lines had been committed to paper he was interrupted by that bothersome person on business from Porlock. An hour later he was able to resume work only to discover that the memory of his dream had fled; the poem consequently consisted of only fifty-four lines.

This is the tale that has long been accepted and which, in that Romantic Age, proved the ideal promotional gimmick! Yet the truth as suggested by Molly Lefebure in her brilliant study *Samuel Taylor Coleridge: A Bondage of Opium* is likely to have been rather different. When 'Kubla Khan' was published in 1816

Coleridge was just surfacing from the trough of his addiction and he was not the sort of person who could keep anything he had written under wraps for so long. Miss Lefebure dubs the presentation of 'Kubla Khan': 'a small masterpiece of trickery on Samuel Taylor Coleridge's part'.

That is not to denigrate the poem but rather to restore it to the position where we can comprehend just how difficult is the act of creation. He may well have dreamed snatches but the finalized work, composed sometime between 1797 and 1816, was the result of painstaking concentration and skill, probably requiring draft after draft until perfection was achieved. For further proof read the doggerel that even so lyrical a poet as Coleridge penned in his notebook under opium's influence. Then re-read 'Kubla Khan'.

Thomas de Quincey was less reticent about his addiction than Coleridge. Indeed, he enhanced his reputation by making a clean, if literary, breast of to what heights and depths the opium had led him—but his was quite a different character: a rebel who had known what it was to starve on the London streets as a runaway teenager. In adulthood somehow he managed to combine drop-out, opium-eater, literary figure, and kind, generous, and chivalric family man into one personality.

If you want to get inside the philosophical and talented skin of an addict, turn to de Quincey's *Confessions of an English Opium-Eater* (which first appeared in the *London Magazine* in 1821) but remember that it was intended to be read by the public; this bearing of a soul is couched in elegant language, unlike Coleridge's despairing records of his nightmares confided in a notebook and intended for no other eyes save his own. *Confessions* is a masterly evocation of the pleasures and torments of opium and provides an important picture of the drug in its contemporary setting, as well as a glimpse of what nowadays we term 'the underground'.

Like the psychoanalysts of a later age, de Quincey recognized that the mind forgets nothing and, in giving us his autobiographical details, we are able to trace how later the most traumatic memories were woven into his worst dreams.

He came to opium at the age of nineteen, when he died at seventy-four he was still on controlled doses of the drug. Excruciating toothache had introduced him to laudanum in 1804; he became aware that its intoxicating delights far outshone anything produced by alcohol but he dismissed its perils. 'Thou hast the keys to Paradise, oh just, subtle and mighty opium!'

And hell, too, but that took longer to discover.

De Quincey did point out, however, something that drug experimenters of every age have acknowledged—that the way in which the substance affects the imagination depends on the individual. 'If a man whose talk is of oxen should become an opium eater,' he wrote, 'the probability is, that (if he is not too dull to dream at all) he will dream about oxen.' Drugs draw on what is within the personality; they do not provide the imagery or thoughts, only the keys to unlock the chest in which they are stored . . . and the container is granted an opportunity of becoming a genuine Pandora's box!

For eight years de Quincey used laudanum intermittently, but only to heighten his senses. Then, in 1813, he was attacked by an appalling stomach irritation, possibly caused by a peptic ulcer resulting from that youthful starvation period. He began to take a surfeit of opium and until then was 'ignorant and unsuspicious of the avenging terrors which opium has in store for those who abuse its lenity'.

By 1817 he was completely shackled, the old excitation replaced by terrible inertia.

> The opium eater loses none of his moral sensibilities, or aspirations . . . but his intellectual apprehension of what is possible infinitely outruns his power not of execution only but even of power to attempt. He lies under the weight of incubus and nightmare.

The splendid dreams were transformed into magnificent nightmares. Any sufferer will immediately recognize the sensations contained in them, but the images are de Quincey's own, founded on his experiences and the breadth of his reading. He had been an over-imaginative and clever child and was well aware how youngsters can paint shapes on the darkness with their minds and eyes. He quoted one who complained: 'I tell them to go and they go, but sometimes they come when I don't tell them to come.' So it was with Thomas and the fiend.

The nightmares borrowed some of their dramas from his waking but unbiddable imaginings—an uncontrollable frieze of never-ending morbid tales. 'I seemed every night to descend into chasms and sunless abysses, depths below depths, from which it seemed hopeless that I could ever reascend.' The gloom persisted into waking and brought with it suicidal depression. In the 'insufferably splendid' dreams, space was distorted to such an extent that architecture and landscapes were too vast for the eye to encompass; and time expanded so that in one night he felt he had lived eons. 'Over every form, and threat and punishment and dim sightless incarceration brooded a sense of eternity, and infinity that drove me into an oppression of madness.'

The minutest details from childhood and forgotten scenes of later years revived to torment him. Regression meant re-experiencing grief for the sister who died when he was eighteen months, but more particularly for the beloved one who died when he was six, and whose death was in some way linked to the cruelty of a servant. In nightmare, too, he revisited the companions of his down-and-out sojourn in London.

On the itinerant, and probably harmless, Malay, who had once knocked at his Grasmere cottage door, and to whom he had presented opium as a tip, de Quincey laid the blame for directing some of the worst nightmares which transported him to Eastern settings. The scenes depicted are so spectacular it is not easy to comprehend the accompanying terror but de Quincey admitted an irrational fear of all things Oriental for they hinted of unspeakable barbarity.

Most of his bad dreams contained moral and spiritual terrors, presumably as would befit a philosopher, but these exotic fantasies were remarkable for their monstrous livestock—ugly birds, snakes, and crocodiles—the last filling him with abject horror:

> I was buried a thousand years, in stone coffins, with mummies and sphinxes in narrow chambers at the heart of eternal pyramids. I was kissed with cancerous kisses by crocodiles, and laid, confounded with all unutterably slimy things, amongst the reeds and nilotic mud.

Some nightmares contained enormous stretches of water that haunted him until he feared some dropsical condition of the brain was trying to make itself objective. Much more likely, these dreams were trying to compensate for the severe effects that opium had in drying up all the body's secretions.

Nor were his nightmares silent; some contained solemn anthems and, buried beneath seas of guilt, de Quincey was forced to listen to their sonorous strains. Then came all those he loved to bid him everlasting farewells: 'And I awoke in struggles, and cried aloud "I will sleep no more!"'

At last, aware that opium would destroy him if he did not break the habit, de Quincey determined to make the effort to free himself for the sake of those he loved. Like Coleridge, his intake was eventually reduced to a level where he could live and work more or less satisfactorily, although not painlessly or easily. Even then, his dreams did not return to perfect calm. 'The dread swell and agitation of the storm have not wholly subsided, the legions that encamped in them are drawing off, but not all departed ...'

I wish we could dismiss the drug-induced nightmare along with the other ills of the past. Unfortunately that is not possible. Opium is neither readily available nor attractive to most Westerners but this century's chronic use of barbiturates, hypnotics, and the major and minor tranquillizers can similarly charm nightmares into existence. Used in large amounts and over any length of time such substances can cause bad dreams, although the nasties of the species manifest after the drug is withdrawn.

How paradoxical that the same pills people take to help regulate their sleep do produce profoundly disturbed sleep patterns; a large percentage of those complaining of insomnia are, in fact, suffering from the habitual use of sleeping pills. The trouble with most of these pills is that they do work—magically—at first. Once you are accustomed to the dose it has to be increased if the old charm is to be recaptured. Thus a tolerance is established and it forms as vicious a circle of torture as anything attributed to the nightmare demons of old. If you are a regular user of sleeping pills you might be surprised to learn that your sleep is not particularly restful or normal. Tests on barbiturate addicts reveal many awakenings throughout the night, with little REM sleep, and with the descent into Stages 3 and 4 being either repressed or diminished. When medication is discontinued the REM sleep rebounds as if the mechanism were trying to make up for lost opportunity. So the person who stops the pills not only encounters a problem in falling asleep, but when this eventually happens it is highly disturbed and usually punctuated with visits from the nightmare making full use of increased REM sessions. Understandably, the sufferer decides that insomnia is still the problem and returns to sleeping pills.

We have to face a somewhat self-evident fact that most of those taking barbiturates and tranquillizers over any extended period must have some psychological disorder which is likely to erupt in nightmare given encouragement. The medicines only alleviate the symptoms, the root cause requires recognition before it can be treated. Many of those suffering from anxiety, depression, and insomnia have the additional burden of dreading sleep lest it contain the nightmare. Studies suggest that such patients are often more consciously worried about death and dying, which colours their darkest dreams, and have probably been exposed to the death of a close friend or relative far earlier or more often than those who *seem* to have few brushes with the fiend.

I must emphasize the word '*seem*'. Some of us are apparently better at repressing the frightening contents of our dreams. That does not mean we do not have nightmares; we just cannot usually recall them. Anxiety-prone individuals who find this unconscious repression technique difficult, *seem* to suffer more nightmares than most simply because they cannot avoid remembering them.

Treating someone for drug dependence insomnia entails a gradual withdrawal from the medication, or its replacement with a tranquillizer or non-barbiturate hypnotic which, however, does not eradicate the psychological reliance problem. It is extremely hazardous to attempt either total withdrawal, or even a substantial cut in dosage, where a subject is accustomed to taking a lot of sleeping medicine for, as well as highly unpleasant physical symptoms, this may well produce hallucinations, severe nightmares, and sometimes convulsions. It is always sensible to consult a doctor before contemplating any tailing-off of medicine regularly used.

Yet the most careful reduction can still lead to nightmares and it is often difficult to treat people who believe that any lessening of their medication will leave them sleepless. Nor do they really accept that stopping the pills will help. If you are someone caught in this snare let me assure you that the sleep experts promise that once complete withdrawal has been effected not only will you experience improved sleep, you will also feel much better than you have done for ages.

However, unless the individual's way of life, surroundings, and ability to cope with situations are improved once the system is emptied of the drug, he or she is likely to feel the need to return to the old poison. After all, the basic problems have not been eliminated. It is especially hard to withdraw the middle-aged woman successfully from these drugs since her real troubles are probably not being examined either by herself or those meant to be helping her. For her, the sleeping pills are a way of sweeping everything under the carpet—until the house decays.

Another hazard for those dependent upon sleeping pills is that sometimes they drink alcohol to encourage sleep, just as alcoholics frequently resort to the random use of sleeping pills. Alcohol, hypnotics, and tranquillizers share certain physical effects. Heavy drinkers develop tolerance for these pills and need more than a normal dose to get them to sleep. However much tolerance is developed, the fatal dose for pills and alcohol does not vary. Of course the other danger is that excessive alcohol, just like barbiturates, breeds the ideal climate for the nightmare.

The use of alcohol, particularly as a regular nightcap, decreases REM sleep, and really heavy indulgers may well suffer nightmares and disturbed rest under the drug's influence. It has been pointed out that nightmares are not only associated with this phase; those that occur during NREM (particularly Stages 3 and 4) do not have vivid hallucinatory contents but are profoundly disturbing for their almost unidentifiable horror, which is less easy to cope with, and similar to the *pavor nocturnis* (night terrors) experienced by very young children.

People who get their drug from the liquor store rather than on prescription usually have some psychological burden which they are trying to stifle. Unfortunately the alcohol may unleash the problem in sleep, escorted by the nightmare. One girl, heading for a total breakdown, was hitting the spirit bottles very heavily to try to obtain some relief from memories and difficulties that seemed insurmountable. Her waking life was purgatory. From her viewpoint there was a barrier between herself and the rest of the world: nobody seemed able to help, understand, or care. The surfeit of alcohol which would drug her into sleep turned the nights into another kind of torment: one particular nightmare image kept recurring—a sinister figure of a monk in a cowled habit, with spikes where his face should have been.

At least this story has a happy ending. A suicide attempt led to psychiatric treatment which, in turn, initiated a new hopeful life style, less necessity to drink, and the routing of the monk without a face.

But it is during the period when those suffering from acute alcoholism are being 'dried out' that the nightmare really manifests with a vengeance. Here the REM rebound may account for one hundred per cent of total sleep at the first sleep stage! *Delirium tremens* appears to be the continuation of the nightmare into the wake-up state: in other words, the backlash of REM is so tremendous it can intrude in the conscious psyche in the form of hallucinations.

Dreaming has been dubbed the prototype of hallucination and perhaps it is as near as many of us ever get to that experience. Of course some drug experimenters go out of their way to achieve hallucinations but they are hoping for some ecstatically mind-blowing revelation from hallucinogenic substances. The effect of LSD in sleep increases the REM phases slightly and diminishes the intervals between but there is no sign that it induces nightmares. Nor can an acid trip be compared with a bad dream. However, the 'bummer' or real 'freak-out' may contain some or all of the negative elements we have encountered in our pursuit of the nightmare.

Like the nightmare's victim, the acid user may be overwhelmed with confusion, terror, and a sense of persecution when encountering the weird and powerful expressions emanating from his or her own mind. Deeply repressed memories surface to prove unbearable. Time may seem stretched to infinity: recall how de Quincey felt during his worst dreams. Imagine horror and shame without any apparent end. Utter depression, the annihilating awareness that everything is without meaning, and even the certainty of the self's imminent death are characteristics of the nightmare as well as the 'bum' acid trip.

At its very worst, a 'freak-out' involves complete loss of emotional control where the victim feels so under attack that he or she must try to escape by whatever means, or destroy whomever seems to be the threat. Only rarely do people resort to self-destruction or murder on acid; and the same applies to nightmares. However, it can and does happen and obviously makes the headlines. An American teenage girl, Jo Ann Kiger, who was a habitual sleepwalker and nightmare sufferer, dreamed that burglars were in the home. She seized two revolvers, fired ten times, killed her father and six-year-old brother, and wounded her mother. Her offence was not regarded as a criminal problem but a medical one for she had murdered in her sleep . . .

Whether or not we like it, this is a drug-using society; we have to learn how best to live with substances that can help, but whose uncontrolled application results in further complications. Although the medical profession is researching and developing new treatments with fewer dependency side-effects, there are always going to be those who abuse whatever substance they get their hands on—just as there are always going to be nightmares.

Before you swallow your next pill, or fix your next drink, consider. Do you really need it? Remember, enslavement to any psychoactive substance may mean accepting the nightmare as your master. That is the cruellest of bondage.

# Escape

> Let him that thinketh he standeth take heed lest he fall. There hath no temptation taken you but such as is common to man: but God is faithful, who will not suffer you to be tempted above that ye are able; but will with the temptation also make a way to escape, that ye may be able to bear it.
>
> II CORINTHIANS X : 12

Widely divergent societies and centuries may have ascribed a host of differing causes and shapes to the nightmare but all have sought one thing from their magic, religion, and medicine: a mightier force to do battle with the fiend, either entirely to prevent its manifestation or to rescue the victim during an attack. It says something for the nightmare's grim potency that we are still as disturbed by it as were our more impressionable forebears —and just as anxious to find some definitive escape route.

We may not be able to argue or bludgeon the fiend out of existence but we do not have to court its presence. So if you believe that some of your bad dreams are the product of physical causes already cited, avoid sleeping on your back . . . or indulging in protein-rich banquets late into the night . . . or getting irrevocably hooked on some psychoactive substance which plays havoc with your sleep pattern. Despite these subterfuges you may still be forced to bear the stifling shapeless company of the incubus in your NREM sleep or be chased from the quiet haven of rest by the hot and bloody dramas of the REM nightmare. Therefore we must look for some positive banishing method.

Perhaps you favour the idea of natural cures, in which case you can always try those prescribed to our ancestors: Macedonian parsley, wild carrot, the black seeds of the male peony, or that magical herb, *ephialton*. Other physical discouragements include: bleeding your ankles, shaving your head, or making little cuts in your throat. Though I daresay your nearest and dearest would find it hard to believe that you are only trying to combat nightmares when you go to bed totally bald, or scratched and bandaged!

The Azande people use body medicines to counteract the witches who bring the nightmare. Everybody has their own preferred version and a father will apply his to a child soon after birth. Another Azande ruse is to place a spear across the threshold so that the witch's soul will be injured as it tries to enter the house, which means that whoever is doing the bewitching will be made ill. Sharp, pointed objects—whatever Freud had to say about their phallic symbolism in dreams—are quite popular in folk customs to block an invasion by evil spirits. Many Brazilians keep a 'Sword of St Anthony' plant beside the front door against such an eventuality.

Another Azande nightmare remedy—blowing whistles to scare away the witches—somewhat resembles a therapy practised at a Chicago Research Centre where Dr Rosalind Cartwright, a psychologist, treats female nightmare sufferers by encouraging them to understand that, whatever the logical psychological reasons behind their worst dreams, they are still only dreams, and she teaches them to give the nightmare a happy, positive finale.

The subject goes to sleep in a special cubicle with a microwave switch in her right hand, which she must press the minute the nightmare arrives. When the buzzer sounds Dr Cartwright waits for the dreamer to wake up and then, before the details are forgotten, records the nightmare's plot.

You must have noticed from your own experience how the nightmare's action always stops short at the most fateful moment, as you sink beneath the waves, or fall from that sky-scraper, or that monstrous attacker grabs you. You wake abruptly ... terrified ... but relieved to be in one piece and out of danger. The fear remains unresolved because it is never faced. You do not know what happens next in your dream. Quite likely you do not want to because you can only envisage the worst: suffering and annihilation.

However, with Dr Cartwright's method the patient is helped towards inventing a successful culmination to the dream: you swim safely to the shore . . . you float effortlessly onto a deliciously soft feather bed . . . you turn round and slay that monster. So the next time the subject signals her bad dream has just arrived on the scene there is an answering bleep from the psychologist's buzzer to remind her to carry on dreaming but to move on to that planned ending. The nightmare is chased away to become an ordinary pleasant dream and the dreamer is made to understand that even in sleep she can control her fantasies. Once the technique is mastered in a clinical setting it can be practised in the individual's bedroom. Although microwave buzzers and research centres sound a long way from the Azande witch whistles the intention behind them is much the same.

Most mythologies have their own god and goddess to be invoked against the nightmare. In Teutonic folklore, Odin—doubtless because he was considered the horse god supreme—was reputed to possess the magic formula for warding off the fiend that so often rode horses or adopted equine form to indulge in its nastier habits.

If you tend to be suspicious you might regard Odin as a possible case of 'poacher turned game-keeper': because he was responsible for procuring the nightmare he had the knowledge to send it packing! As leader of the Wild Hunt—a company of riding souls—Odin was originally considered a bringer-of-death-by-night. The Hunt also pursued an animal or a lady who, according to certain traditions, could transform herself into a horse—perhaps the Teutonic *mara*. This somehow suggests that the roles of hunter and hunted were interchangeable—which is scant consolation to ancient or modern victims.

The horse god cults that have left traces in the shape of horses cut into hillsides have their beginnings in the worship of Odin and we might speculate whether or not dreamers in those distant times sometimes looked towards the great white horse etched into the green turf as a possible protection against the nightmare. The Anglo-Saxons particularly revered Odin so it is not surprising that he is the 'man of power' mentioned in this fourteenth-century English North Country 'Charm against the Night Mare':

> *Tha mon o' micht, he rade o' nicht*
> *Wi' neider swerd ne ferd ne licht.*
> *He socht tha Mare, he fond tha Mare,*
> *He bond tha Mare wi' her ain hare,*
> *Ond gared her swar by midder-nicht*
> *She wolde nae mair rid o' nicht*
> *Whar aince he rade, thot mon o' nicht.*

If you do not relish invoking a pagan deity to defend you against the fiend, Odin's powers under Christianity were transferred to St Swithold:

> *Swithold footed thrice the wold.*
> *He met the Night-Mare and her nine-fold,*
> *Bid her alight and her troth plight,*
> *And aroynt thee, witch, aroynt thee!*

To the modern mind all these charms and herbs may seem only fit for the superstitious or primitive who see dreams as particularly significant but it is from a so-called primitive tribe that we can actually acquire one of the most effective techniques for teaching ourselves—and more importantly, our children—how to cope with the nightmare as well as how to value the dream.

The Senoi people of Malaysia have astonished researchers by their non-violent, co-operative life-style. They are a tolerant and creative people with flexible attitudes towards marriage and sexuality, and are singularly free of neuroses and anxiety and *nightmares*. It must be gratifying for psychoanalysts to find a group that has so clearly benefited from learning to understand, control, and use their dreams.

From the earliest age Senoi children learn how important is the dream to the individual, the family, and the community. Like all other youngsters they are not immune from nightmare attacks but they are luckier than most since it is inherent in their culture for the adults to educate the young in skills which eliminate the bad dream and transform it into something positive and rewarding. By the time a Senoi reaches adolescence the nightmare is entirely vanquished and it is seen as a sign of maturity when a person can exercise complete control over dream characters and situations.

For the Senoi a dream's frightening contents point to aggressive factors within the self, which must prove destructive to the personality as well as other people if allowed to flourish. Like those who favour Gestalt methods of therapy these people regard aspects in the dream as parts of the self requiring integration.

Being taught to shape the dream by those in authority has a profound effect on the personality, for the child is learning to modify its behaviour during dreams; this is gradually carried over into waking life, helping it towards adulthood and the ability to co-exist with others. When you can confront the dangers in your worst dreams it is much easier to deal with those arising in daily life and you are then more likely to be a self-aware and self-reliant individual.

If you think shaping a dream to a given authority's direction is an exaggerated description of some hit-and-miss custom, let me assure you it is not. Those being treated according to the various psychoanalytical schools tend to dream in Freudian, Jungian, Adlerian, or other symbols. It is not merely interpretation that conditions the dream but the particular therapy influencing the unconscious to spell out its messages in corresponding terms. In fact, with patience, concentration, and above all willingness, you can learn to dream about the subjects you prefer—others have.

The most important lesson the Senoi child receives—which we can try to learn too—is not to run away from the danger in the nightmare, whether it is a monster, a fierce animal, a bad person, or some amorphous threat. Only when the terror is confronted can it be conquered. While the dreamer keeps on fleeing the nightmare will reappear to grow fat, complacent and faithful. So the child is instructed that when this bad dream next manifests it must stand and fight back, summoning other dream images to its aid. All those who refuse help should be viewed as enemies, as are all those the dreamer fears.

The child is told to fight the attacker to the death if needs be—this releases the positive force from that part of the psyche which initiated the hostile image. The destroyed enemy will become a helpful ally. We have already met the Gestaltists' 'topdog' and 'underdog' analogy: where the attacker is 'underdog' it usually ceases to be dangerous the moment it is confronted for it only wants the acceptance that the 'topdog' is denying it; however, where the aggressor is 'topdog' it is a much more implacable foe, and will do battle to the last, but has to be defeated for the sake of the self's development.

A child learns that even if it is killed in its dream the attacker will be rendered harmless (rather like an insect that dies after losing its sting) and the dreamer must at once be reborn but in an improved form, so profiting from the nightmare.

Nowadays therapists working with children who suffer recurring nightmares employ techniques rather similar to the Senoi. A youngster will be urged to turn round and tell its nightmare horrors to go away and stay away! The child finds this novel approach appealing and quickly absorbs it for now the individual is master in his or her own dream. It works too, which is a clear example of an accepted authority restructuring a dream scenario.

Remember Max in *Where the Wild Things Are*? His story is of a 'successful' nightmare. The antics so disapproved of by mother were projected on to a band of fierce wild beasts but Max's dream allowed *him* to dominate and punish them, that is, to gain control over his own 'untamed' impulses rather than be their victim.

It has been proved that where any child is told merely to ignore its bad dreams these will take far longer to vanish than those whose nightmares are dealt with promptly. If the fear is an objective one, say of water or machinery, it is particularly beneficial for a child—or better still a group of children—to be taken to visit the source of terror so that it may be understood and examined. Gradually familiarity breeds not contempt but reassurance that there is nothing to fear, nothing the individual cannot cope with.

The Senoi child also learns to advance its dream to an enjoyable and successful conclusion. All the activities within dreams must be completed. So those horrible falling nightmares become incredible flying adventures where not only is the experience delicious and to be encouraged but the dreamer visits marvellous new places to be described afterwards in waking life.

For the Senoi there are no shameful, incestuous, or tabooed images in dreams and consequently none of those distressing nightmares whose libidinous contents the individual dreads to recall, let alone relate to another person. Love dreams are reckoned so delightful that you cannot have enough of them and the Senoi children are taught that pleasurable sexual intercourse, and erotic play, occurring in their dreams should culminate in orgasm.

Perhaps the most endearing facet of the Senoi lesson in ousting the nightmare is that the dreamer has to force its subjugated one-time oppressor into giving it a present, preferably without striking any bargain. The gift can be a beautiful image, a poem, a song, a tale, a new design, the practical solution to some problem, or a useful new idea. Whatever it is this token must have recognizable value in the waking context so that other people can esteem its worth. Westerners who have experimented with Senoi dream tactics have been delighted by some really worthwhile results, including the banishment of their nightmares and the receipt of dream presents.

If you want to try to control your dreams and eradicate the bad ones, by Senoi means or any other, you must first do what all dream therapists recommend: keep a note book or cassette player at your bedside. Once you begin noting down both the pleasant and uncomfortable dreams you will be surprised at how little a chore it is, and may even find yourself waking in the night at the end of a REM phase just to record the last vivid drama, and then go straight off to sleep without any ensuing discomfort or fatigue. Those who insist they never recall dreams will be amazed to discover that they can when they decide to commit them to paper.

Mastering the images will not happen overnight—only by trial and error—but if you think examining your dreams in broad daylight can help, why not try it? As to interpretation, choose whatever system seems appropriate. This may alter with circumstances. It is more important that the school of thought answers your current needs rather than remains grimly faithful-until-death to one when it is no longer appropriate.

Remember, the dream is a piece of you—composed of your hopes, fears, problems, and memories which, in turn, reflect all those ever known to human beings; if you want to understand yourself why let certain aspects lurk in the shadows of your mind to make you needlessly miserable?

A word of caution to anyone who has bad recurrent nightmares that cast a very negative shadow over your whole life: seek professional advice rather than suffer in silence. Do not allow yourself to remain the fiend's plaything.

You may, of course, turn away from all this with a shrug and say: 'Why the fuss? . . . everyone has nightmares at some time . . . most grow out of them . . . it's part of the human condition . . . and, anyway, the nightmare can't really damage you, or anyone else . . .' As a generalization these remarks are true; but when they are not the harm done to the individual may be inestimable. We have already seen how adults can be psychologically scarred as a result of the mishandling of their bad dreams in childhood. There are even more extreme examples where the nightmare takes over and kills the dreamer or someone else.

No doubt you accept that people do walk and talk in their sleep. Sometimes somnambulism in conjunction with a dream's contents leads to death. The enthusiastic twelve-year-old swimmer who 'dived' sixty feet out of a window to die in a London street was fast asleep at the time. In spring 1978 Lynda Hughes was exonerated at Preston Crown Court of trying to kill her husband. In her sleep she had stabbed him fifteen times with a potato knife. Also while asleep Francis Stockwell, a quiet Englishman, murdered and dismembered his wife. On waking he was so shattered by his actions he had to be committed to a mental hospital. There is the macabre case of the famous French detective Robert Ledru who found his own footprints on a beach at Le Havre where the victim had been shot. Ledru was the murderer. Some individuals, so traumatized by war experiences which recur in nightmare form, may try to kill those they love, believing themselves to be under attack by the old enemy . . .

These cases, like those of ostensible precognition, are rare but that does not mean we can ignore that sometimes the nightmare is capable of taking complete control of its victim. Nobody has yet found a cure for people who in sleep act out the impulses of their worst dreams. The only practical precaution for those who share their lives is to ensure that the sleepwalker can neither harm him or herself, nor anyone else, and that the causes behind recurring nightmares are resolved as soon as practicable.

Although we have examined ways of eliminating our worst dreams, and there are those lucky few who claim never to suffer any, it looks highly unlikely the nightmare will ever be wholly banished from the continent of sleep. Its roots are too deep within the human psyche together with our highest and basest impulses.

Perhaps this product of mind and physiology is a residual alarm system. Certainly it is often our first instructor in terror.

If there is no escape let us turn its unsolicited visit into a postive experience. By learning to understand the reasons behind our nightmare we may gradually outwit it for we can begin to expel much suppressed fear and anxiety from our waking existence that erupt in unlovely images during that nightly journey into sleep.

# Acknowledgements

May I say thank you for the enthusiastic help I received in researching material for the chapter entitled 'The Dark Prophet' to the College of Psychic Studies, and the Society of Psychical Research, who were kind enough to allow me to quote from copies of the Society's *Proceedings* and *Journal*, details of which are given in the bibliography. It makes the author's task a pleasant one when she is shown such interest by specialist libraries.

# Bibliography

Aaronson, B.S. and Osmond, H. *Psychedelics* (1971)
Arnold Foster, M. *Studies in Dreams* (1921)
Besterman, A. *On Dreams* (1935)
Bigland, E. *Mary Shelley* (1959)
Blum, H. and E. *The Dangerous Hour* (1970)
Bonaparte, M. *Life and Works of Edgar Allan Poe* (1949)
Boss, M. *Analysis of Dreams* (1957)
Brasch, R. *How Did it Begin?* (1965)
Breger, L. *Effect of Stress in Dreams* (1971)
Castaneda, C. *The Teachings of Don Juan: Yaqui Way of Knowledge* (1971), *A Separate Reality: Further Conversations with Don Juan* (1971), *Journey to Ixtlan: Lessons of Don Juan* (1973)
Coxhead, D. and Hiller, S. *Dreams: Visions of the Night* (1976)
Crooke, W. *Popular Religion and Folklore of North India* (1894)
Davies, T.W. *Magic, Divination and Demonology among Hebrews and Their Neighbours* (1898)
De Becker, R. *The Understanding of Dreams: the Machinations of the Night* (1968)
Dement, W. *Some Must Watch While Some Must Sleep* (1974)
De Quincey, T. *Confessions of An English Opium-Eater* (1822)
Devereux, G. *Dreams in Greek Tragedy: An Ethno-analytical Study* (1976)
Diamond, E. *The Science of Dreams* (1962)
Dunlap, J. *Exploring Inner Space* (1961)
Dunne J. W. *An Experiment with Time* (1927)
Ebon, M. *Prophesy in Our Time* (1968)
Eliade, M. *Myths, Dreams and Mysteries* (1960)
Ellis, H. *The World of Dreams* (1911)
Elwin, H. V. *Religion of an Indian Tribe* (1955)
Evans, J. I. *Your Sleeping Life* (1970)
Evans Pritchard, E. E. *Witchcraft and Magic among the Azande* (1937)
Faraday, A. *The Dream Game* (1975)
Freud, S. *The Interpretation of Dreams* (1955)

## BIBLIOGRAPHY

Garfield, P. *Creative Dreaming* (1976)
Grant, A. H. *Literature and Curiosities of Dreams* (1865)
Grant, K. *Cults of the Shadow* (1975)
Graves, R. *Greek Myths* (1955), *The White Goddess* (1961)
Gurney, Myers, and Podmore *Phantasm of the Living* (1886)
Harms, E. *Problems of Sleep and Dream in Children* (1964)
Hartmann, E. *Biology of Dreaming* (1967), *Functions of Sleep* (1973)
Hill, B. *Such Stuff as Dreams* (1967)
Jahoda, G. *The Psychology of Superstition* (1956)
James, H. *Autobiography* (1956)
Jastrow, J. *Fact and Fable in Psychology* (1901)
Jones, E. *On the Nightmare* (1931)
Jones, R. M. *The New Psychology of Dreaming* (1970)
Jung, C. G. *Modern Man in Search of a Soul* (1933), *Integration of the Personality* (1948), *Two Essays on Analytical Psychology* (1953), *Memories, Dreams, Reflections* (1963)
Kaplan, J. *Mister Clemens and Mark Twain* (1967)
Kerouac, J. *Book of Dreams* (1961)
Kleitman, N. *Sleep and Wakefulness* (1963)
Lamb, C. *Essays of Elia* (1823)
Laughlin, R. M. *Of Wonders Wild and New* (1976)
Lefebure, M. *Samuel Taylor Coleridge: A Bondage of Opium* (1974)
L'Estrange Ewan, C. L. *Witchcraft and Demonianism* (1970)
Lincoln, J. S. *The Dream in Primitive Cultures* (1935)
Lowes, J. L. *The Road to Xanadu: A Study in the Ways of the Imagination* (1927)
Luce, G. and Segal, J. *Sleep* (1967), *Insomnia* (1969)
Mack, J. E. *Nightmares and Human Conflict* (1970)
Mackay, C. *Extraordinary Popular Delusions and the Madness of Crowds* (1956)
Mackenzie, A. *Frontiers of the Unknown* (1968), *Riddle of the Future* (1974)
Mackenzie, N. I. *Dreams and Dreaming* (1965)
Malcolm, N. A. *Dreaming* (1955)
Maple, E. *Superstitions and the Superstitious* (1971)
Masters, R. and Houston, J. *The Varieties of Psychedelic Experience* (1967)
Megroz, R. L. *The Dream World* (1939)
Michaux, H. *The Effect of Drugs* (1974)
Noone, R. *In Search of the Dream People* (1972)
Oswald, I. *Sleep* (1966)
Parrinder, G. *Witchcraft: European and African* (1962)

Petre-Quadens, O. and Schlag, J. O. *Basic Sleep Mechanics* (1974)
Potter, S. (ed) *Samuel Taylor Coleridge: Selected Poetry, Prose, Letters* (1971)
Powell, N. *Fuseli's 'The Nightmare'* (1973)
Priestley, J. B. *Man and Time* (1966), *Over the Long High Wall: Some Reflections and Speculations on Life, Death and Time* (1972)
Ratcliff, A. J. J. *A History of Dreams* (1923)
Rivers, W. *Conflict and Dream* (1923)
Robbins, R. *The Encyclopedia of Witchcraft and Demonology* (1959)
Saggs, H. W. F. *The Greatness that was Babylon* (1962)
Sendak, M. *Where the Wild Things Are* (1963)
Shulman, S. *Dreams* (1970), *A Guide to Drugs. Use, Abuse and Effects* (1974)
Spearing, A. C. *Mediaeval Dream-Poetry* (1976)
Stekel, W. *The Interpretation of Dreams* (1943)
Stevens, W. O. *Mystery of Dreams* (1950)
Stevenson, R. L. *Across the Plains* (1892)
Stoehr, T. *Dickens: the Dreamer's Stance* (1966)
Symonds, J. A. *Sleep and Dreams* (1875)
Tart, C. T. (ed) *Altered States of Consciousness* (1969)
Tylor, E. B. *Researches into the Early History of Mankind and the Development of Civilization* (1964)
Ullman, M. and Krippner, S. with Vaughan, A. *Dream Telepathy* (1973)
Vallentin, A. *This I Saw: the Life and Times of Goya* (1951)
Vaughan, A. *Patterns of Prophecy* (1974)
Wasiolek, E. *The Notebooks for 'Crime and Punishment'* (1967)
Weidhorn, M. *Dreams in 17th Century English Literature* (1970)
Weinstein, E. A. *Cultural Aspects of Delusions* (1962)
Williams, R. L. and Karracan, I. *Pharmacology of Sleep* (1976)
Wilson, C. *The Occult* (1971)
Zimmels, H. J. *Magicians, Theologians and Doctors* (1952)

*Periodicals, Pamphlets, and Newspapers*

*International Journal of Parapsychology* (R. K. Greenbank; 1960)
*Journal of the Society for Psychical Research 15* (1912), *43* (1965), *44* (1967)
*Proceedings of an International Conference*—a Century of Psychical Research held in St Paul de Vence (1970)
*Proceedings of the Society for Physical Research 26* (1912–13)
*The Daily Mail* (12.4.78)
*The Sunday Times* (7.5.78)

# Index

Aberfan disaster, 180-2
*Across the Plains*, 75, 76, 111, 112
Africa, 31, 41, 50, 53, 144, 145
African bushman, 40
alcohol, 14, 21, 201, 202
'alp', 38
'Ancient Mariner', 117, 118
animal-headed humans, 36, 37, 53
anti-biotics, 190
anxiety dreams, 28, 80, 86, 96, 98, 102, 106, 109, 200
apnoea, 21
apocalyptic nightmare, 65, 66
Apollo, 39
Aquinas, T., 47, 50
archetypes, 75, 105, 106, 147, 168
Aristotle, 82, 83
art: Chinese, 37; pre-historic, 37, 42
Artemidorus of Daldus, 143-7
Aserinsky, E., 18
assassination nightmares, 168-71
Assyria, 144
Assyrian clay tablets, 10
Aubrey, J., 136
Australian aborigines, 41
Azande remedies, 206, 207
Aztecs, 183

Babylon, 47, 144
Babylonian banishing ritual, 13, 39; clay tablets, 10
barbiturates, 21, 199, 200
Barker, Dr, 180-2
belladonna, 191
Bessant, M., 168
Bible, 47, 205
black magic, 54
blood, 60, 63, 64
Bond, Dr J., 83, 84, 98
British Premonitions Bureau, 182
Brognolus, C., 46
Brontë, E., 137, 138
burglars, 29, 78
Burke and Hare, 73
Burton, R., 83
Byron, Lord, 124, 153

Cabbalistic teaching, 47
Calpurnia, 170, 171
cannibalism, 63, 64
Cartright, Dr R., 206, 207
cauchemar, 12
Caxton's Chronicle, 31
Cayce, E., 183
Central Premonitions Registry, 182
Chatterton, T., 136
children's nightmares, 24, 28, 29, 50, 53, 73-80, 86, 105-11, 141, 142, 181, 208-11
Christianity, 31, 42-7, 49, 50
Cicero, 58, 164, 168, 170
Circadian rhythm, 24
circumcision, 26
*Civilization in Transition*, 101
Clive of India, 193
Coleridge, S. T., 40, 55, 106, 116-19
combat nightmares, 108, 112, 113
conflict as cause of nightmare, 13, 84, 85, 104, 109, 132, 143, 148
Cortes, H., 183
*Crime and Punishment*, 134, 135

Darwin, E., 127, 128
death in nightmares, 33, 35, 56, 59-61, 64, 68, 78, 79, 159, 161-3, 165, 168, 174-80, 183, 210
Defoe, D., 135
*déjà vu*, 167
deliriants, 191
*delirium tremens*, 202
Dement, W., 18
demon, 11, 23, 38, 44, 46, 47, 82
demon lover, 41, 42, 50
de Quincey, T., 188, 192, 194, 196-9, 202
Dostoevsky, F., 85, 134, 135, 138
Drayton, M., 135, 136
dream books, 10, 92, 144, 145
dreams, 36, 86, 88-94, 101-7
  amplification in, 103
  condensation in, 94, 112
  displacement in, 94
  as 'guardians of sleep', 9, 86, 92

221

# INDEX

of newborn babies, 24, 25
predictive, 104, 164, 165
symbolization in, 90, 95, 102, 105, 112, 144, 145
as wish-fulfilment, 86, 92, 100, 103
drugs, effect on nightmare, 188-204
Dunne, J. W., 178, 179

EEG, 18, 19
Egypt, 47, 78, 144
Eliot, T. S., 82
embarrassment in nightmare, 72
EMG, 18
EOG, 18
Ephialtes, 38, 39, 92

Fairley, P., 180, 182
fairy tales, 11, 99, 105, 106
fatal woman, 48
'Fiddler on the Roof', 138
flying ointment, 191
Freud, S., 86-98, 100-3, 129, 144, 147, 148, 151, 154, 156, 160, 162, 173, 206; on nightmares, 96-8
Fuseli, H., 125-30, 189

Galen, 13
Gervais of Tilbury, 48
Gestalt therapy, 147, 150, 161, 209
ghost, 36, 37, 59, 75, 78, 111, 143, 144
goblin, 12, 75
Godwin, M., 124, 125
Godwin, W., 125
Goya, F., 130-2
graveyard, 64, 65
Greece, 38
Greek remedy against nightmare, 39
guilt, 12, 99, 104, 194, 199

Haggard, H. R., 174
hallucination, 20, 21, 24, 28, 97, 200, 202, 203
hell, 66
henbane, 191
Hera, 47
Heracles, 39
herbal remedies, 206
heroin, 191
Hippocrates, 13
Hobbes, T., 44, 49, 83
Homer, 167
horse god cults, 207, 209
Hughes, Mrs L., 212
hypersomnia, 21
hypnotics, 190, 199, 200, 201

Icelandic tradition, 12
incestuous desires, 99
incubation, 16

incubus, 12, 29, 38, 40-2, 44-7, 98, 99, 143
India, 40, 41
indigestion, 13, 23, 118, 119
*Interpretation of Dreams*, 89
Ireland, 16

James, H., 123
James, M. R., 136, 137
Jews, Jewish customs, 32, 47, 49
Johnson, Dr S., 127
Jones, E., 98, 99, 100, 129
Jones, E. M., 181
*Journal of SPR*, 180, 181, 184
Jung, C. G., 75, 100-7, 129, 130, 144, 149, 150, 156, 185; on nightmares, 105-7
Juno Lacinia, 58
Jupiter, 58

Kennedy, R., 169
Kerouac, J., 132
Kiger, J. A., 203
Kleitman, N., 18
Koin, 41
Krippner, Dr S., 168, 169
*Kubla Khan*, 195, 196

Lamb, C., 75, 77
Lambert, G. W., 184
Lamia, 47, 48
Lanyi, Bishop, 170
La Plata, 179
laudanum, 192
Lawrence, D. H., 14
*Lear, King*, 40
Ledru, R., 213
Le Fanu, S., 137
Lefebure, M., 195, 196
Lilith, Lilitu, 47
Lincoln, A., 171
LSD, 14, 203

*Macbeth*, 15, 132, 133
Macnish, R., 74
Maimonides Dream Laboratory, 168, 169
Mara, 12, 40, 99, 207
Mare, 12, 32, 98
mare, 12, 98
Marten, M., 171, 172
masturbation, 12
Maury, A., 23
*Memories, Dreams, Reflections*, 105
menstrual cycle, 26, 85
Mesopotamia, 47
Mexico, 35, 53, 183
misogny, 49
Monoamine oxidase inhibitors, 21

# INDEX

monsters, 11, 35, 44, 58, 99, 107, 108, 110, 141, 143
Montezuma, 183
murder, 60, 61, 62, 73, 79, 132, 203, 213
mythology, 105, 106, 153, 207
  Greek, 38-40, 47, 48
  Nordic, 40
  Teutonic, 12, 38, 207

Napoleon, 61
narcolepsy, 21, 22, 29
nightmare of:
  Algerian clerk, 32
  Archer, W., 72
  author, 71, 151, 152
  Axford, H., 73
  Beddoes, T. L., 64
  Benson, E. White, 72
  blind and deaf, 81
  Bunyan, J., 79, 80
  Caligula, 57, 58
  Carlyle, T., 68, 69
  Clare, J., 71
  Dee, Dr J., 65
  de la Mare, W., 60, 61
  Dougal, H., 73
  Eddy, M. Baker, 63
  Flaubert, G., 63, 64
  Godwin, M., 124
  Hannibal, 58
  Hardy, T., 154
  Haynes, E. S. P., 56
  Hebbel, F., 65
  Heine, H., 71, 72
  Hitler, A., 67
  Hood, T., 72
  Ibsen, H., 65, 66
  Jerome K. Jerome, 55, 56
  Jung, C. G., 105
  Keller, H., 81
  Kilvert, F., 62, 63
  Lamb, C., 73-5
  Lodge, O., 160
  Lucian, 80
  Macaulay, T. B., 72
  Marten, Mrs, 171, 172
  Middleton, J. C., 167
  Nero, 57
  Patmore, C., 59, 60
  Pepys, S., 60
  Richard III, 67, 68
  Rossetti, C., 64
  Ruskin, J., 59
  St Anthony of Egypt, 45
  St Hilary, 45
  St Hippolytus, 45
  St Margaret of Cortona, 45
  Shaw, G. B., 159

Shelley, P. B., 152, 153
Siddons, S., 155
Sister Marie-du-St-Sacrament, 46
Southey, R., 61, 79
Stevenson, R. L., 75, 76, 111, 112
Swedenborg, E., 66
Symonds, J. A., 78, 79
Walpole, H., 68
*On the Nightmare*, 98
*The Nightmare*, 125-30, 189
North Borneo, 40
NREM, 18-20, 22, 24, 25, 27, 28,, 168, 202, 205

Octavian, 164
Odin, 207, 208
ogre, 40, 107, 108, 143
*Oneirocritica*, 143-7
opium, 191-9

Palmer, Miss, 79
Paracelsus, 46, 85
paralysis, 19, 29
*pavor nocturnus* (night terror), 28, 53, 97, 202
penicillin, 190
Pepys' diary, 60, 72
*Pilgrim's Progress*, 79
Plato, 13
Plutarch, 170
Poe, E. A., 123
pregnancy, 26
pre-menstrual tension, 26
Prierias, S., 42
primordial images, 104, 105
prodromic nightmares, 172, 173
prophetic nightmares, 164-87
  of Aberfan, 180, 181
  of death of Henry Clemens, 179
  of death of Lincoln, 171
  of death of General Toutschkoff, 178
  of derailment of Flying Scotsman, 178
  of murder of Julius Caesar, 170
  of murder of Franz Ferdinand, 170
  of murder of R. Kennedy, 169
  of murder of Spencer Perceval, 169
  of sinking of La Plata, 179
  of sinking of Titanic, 166, 174, 177
psychosis, 21, 82, 86, 97, 111, 114

Radcliffe, A., 118, 119
recurring nightmares, 62, 98, 111, 112, 159, 212
'Red Barn' affair, 171
REM, 18, 29, 168, 189, 200, 202, 203, 205
Reserpine, 21
*Richard III*, 67, 68, 133, 134

# INDEX

*Robinson Crusoe*, 135
*Romeo and Juliet*, 135

St John's Eve, 16
St Swithold, 208
Satan, 48, 65, 130
schizophrenia, 86
Sendak, M., 141
Senoi attitude to nightmare, 208-11
sexual associations of nightmare, 11, 12, 42-50, 54, 84, 85, 96-100, 108, 117, 123, 132, 147, 148, 151, 156, 159, 161
Shakespeare, W., 15, 40, 132, 133, 170
shamans, 37, 38, 40, 53
Shelley, M., 152
Shelley, P. B., 124, 152, 153
sleep, 15-30
  of animals, 24, 25
  deprivation, 20, 21
  de-synchronized, 18
  laboratory, 13, 18, 20, 21
  of newborn, 25
  requirement, 26
  synchronized, 18
  talking, 28
somnambulism, 28, 152, 202, 212, 213
spermatorrhoea, 122
Stead, W. T., 177
Stevenson, R. L., 75, 76, 79, 119, 120
Stockwell, F., 213
succubus, 41, 42, 45, 47
suicide in nightmare, 173, 185

telepathy in nightmares, 167, 173, 174, 177, 184
Thackeray, W. M., 135
thalidomide, 190
thornapple, 191
Titanic, 166, 174, 177, 182
Titans, 39
'top dog', 150, 154, 161-3, 210
train disasters, 10, 68, 178
tranquillizers, 190, 191, 199-201

trauma, 112, 113, 147, 153
tryptophan, 189, 190
Twain, M., 120, 123, 179, 180, 185
typical nightmares, 143-63
  being chased, 78, 79, 97, 148, 149
  climbing, 112, 159, 160
  crawling through tunnels, 153
  death, 161-3
  examinations, 80, 158, 159
  falling, 150, 151, 211
  losing teeth, 155, 156
  missing trains, 160, 161
  nudity, 71, 154
  punishment, 97, 161
  water, 77, 151-4

Ullman, Dr M., 168
'underdog', 150, 161, 210

vampires, 11, 44, 98, 107
Vaughan, A., 169

Wedgewood, T., 117
werewolves, 11, 12, 44, 98
West Cameroon, 50
*Where the Wild Things Are*, 141, 210
wild beasts, 76, 77, 78, 210
Wild Hunt, 207
Wilberforce, W., 193
William Rufus, 171
Williams, E. and J., 152, 153
Williams, J., 169
witchcraft, 48, 49, 50, 52, 53
Witch of Endor, 74
witches, 11, 12, 38, 41, 44, 47, 48, 98, 108, 143
*Witches and Other Night Fears*, 74, 77
Wollstencraft, M., 125
wolves, 76, 77, 81, 97, 109
Wordsworth D. and M., 117

Zeus, 47
Zinacantecs, 35, 53